THE CLOISTER

A DISSERTATION

Submitted to the Faculty of Sacred Sciences
of the Catholic University of America
in partial fulfilment of the requirements for the Degree of

DOCTOR OF CANON LAW

BY

VALENTINE THEODORE SCHAAF, O. F. M., J. C. L.

Of the Province of St. John Baptist
Cincinnati, Ohio

St. Anthony Messenger,
Cincinnati, Ohio.
1921

Nihil Obstat.

FR. HUGO STAUD, O. F. M.,

Censor Deputatus.

Imprimi Potest.

FR. FLAVIANUS LARBES, O. F. M.,

Custos Prov. S. Joannis Bapt.

Cincinnati, Ohio, die 31 Maii 1921.

Nihil Obstat.

FR. FULGENTIUS MEYER, O. F. M.,

Censor Deputatus.

Imprimatur.

†HENRICUS MOELLER,

Archiep. Cincinnatensis.

Cincinnati, Ohio, die 2 Junii 1921.

PREFACE.

THE promulgation of the new Code of Canon Law has revived interest in ecclesiastical legislation, partly due to the simple arrangement of the Code, principally, however, to the numerous changes introduced. A number of these changes bear upon the cloister of religious. While most of them are comparatively slight, some are quite important in their practical aspect, others clear up points disputed under the former legislation. To explain the prevailing legislation on the cloister, as contained in the Code, is the purpose of the present study.

To the commentary of the canons dealing with the cloister an historical introduction has been prefixed. The history of the cloister has not been written. The author's first impulse was to undertake the task of supplying this want. But a cursory survey of the field convinced him that within the short space of time at his disposal it would be impossible to make more than a beginning, especially since the material was not easily accessible. The same difficulty did not exist, as far as the law of the cloister was concerned.

For a better understanding of the subject it was necessary to trace its earliest vestiges in Eastern monasticism. For through translations of the rules and lives of Egyptian and other Eastern monks by Jerome, Rufinus and John Cassian, Western monastic founders, among them St. Benedict, had become acquainted with those solitaires and cenobites and had profited by their experience. As to Western monasticism it was sufficient to describe the development of the cloister in Benedictine monachism, since it was the Benedictine Order more than any other that established the general forms which every religious institute must adopt. Although for several centuries other orders existed in the Western Church, especially in Gaul and Ireland, side by side with the great Benedictine family, they have hardly entered into this monograph, since they contributed to the canonical legislation of the cloister little that is distinctive.

From the development of the enclosure in monastic rule and custom we pass to the ecclesiastical legislation. There it will be found that pre-Tridentine particular laws paved the way for the later general legislation which in turn is revised and reenacted by the new Code of Canon Law.

The method which is followed in discussing the canons that deal with the cloister calls for an explanation. A glance at any page of the second part of this study will reveal the fact that it does not contain a bare commentary of the present legislation, but that it is interspersed with numerous historical data. After a somewhat lengthy historical sketch of the cloistral legislation this may appear superfluous. However, two considerations seemed to justify that arrangement. While the preceding chapters present the development of the cloistral legislation as a whole, the historical note introducing each point of the law shows its origin and gradual evolution. In the second place these historical notes serve for the better elucidation of the various canons; for the Code is not new in the sense that it is a complete departure from the former legislation; it is rather the latest revision of it. Therefore, whether the Code restates or revises the previous laws, they must be consulted for light on the meaning and extent of the present legislation. This procedure in the commentary finds approbation in canon 6 of the Code as well as in the two instructions of the Sacred Congregation of Seminaries and Universities regarding the method to be followed in expounding the canons of the Code in seminaries and the examination of candidates for higher degrees in the Sacred Sciences[1].

The author takes this occasion to acknowledge his indebtedness to his professor, the Rt. Rev. Filippo Bernardini, J. U. D., under whose direction this monograph was written. He likewise desires to express his sincerest gratitude to his confrere, Rev. Edwin J. Auweiler, O. F. M., Ph. D., for his careful revision of the manuscript in preparing it for the press.

[1] S C. de Seminariis et Studiorum Universitatibus, 7 Aug. 1917 et 31 Oct. 1918, A. A. S. IX 439 et XI 19.

BIBLIOGRAPHY.

Usually the following works will be quoted by the name of the author only. Whenever any other method of citation is employed, it will be prefixed to the title of the work.

Codex Juris Canonici Pii X Pontificis Maximi jussu digestus Benedicti Papae XV auctoritate promulgatus, Romae 1917.

As far as possible the canons of the Code will be quoted from:

Canonical Legislation concerning Religious. Authorised English Translation, Rome 1918.

A. A. S.=*Acta Apostolicae Sedis,* Romae 1909—.

A. S. S.=*Acta Sanctae Sedis,* 41 vol., Romae 1865-1908.

Acta Pii IX Pontificis Maximi, pars I vol. III.

Acta SS.=*Acta Sanctorum Bollandiana.*

Appeltern, Victorinus ab, *Compendium Praelectionum Juris Regularium Adm. R. P. Piati Montani, O. M. Cap.,* Tornaci 1903.

Arndt, Augustin, S. J., *Die Kirchlichen Rechtsbestimmungen für die Frauen-Congregationen,* Mainz 1901.

Ayrinhac, H. A., S. S., *Penal Legislation in the New Code of Canon Law,* New York 1920.

Bachofen, P. Augustinus, O. S. B., *Compendium Juris Regularium,* Neo-Eboraci 1903.

Ballerini, Antonius, S. J., *Opus Theologicum Morale edidit Palmieri, S. J.,* vol. IV et VII, Prati 1891-1893.

Bastien, Peter, O. S. B., *Kirchenrechtliches Handbuch für die Religiösen Genossenschaften mit Einfachen Gelübden, übertragen von Konrad Elfner, O. S. B.,* Freiburg im Breisgau 1911.

Benedictus XIV, *Opera Omnia,* 17 vol., Prati 1839-1847.

Biederlack, Josephus, S. J., *De Religiosis Codicis Juris Canonici libri II pars II (Can. 487-681) . . . . denuo recognovit Maximilianus Führich, S. J.,* Oeniponte 1919.

Bizzarri, Andreas, *Collectanea in usum Secretariae Sacrae Congregationis Episcoporum et Regularium edita,* Romae 1885.

Blair, D. Oswald Hunter, O. S. B., *The Rule of St. Benedict edited with an English Translation and Explanatory Notes,* 2. ed., Fort Augustus 1906.

Blat, Albertus, O. P., *Commentarium Textus Codicis Juris Canonici. Liber II: De Personis,* Romae 1919.

Bonacina, *De Clausura etc.,*=Bonacina, Martinus, *Opera Omnia,* 3 vol., Venetiis 1687. (Tractatus *De Clausura etc.*)

Bouix, D., *Tractatus De Jure Regularium,* 2 vol., 2. ed., Parisiis 1867.

Brandys, P. Maximilian, O. F. M., *Kirchliches Rechtsbuch für die Religiösen Laiengenossenschaften der Brüder und Schwestern nach dem neuen Gesetzbuch der Hl. Kirche,* 2. ed., Paderborn 1920.

Bullarium Franciscanum, 7 vol., Romae 1759-1908. *Supplementum,* Apud Claras Aquas 1908.

Bullarium Ordinis Praedicatorum, vol. VII, Romae 1739.

Butler, *Benedictine Monachism*=Butler, Cuthbert, O. S. B., *Benedictine Monachism,* New York 1919.

Butler, *Lausiac History*=Butler, Cuthbert, O. S. B., *The Lausiac History of Palladius*, in *Texts and Studies VI*, 2. vol., Cambridge, 1898-1904.

Cappello, *De Censuris*=Cappello, Felix M., S. J., *De Censuris juxta Codicem Juris Canonici*, Augustae Taurinorum 1919.

Cappello, *De Visitatione*=Cappello, Felix M., S. J., *De Visitatione Sacrorum Liminum et Dioeceseon*, 2 vol., Romae 1912-1913.

Catholic Encyclopedia, 15 vol., New York 1907-1912.

Cavigioli, Johannes, *De Censuris latae sententiae quae in Codice Juris Canonici continentur Commentariolus*, Torino 1919.

Cerato, Prosodocimus, *Censurae vigentes ipso facto a Codice Juris Canonici excerptae cum suspensionibus ferendae sententiae, poenis vindicativis, remediis poenalibus, poenitentiis et irregularitatibus*, Patavii 1918.

Charles Augustine, Rev. P., O. S. B., *A Commentary on the New Code of Canon Law*, 6 vol., St. Louis 1918—.

Collectanea Sacrae Congregationis de Propaganda Fide, 2 vol., Romae 1907.

Coll. Lac.=*Acta et Decreta Sacrorum Conciliorum recentiorum Collectio Lacensis*, vol. II, Friburgi Brisgoviae 1876.

Corpus Juris Canonici, editio Lipsiensis II post Aemilii Ludouici Richteri curas ad librorum manu scriptorum et editionis Romanae fidem recognovit et adnotatione critica instruxit Aemilianus Friedberg, 2 vol., Lipsiae 1879-1881.

D'Annibale, *Comment.*=D'Annibale, Josephus, *In Constitutionem "Apostolicae Sedis" qua Censurae latae sententiae limitantur Commentarii*, 4. ed., Prati 1894.

D'Annibale, *Theologia Moralis*=D'Annibale, Josephus, *Summula Theologiae Moralis*, pars III, 4. ed., Romae 1897.

Decreta Authentica Congregationis Sacrorum Rituum ex actis eiusdem collecta eiusque auctoritate promulgata sub auspiciis SS. D. N. Leonis XIII, 6 vol., Romae 1898-1912.

Delatte, Paul, O. S. B., *The Rule of St. Benedict, a commentary translated by Justin McCann, O. S. B.*, London 1921.

Egger, Augustin, O. S. B., *Das Neue Ordensrecht für die Religiösen Genossenschaften mit Einfachen Gelübden*, Freiburg im Breisgau 1919.

Fanfani, Ludovicus, O. P., *De Jure Religiosorum ad normam Codicis Juris Canonici*, Augustae Taurinorum 1920.

Ferraris, F. Lucii, O. M. Reg. Obs. Sti Francisci, *Bibliotheca Canonica, Juridica, Moralis, Theologica nec non Ascetica, Polemica, Rubricistica, Historica*, 9 vol., Romae 1885-1892. (v. *Conventus* III 14= verbum *Conventus* articulus III numerus 14.)

Ferreres, Joannes B., S. J., *Compendium Theologiae Moralis*, 2 vol., 9. ed., Barcinone 1918-1919.

Forcellini, Aegidius, *Totius Latinitatis Lexicon*, 4 vol., Schneebergae-Lipsiae 1831-1839.

Gasquet, Francis Aidan, O. S. B., *English Monastic Life*, 3. ed., New York 1905.

Hefele, Carl Joseph, *Conciliengeschichte*, 9 vol., 2. ed., Freiburg im Breisgau 1873-1890.

Heimbucher, Dr. Max, *Die Orden und Kongregationen der Katholischen Kirche*, 3 vol., 2. ed., Paderborn 1907-1908.

Hilarius a Sexten, O. M. Cap., *Tractatus de Censuris Ecclesiasticis cum appendice de Irregularitatibus,* Moguntiae 1898.

Hollweck, Dr. Joseph, *Die Kirchlichen Strafgesetze,* Mainz 1899.

Kirchenlexikon, 12 vol., 2. ed., Freiburg im Breisgau 1882-1901.

Koeck, Johann, *Die Kirchlichen Censuren latae sententiae,* Graz 1902.

Ladeuze, Paulin, *Etude sur le cénobitisme Pakhomien,* Louvain 1898.

Lanslots, D. I., O. S. B., *Handbook of Canon Law for Congregations of Women under Simple Vows,* 8. ed., New York 1919.

Lehmkuhl, Augustinus, S. J., *Theologia Moralis,* 2 vol., 11. ed., Friburgi Brisgoviae 1910.

Leipoldt, Johannes, *Schenute von Atripe und die Entstehung des National-Aegyptischen Christentums* in *Texte und Untersuchungen zur Geschichte der Altchristlichen Literatur,* N. F. Bd. X, Hft. I, Leipzig 1903.

Leitner, Dr. Martin, *Handbuch des Katholischen Kirchenrechts auf Grund des Neuen Kodex vom 28. Juni 1917,* Regensburg 1918-1919.

Lucidi, Angelus, *De Visitatione Sacrorum Liminum Instructio S. C. Concilii edita jussu S. M. Benedicti XIII exposita et additionibus aucta per P. Josephum Schneider, S. J.,* 3 vol., 3. ed., Romae 1883.

Lutz, Franz Joseph, *Die Kirchliche Lehre von den Evangelischen Räten mit Berücksichtigung ihrer sittlichen und sozialen Bedeutung,* Paderborn 1907.

MPG=Migne, *Patrologia Graeca.*

MPL=Migne, *Patrologia Latina.*

Matthaeucci, Augustinus, O. M. Reg. Obs. Sti Francisci, *Officialis Curiae Ecclesiasticae ad praxim pro foro ecclesiastico, tum saeculari tum regulari, utiliter aptatus,* Venetiis 1736.

Moochegiani, Petrus, O. F. M., *Jurisprudentia Ecclesiastica ad usum et commoditatem utriusque cleri,* 3 vol., Ad Claras Aquas 1904-1905.

Monacelli, Franciscus, *Formularium Legale practicum fori ecclesiastici,* 4 vol., 3. ed. Romana, Romae 1844.

Montalembert, Charles Count de, *The Monks of the West from St. Benedict to St. Bernard,* 2 vol., Boston.

Morison, E. F., *St. Basil and His Rule,* London 1912.

Ojetti, Benedictus, S. J., *Synopsis Rerum Moralium et Juris Pontificii,* 4 vol., 3. ed., Romae 1909-1914.

Oliger, P. Livarius, O. F. M., *De Origine Regularum Ordinis S. Clarae,* in *Archivum Franciscanum Historicum,* vol. II, Ad Claras Aquas 1912.

Pallottini, Salvator, *Collectio omnium conclusionum et resolutionum . . . S. C. Concilii,* 17 vol., Romae 1868-1893.

Paschalis de Siena, *Commentarius in Constitutionem "Apostolicae Sedis",* Romae 1902.

Pennacchi, Joseph, *Commentaria in Constitutionem "Apostolicae Sedis",* 2 vol., Romae 1883.

Piatus, *Comment.*=Piatus, F., Montensis, O. M. Cap., *Commentarius in Constitutionem "Apostolicae Sedis",* Tornaci 1881.

Piatus, *Praelectiones*=Piatus, F., Montensis, O. M. Cap., *Praelectiones Juris Regularis,* 2 vol., Tornaci 1888.

Poeschl, Dr. Arnold, *Kurzgefasstes Lehrbuch des Katholischen Kirchenrechts auf Grund des Neuen Kirchlichen Gesetzbuches,* Graz 1918.

Pruemmer II=Pruemmer, P. Fr. Dominicus M., O. P., *Manuale Juris Ecclesiastici, Tomus II: Jus Regularium Speciale,* Friburgi Brisgoviae 1907.

Pruemmer[2]=Pruemmer, Dominicus M., O. P., *Manuale Juris Ecclesiastici in usum clericorum praesertim illorum qui ad ordines religiosos pertinent. Editio altera aucta et secundum Codicem Juris Canonici recognita,* Friburgi Brisgoviae 1920.

Quaranta, Stephanus, *Summa Bullarii,* Venetiis 1622.

Reiffenstuel, Anacletus, O. F. M. Ref., *Jus Canonicum Universum edidit Victor Pelletier,* 5 vol., Parisiis 1868.

S. Alphonsus Maria de Ligorio, *Theologia Moralis, edidit P. Leonardus Gaude, C. SS. R.,* vol. IV, Romae 1912.

Schiwietz, Dr. Stephan, *Das Morgenländische Mönchtum. Bd. I: Das Ascetentum der drei ersten christlichen Jahrhunderte und das aegyptische Mönchtum im vierten Jahrhundert,* Mainz 1904.

Schlosser, Julius, *Die Abendländische Klosteranlage des früheren Mittelalters,* Wien 1889.

Schmalzgrueber, R. P. Franciscus, S. J., *Jus Ecclesiasticum,* 6 vol., Romae 1843-1845.

Schuppe, F., *Das Wesen und die Rechtsverhältnisse der neueren Religiösen Frauengenossenschaften,* Mainz 1868.

Seraphicae Legislationis Textus Originales (photographice), Romae 1901.

Sleutjes, Michael, O. F. M., *Commentarius in Constitutiones Generales Fratrum Minorum,* vol. I, Ad Claras Aquas 1915.

Sole, Jacobus, *De Delictis et Poenis. Praelectiones in librum V Codicis Juris Canonici,* Romae 1920.

Spreitzenhofer, Ernest, O. S. B., *Entwicklung des alten Mönchtums in Italien von seinen ersten Anfängen bis zum hl. Benedikt,* Wien 1894.

Ss. Conc.,=Labbeus, Philipus et Gabriel Cossart, S. J., *Sacrosancta Concilia ad Regiam Editionem exacta,* 15 vol., Lutetiae Parisiorum 1671-1672.

Stadtmueller, Raphael Maria, O. P., *Das Neue Ordensrecht,* Duelmen i. W. 1919.

Studien und Mitteilungen=Studien und Mitteilungen aus dem Benediktiner- und Cisterzienserorden mit besonderer Berücksichtigung der Ordensgeschichte und Statistik, Bruenn 1880—.

Suarez, Franciscus, S. J., *Opera Omnia,* vol. XVI, Parisiis 1866.

Vermeersch, *De Religiosis*=Vermeersch, A., S. I., *De Religiosis Institutis et Personis tractatus canonico-moralis,* 2 vol., 2. ed., Brugis 1902-1904.

Vermeersch, *Summa*=Vermeersch, A., S. I., *Summa Novi Juris Canonici Commentariis aucta,* 2. ed., Mechliniae 1919.

Wernz, Franciscus, S. J., *Jus Decretalium,* vol. III p. II, 2. ed., Romae 1908.

Zamboni, Joh. Fortunatus de Comitibus, *Collectio Declarationum S. C. Concilii,* 7 vol., Mutinae 1815-1816.

Zeitschrift für Christliche Kunst, vol. XIV, Duesseldorf 1901.

Zoeckler, D. Otto, *Askese und Mönchtum,* 2. ed., Frankfurt a. M. 1897.

PAPAL DECREES.

For all papal decrees not contained in the following list references will be given in their proper places.

Bonifacius VIII, const. *Periculoso*—c. un., *de statu regularium,* III, 16, in VI°.
S. Pius V, const. *Circa pastoralis,* 29 Maii 1566—Lucidi III 444-448.
S. Pius V, const. *Regularium,* 24 Oct. 1566—Quaranta 403-405.
S. Pius V, const. *Decori,* 1 Feb. 1570—Lucidi III 448-451.
S. Pius V, const. *Decet,* 16 Julii 1570—Ferraris, v. *Conventus,* III 24.
Gregorius XIII, const. *Deo sacris,* 30 Dec. 1572—Lucidi III 451-457.
Gregorius XIII, const. *Ubi gratiae,* 13 Junii 1575—Quaranta 447-449.
Gregorius XIII, const. *Dubiis,* 23 Dec. 1581—Quaranta 447.
Sixtus V, const. *Cum de omnibus,* 26 Nov. 1587—Vermeersch, *De Religiosis,* II 266-270.
Sixtus V, const. *Ad Romanum spectat,* 21 Oct. 1588—Vermeersch, *De Religiosis,* II 270-274.
Clemens VIII, decr. *Sanctissimus Dominus Noster,* 29 Maii 1593—Quaranta 423-424.
Clemens VIII, decr. *Nullus omnino,* 25 Julii 1599—Vermeersch, *De Religiosis,* II 308-312.
Gregorius XV, const. *Inscrutabili,* 5 Feb. 1622—Vermeersch, *De Religiosis,* II 689-691.
Alexander VII, const. *Felici,* 20 Oct. 1664—Lucidi III 477-481.
Innocentius XIII, const. *Apostolici ministerii,* 23 Maii 1723—Lucidi III 279-296.
Benedictus XIII, const. *In supremo,* 23 Sept. 1724—Lucidi III 296-297.
Benedictus XIV, ep. encycl. *Cum sacrarum,* 1 Julii 1741—*Opera omnia* XV 69-70.
Benedictus XIV, const. *Regularis disciplinae,* 3 Jan. 1742—*Opera omnia* XV 125-128.
Benedictus XIV, const. *Salutare,* 3 Jan. 1742—*Opera omnia* XV 128-131.
Benedictus XIV, const. *Ad militantis,* 30 Martii 1742—*Opera omnia* XV 164-172.
Benedictus XIV, ep. *Per binas,* 24 Jan. 1747—*Opera omnia* XVI 163-164.
Benedictus XIV, const. *Quamvis justo,* 30 Aprilis 1749—*Opera omnia* XVII pars I 49-61.
Benedictus XIV, ep. encycl. *Gravissimo,* 31 Oct. 1749—*Opera omnia* XVII pars I 85-86.
Pius IX, ep. *Quo graviora,* 8 Julii 1862—*Acta Pii IX* p. I vol. III 463-469.
Pius IX, const. *Apostolicae Sedis,* 12 Oct. 1869—*Collectanea S. C. de Prop. Fide,* n. 1348.
Leo XIII, const. *Conditae a Christo,* 8 Dec. 1900—A. S. S. XXXIII 341-347.
S. C. Ep. et Reg., declaratio, 4 Oct. 1588—Ferraris, v. *Conventus* III 8; translated into Latin: Pennacchi I 768-769.
S. C. Ep. et Reg., *Americana votorum,* 2 Sept. 1864—A. S. S. I 708-739.
S. C. de Prop. Fide, decr. *Cum deceat,* 26 Aug. 1780—*Collectanea S. C. de Prop. Fide,* n. 545.
S. C. Ep. et Reg., declaratio eiusdem decr., 5 Martii 1787—*Collectanea S. C. de Prop. Fide,* n. 587.
S. C. Ep. et Reg., *Normae secundum quas S. C. Ep. et Reg. procedere solet in approbandis novis Institutis votorum simplicium,* 28 Junii 1901—Vermeersch, *De Religiosis,* II 118-167.
C. Vaticanum, schema const. *De Clausura*—*Coll. Lac.* V 680-682.

TABLE OF CONTENTS.

VI. PAPAL CLOISTER OF NUNS.

VII. EPISCOPAL CLOISTER.

VIII. EGRESS AND VISITS OF RELIGIOUS.

CHAPTER I.

The Cloister.

1. Definition.

THE Latin word "claustrum," pl. "claustra," was employed very early in monastic rules to designate the enclosed area which was set apart for the sole use of the religious. Later the word "clausura" became more frequent. Derived from "claudere," "to close," these words signify in their original meaning a key, lock or barrier, by means of which anything is closed; in a wider sense they denote the place that is closed off by that lock or barrier[1]. In both these meanings the Latin "claustrum," "claustra," and "clausura" and their English equivalents "cloister" and "enclosure" are employed in monastic rule and life.

Materially the cloister embraces all those buildings and all that space, which are reserved for the exclusive use of the religious, where they reside and which they may not leave except for a good reason and with lawful permission; and within which those who do not belong to the religious community are not permitted save by way of exception.

From this meaning the word "cloister" or "enclosure" is applied to the legal barrier that closes the monastery upon its inhabitants and against all others. Formally, then, the cloister is the law by which religious are bound to live within the limits of their monastery and not go beyond them except as permitted by that law; and by which those not belonging to the religious body are excluded from the monastery.

In architecture the word "cloister" is applied in a technical sense to the vaulted portico around the inner court, which early became a feature of most monasteries of the Benedictine Order. The various monastic buildings were grouped so as to leave an open court in the center. Usually the chapel occupied the northern tract, with the monks' choir in the transept towards the East. In the eastern tract were the

[1] Cfr. Forcellini, v. *claustrum, clausura.*

chapter-house and auditorium, not the parlor for visitors, but the office, one might almost call it, where the abbot and prior met the individual monks, the calefactorium and lavatory; above these was the dormitory. In the southern tract were situated the refectory and kitchen. In the western tract were store-rooms and parlors for visitors, with the entrance to the monastery near the chapel; in the upper story of this wing were the apartments of the abbot. Along the sides of the quadrangle formed by these buildings there ran a sort of corridor covered with a vaulted roof. This was called the "cloister." It was intended not merely, or even primarily, as an ambulatory; it was rather the scene of most of the activities of the monks. Here the greater part of the monks' waking hours, outside of the time taken up in choir, were spent; here the monks read the Scriptures and other books; here the copyists transcribed the prized manuscripts; here the younger monks received their education; here the religious spent their few and brief recreations. Later, especially in colder climates, study and work had especially appointed rooms[2]. This arrangement of the different quarters offered many striking advantages. The choir was so placed, that the monks could enter quickly from the cloister for the day office as well as from the dormitory for Matins and Prime. The refectory and kitchen were situated farthest from the chapel, in order that the odor of cooking victuals might not penetrate to it. The store-rooms were to the front of the monastery and away from the place where the monks were at work or study in order that unavoidable noise might not disturb them. For a similar reason the abbot had his quarters in the same section, lest the visits that he must receive interrupt the work or study of the monks in the cloister. Thus careful study had mapped out a plan for the monastery, that served at once the monks' greater convenience and safeguarded them against all intrusion from without.

When that general plan was adopted is difficult to say. It is possible that in its general lines it was already employed by St. Benedict in his monastery at Monte Cassino. It is certain that by the ninth century it was almost exclusively followed

[2] Cfr. Gasquet 13-36.

in Benedictine abbeys. Of course, circumstances, especially the lay of the land, at times made a modification of that plan necessary, as for example at Fontanella, where the chapel lies towards the south instead of the north. But for the rest the plan was carried out as nearly as possible[3]. In this study the word "cloister" will not be used in the sense proper to architecture, unless expressly stated. It will be employed to signify the space reserved for the religious as well as in the legal sense.

Finally the word "cloister" is frequently employed to designate the religious state itself in such phrases as "life in the cloister," "to enter the cloister."

2. Division.

As a law the cloister can be divided into papal and episcopal. *Papal* enclosure is that which is governed in all its details, including the penalties for its violation, by the general law of the Church; formerly it was regulated by the Council of Trent and the constitutions of various Popes and the decrees of the Sacred Congregations; today by the Code. It is binding upon all regulars, both men and women, with solemn vows. Except for its enforcement in nuns' convents, it is entirely withdrawn from the jurisdiction of the bishops. Papal cloister imposes stricter obligations upon nuns than upon male regulars. The former are not allowed to leave their convent except for a very great necessity or with a dispensation of the Holy See; whereas the latter may leave their monastery for a short time, if they have a good reason and obtain the permission of their superior. Again no one, neither man nor woman, may enter the enclosure of nuns except with the approval of the Ordinary of the place in the cases specified in the law. Admission of women into men's convents is absolutely forbidden; but the papal laws do not contain any prohibition of men entering the enclosure of male regulars, though the rule or constitutions of the order may place some restrictions.

---

[3] Cfr. Hager, *Zur Geschichte der abendländischen Klosteranlage,* in *Zeitschrift f. chr. Kunst,* XIV 97-106, 139-146, 167-186, 193-204; Heimbucher I 213; Schlosser, *Die abendländische Klosteranlage des früheren Mittelalters,* Wien 1889.

By the general law of the Church papal enclosure is obligatory only in houses of regulars; nevertheless there are some religious congregations with only simple vows, in which it is observed because of a special law[4]. Otherwise religious congregations observe an enclosure that is modified to accommodate it to the purposes of the institute. Formerly it was imposed by the constitutions and could very well be styled *disciplinary*. It lay within the power of the bishop to impose an obligation of cloister that did not conflict with the constitutions of the congregation concerned. If the bishop exercised his authority in this respect, the enclosure was called *episcopal*. This name can well be retained under the present legislation to designate the enclosure that is binding in all houses of congregations to distinguish it from the papal enclosure[5]. The Code itself imposes the modified cloister upon all congregations without determining any penalties for its violation and commits the care for it even in exempt clerical congregations in a special manner to the bishop.

With reference to its extent the cloister is either total or partial. It is *total*, if the entire convent, excepting the public church, the parlors and the guest-house, is subject to the law of enclosure. If only a part of the religious house is subject to it, the remaining being set aside for school purposes and the like, as provided in canon 599, the enclosure is *partial*.

3. Purpose.

The cloister, however, is not so much a law imposed upon religious by the Church as an institution intimately connected with monasticism and developed within it prior to any general legislation of the Church. It is far from being the end and aim of the religious state, but only a means to the end to which that life tends. To understand it fully, one must be well versed in the spiritual life. The goal of religious life is that perfection which culminates in the union with God by perfect love. But the world presents countless cares and distractions as so many obstacles to a generous service and love

[4] Vide infra pp. 58-59, 105-106.
[5] Leo XIII, const. *Conditae a Christo,* 8 Dec., 1900; Ferraris, Supplementum, v. *Clausura,* 1; Ojetti, v. *Clausura,* n. 1162; Brandys 66.

of God. To deliver themselves from these bonds that shackle them to the world, the religious renounce, as far as possible, all that it can offer them, in order to follow the more freely and securely in the footsteps of the Master[6]. They heed His invitation, as though it were addressed to themselves: "If thou wilt be perfect, go sell what thou hast, and give to the poor, and thou shalt have treasure in heaven: and come follow me"[7]; they have grasped the Master's word and have made themselves eunuchs for the kingdom of heaven[8], in order to become the spouses of the Spotless Lamb; they have denied themselves and taken up their cross to follow the Saviour by placing upon their shoulders the yoke of obedience[9]. What more natural than that they who, for Christ's sake, have renounced all earthly possessions, the right to lawful pleasures and their own free will, should retire from the world, as far as possible, and unite for mutual assistance and encouragement? The religious have given up all earthly goods, to become poor with the poor Jesus: their place is not with those who bargain in them. They forego marriage to become pure and chaste spouses of the spotless Lamb of God: their place is not among those who marry and give in marriage. They subject themselves to the will of another in all that is good and holy, to become obedient as the Son of God: their place is not with those who seek their own preferments. Such is the *ideal* of the monastic or religious world-view.

The claim is often made that the retirement of Christian monks owes its origin to pagan sources and is based on the same un-Christian principles as pagan monasticism. There is no denying some similarity between the two forms of monasticism, but that is not sufficient to prove that the one is derived from the other. Historical contact between them has not been established[10]. The resemblances themselves lie on the surface. In both pagan and Christian monasticism the outward expressions run much along the same lines. This is not surprising. For all men feel an overwhelming sense of a

---

6 Montalembert I 7-15.
7 Matthew XIX 21.
8 Matthew XIX 12.
9 Matthew XVI 24.
10 Hastings, v. *Monasticism, Christian,* VIII 783.

debasing subjection to the material world and yearn to free themselves from its thraldom by rising superior to it in voluntary renunciation of the things it offers even at the cost of lifelong suffering. But here the resemblances cease. For the principles upon which the two forms of monasticism are built oppose each other diametrically. Pagan monasticism is sprung from some form of dualism. It manifests itself in Hinduism and Buddhism in the desire to escape the misery of an otherwise endless circle of existences by final extinction of being[11]. The Brahman monk strove after the same goal, not by extinction, but by emancipation—final absorption in the absolute effected by a life of rigorous renunciation and devout contemplation[12]. Manichaeans abstained from evil words and unlawful food, from evil actions and from marriage in their endeavor to liberate aeons of light imprisoned in the world which in their view was the creation of the king of darkness[13]. Closely allied to the Manichaeans were the Encratites, a Christian sect which considered marriage unholy, inasmuch as woman was for them a creation of Satan[14].

In comparison with all such forms, how elevated is Christian monasticism built upon the far nobler and grander conceptions of the world in general and of human life in particular! The Catholic religious renounces earthly possessions, not because they are evil; he renounces marriage, not as though it were no more than legalized fornication; he renounces his own free will, not because its aspirations are unholy. Such thoughts are foreign to the Catholic mind. The world, its goods and its pleasures, life itself are all good, because they are the works of an infinitely good God. The possession and enjoyment of them is holy, if they are employed in conformity with the Divine Will. Thus they become a means of salvation. Whether one be rich or poor, married or unmarried, high or lowly, one and all are called to serve God by a holy life. All can and must strive for this end and the state of perfection—

---

[11] Lutz 262-268; Hastings, v. *Monasticism, Buddhist and Hindu,* VIII 797-805; cfr. Ladeuze 158-162.

[12] Hastings, v. *Brahmanism,* II 802; cfr. v. *Nirvana,* IX 376-379.

[13] *Catholic Encyclopedia,* v. *Manichaeism,* IX 591-597; Lutz 269-270; Hastings, v. *Manichaeans,* VIII 394-402.

[14] *Catholic Encyclopedia,* v. *Encratites,* V 412-413.

by which is meant, not that those who enter it or belong to it, are perfect, but that they have obliged themselves to seek perfection by special means—offers no more assurance that this goal is reached or approached than a secular vocation. In fact a person in the world, who is faithful to his duties, might well outstrip a religious who, though not positively unfaithful to his calling, yet falls short in his striving for the common goal[15]. Why, then, renounce the world and what it offers? Because in the enjoyment of the world's goods man is exposed to many dangers that may draw him away from his final end—God, his Creator. Catholic religious resign voluntarily what they might otherwise justly enjoy, in order that they might free themselves from many of the dangers that lurk in the craving and enjoyment of earthly possessions and pleasures and that threaten to check their progress in the love of God and neighbor[16].

Catholic religious, therefore, hide themselves in the cloister out of the sight of men. This cloister is a hedge that separates them from the world. It is an asylum into which they have taken refuge from the temptations and distractions of the world. It is a safeguard that shields them from the dangers that threaten on all sides. It is a prison which their vow of obedience has built. Upon this vow of obedience rests the obligation of the enclosure. The religious have renounced their own will to do the will of another; they have fled from the world and its temptations; they have entered the religious community in order to profit by its example, its guidance, its encouragement, and in return they must serve it, whenever such service is demanded; they must not leave it except with the merit of obedience. This then is the first purpose of the enclosure: to remove them from the cares and distractions of the world and to hold them to the task they have taken upon themselves, that they may advance untrammelled towards their goal—union with God in perfect love. Its sec-

---

[15] Cfr. Leipoldt 64-67.

[16] Montalembert I 166. An exhaustive study of this question lies beyond our present scope. For a more complete treatment of the underlying principles the reader is referred to: Franz Joseph Lutz, *Die kirchliche Lehre von den evangelischen Räten mit Berücksichtigung ihrer sittlichen and sozialen Bedeutung,* Paderborn 1907.

ondary purpose supplements this. Since the religious have left the world, they must not suffer it to follow them and bring its distractions, its temptations, its dangers into the convent. Therefore, the law of the enclosure closes the door against the world. If those of the opposite sex are more rigorously excluded, it is for the greater safeguarding of the vow of chastity. This virtue must always remain the precious pearl of monasticism. But it must be jealously guarded. Too easily its lustre fades and wanes. This was always recognized and every effort was made to protect the religious against all danger of temptation, of scandal and even of suspicion. This purpose was obtained by enactments excluding women from the enclosure of male religious. Subsequently almost the entire ecclesiastical legislation touched only this one point. The explanation lies in the fact that the admission of women was a very fruitful source of violations of the vow of chastity. An excellent remedy lay at hand. It was only necessary to enforce the rule that monasticism itself had laid down. This means the Church adopted and made that rule her law. She made the exclusion of women absolute. If the other prescriptions were not so rigorously enforced by the Church, the reason is obvious. Other abuses could not so easily be traced to a definite source and minute details could not be covered by a general law.

For nuns the rules of various orders as well as the laws of the Church were always stricter than for male religious, until finally the nuns were forbidden to leave their convents or to admit any other persons. The greater severity must be traced to the vocation of nuns. Theirs was primarily a contemplative life not an active one. Such work as would call them from their retreat or bring others in, lay outside their sphere. They sought rather to offer up a more continuous sacrifice of prayer and meditation, for which greater seclusion was required. Therefore, their enclosure is intended not only to guard their chastity, but also to shield them from the many distracting influences from without, that might lessen or destroy their spirit of devotion.

As a monastic institution then the cloister is intended to foster the entire religious life by banishing all distractions and by encouraging and assisting the religious to a closer following of Christ. The laws which the Church has enacted to enforce the observance of the enclosure are designed as an added aid to the entire purpose of the religious life of nuns or to the preservation of the ennobling virtue of chastity of male religious.

CHAPTER II.

Development of the Cloister in Cenobitism.

NO sooner had the Holy Ghost descended upon the disciples of Christ assembled in the cenacle, than His grace began to bring forth abundant fruit. From the first Pentecost we can trace the rise of Christian asceticism. Among the early converts there were those who took the counsels of Christ to heart and sought to put them into practice. While many continued in the pursuit of the ordinary mode of life, some devoted themselves even then more exclusively to the service of the Church[1]. It was quite natural that such as heeded the evangelical counsels of the Master should shrink from the contagion of a sinful world and seek a safe haven in the society of men of the same noble aspirations[2]. Alas, the persecutions prevented any large numbers from taking up the ascetical life in common. Yet, it was a persecution that indirectly lent impetus to its rapid spread. When Decius (c. 250) began to employ new and unheard-of cruelties to root out Christianity, large numbers fled before the storm and sought shelter in the desert[3]. The same took place during the persecution of Licinius[4]. Many of these grew fond of the solitude, where they had found peace and contentment; and, when the fury of the persecution abated, they were loath to quit it, preferring

---

[1] Cfr. Acts XXI 9; I Cor. VII; S. Clemens, *ep. ad Cor.*, c. 38, MPG I 283-286; S. Ignatius, *ep. ad Polycarpum*, c. 5, MPG V 723-724; Justinus M., *Apologia I*, c. 15, MPG VI 329-332; Athenagoras, *Legatio pro Christianis*, c. 33, MPG VI 965-968; Clemens Alex., *Paedagogus*, I 7, II 1, II 2 § 20, MPG VIII 311-324, 377-410, 409-432; *Stromata*, III 6 § 33, VII 1 § 4, VII 12 § 69, MPG VIII 1097-1108, IX 447-450, 495-512; Origenes, in *Jeremiam*, XIX 7 MPG XIII 515-518; *contra Celsum*, I 26, V 49, VII 48, MPG XI 712, 1257-1260, 1489-1492; Tertullianus, *Apologeticus*, c. 9, MPL I 314-327; *de virg. vel.*, c. 10, MPL II 905-906; *de cultu fem.*, II 9, MPL I 1325-1327.

[2] Clemens Alex., *Stromata*, VII 7, MPG IX 470; *Quis dives salvetur?* c. 36, MPG VIII 641.

[3] Eus. *HE* VI 42, MPG XX 613-616.

[4] Eus., *Vita Constantini*, II 2, MPG 979-983; cfr. Butler, *Lausiac History*, I 230; Schiwietz 48-49; Montalembert I 172-175.

to continue their life of penance and mortification, of prayer and contemplation. These must be reckoned among the earliest Christian monks. They were solitaires, each one fashioning his manner of living to suit his individual bent. True, frequently they gathered around some famous hermit, such as St. Anthony, who became their teacher in the spiritual life. But even he did not give his disciples a set rule; he merely acted as a guide to direct their faltering steps, until they felt sufficiently grounded in the way of sanctification to proceed for themselves. Then they parted from the master and took up their abode in some lonely spot, often far from the nearest hermit[5]. St. Athanasius tells us of St. Anthony that he placed his sister in a nunnery before he retired into the desert to begin his eremitic life, but we know no more about it[6].

PACHOMIUS.

The first to unite ascetics into a close-knit body was the Egyptian Pachomius. He was born of pagan parents south of Esneh (Latopolis) in the Upper Thebais about the year 292[7]. At the age of twenty he was drafted into the army recruited by the emperor[8] for a campaign he was planning. An early victory and the cessation of hostilities kept Pachomius from being mustered into the army. During the brief period of training he was struck by the charity of some Christians in caring for the soldiers and, as soon as he was discharged, he retired to a deserted temple of Serapis near Schenesit[9]. Here he spent his time in works of charity and the study of the Christian religion and was baptized soon afterward. When his ministrations to the victims of an epidemic attracted attention, he betook himself to the nearby hermitage of Palaemon who became his spiritual director. After a while Pachomius withdrew further south to Tabennisi in the diocese of

---

[5] Cfr. Schiwietz 1-118; Butler, *Lausiac History,* I 230-234; Zoeckler 136-192.

[6] S. Athanasius, *Vita S. Antonii,* c. 3, MPG XXVI 844.

[7] Ladeuze 240.

[8] Which emperor? Cfr. Schiwietz 150-152 footnote; Zoeckler 194.

[9] Not as a priest of Serapis, whose temple was already destroyed, but as a Christian hermit. Weingarten's "theory" to the contrary "rests on a series of unverified hypotheses." Hastings, v. ***Monasticism, Christian,*** VIII 781; Ladeuze 157-162; Schiwietz 152-153.

Tentyra. It was here that he laid the foundation of the cenobitic life. He had clearly perceived that life in a community offers untold advantages to those striving after perfection over that of a hermit, for in mutual correction and example they would find a strong safeguard and encouragement. His older brother John became his first associate. Soon Pachomius began building his monastery and surrounded it with a wall which at first threatened the harmony between the brothers, but after a short time John was reconciled to it[10]. This monastery was built as early as 328[11]. His institution grew rapidly and before his death, May 9, 346[12], he had established nine monasteries for men and two for women.

In his rule Pachomius minutely regulated every detail of manastic life, as it was to be spent *within the wall* which surrounded his monastery[13]. No monk was allowed to go beyond this enclosure without permission of the "praepositus" (Reg. 84). Neither was anyone free to enter the village, unless he was sent or went on business (Reg. 108). Only the *praepositi* might enter the shops of tradesmen to obtain what was needful (Reg. 111). Nor should anyone be sent without a companion (Reg. 56); the older monks acting as such, should have the authority of superiors; any dissension that might arise among them should be reported and decided upon their return to the monastery (Reg. 189). Neither monks nor relatives were admitted to the infirmary except with permission of the praepositus (Reg. 47).

In the early days of his foundation Pachomius would not allow any of his monks to receive visits from their relatives[14]. But later he relaxed this rule, permitting such visits at the discretion of the praepositus and in the presence of another monk (Reg. 52). He even granted his subjects permission to go in company of one or two other trustworthy monks to visit sick relatives or to assist at their burial (Reg. 53, 55)[15].

---

10 Ladeuze 171; Schiwietz 155, 176; Zoeckler 197.

11 Schiwietz 156.

12 Cfr. Ladeuze 241; Montalembert I 179-180.

13 *Regula Pachomii* translated into Latin, MPL XXIII 61-86; cfr. Schiwietz 184-185.

14 Cfr. *Vita Pachomii*, cc. 22 & 26, Acta SS. Maii III 304-305; Zoeckler 207.

15 Cfr. ep. Ammonis, c. 21, Acta SS. Maii III 354; Schiwietz 218.

But on the journey they were to eat only with clerics or monks, unless necessity compelled them to eat with their relatives (Reg. 54)[16]. In fact, whenever outside the monastery, his monks should observe the same decorum and discipline as within it in conversing among themselves and with others (Reg. 59, 60, 122).

Visitors found shelter within a guest-house, a part of which was reserved for women whom necessity compelled to stay at the monastery over night. Only in this guest-house was the hospitality of the monastery to be shown; no visitors were allowed at the table of the monks (Reg. 50). Priests and visiting monks were received with due reverence and, if they wished, they might take part in the office and other devotions; but beyond this they were not allowed to associate with the monks (Reg. 51). When his friend Dionysius reproached him for this apparent lack of deference to their state, he justified his course by saying that he desired to spare them from being scandalized at the behaviour of the younger monks; for some of them had not yet acquired any knowledge of monastic discipline[17]. Schiwietz[18] and Ladeuze[19] will not admit with Tillemont[20] that article 51 of Pachomius' rule permits women in the oratory of the monks.

His sister having heard of his monastery came to visit him. He would not see her, but sent word by the porter that she should be satisfied to know that he was alive and urged her to follow his example of a retired life. She accepted his advice and soon a community gathered around her as their spiritual mother. Pachomius and his monks erected a monastery for them in the town of Tabennisi. It was separated from the monastery of the monks by a stream[21], for we are told that, if a nun died, her corpse was prepared for burial and brought

---

16 Cfr. *Vita Pachomii*, c. 42, Acta SS. Maii III 312.

17 *Vita Pachomii*, c. 28, Acta SS. Maii III 307. Only on one occasion is it reported that Pachomius admitted two monks within the enclosure. *Paralipomena de SS. Pachomio et Theodoro*, c. 7, Acta SS. Maii III 355.

18 Schiwietz 219.

19 Ladeuze 319 footnote 4.

20 *Memoires pour servir à l'histoire ecclésiastique* (Paris 1706) tom. VII 188.

21 Can this be the Nile, as Zoeckler 208 assumes? Cfr. map of Monastic Egypt in Butler, *Lausiac History*, II p. XCVIII.

to the banks of the stream by the nuns; then the monks crossed over and transported it to their burial place. Pachomius gave the nuns the same rule as the monks observed and appointed one brother Peter of advanced age to visit them occasionally to impart spiritual instruction and with other monks to conduct services for them[22]. In fulfilment of the promise which he had made to his sister, when he invited her to follow him, he despatched monks above reproach to perform all necessary work for the nuns[23]; but they were not allowed to see the nuns nor to receive even their meals from them. If a monk had a sister or other relative in the convent of nuns, he might be permitted to go in company of another monk to visit her in the presence of other nuns[24].

These are the earliest vestiges of enclosure that we find in the history of monasticism. Several anchorites of this and the preceding century had extolled the advantages to be gained by a hermit in his seclusion. Pachomius established this retirement as an obligation for his monks and it is striking that his rule embodied substantially all the legislation of later days. It must not, however, be supposed that these regulations were prescribed by Pachomius from the beginning of his foundation. Some were modified, others were added with the growth of the community, as in particular we are informed regarding visits received and paid by the monks[25].

SCHENUTE (SCHENOUDI).

Towards the end of Pachomius' life there were two other monastic foundations made in the Thebean Desert. The first was that of Pschai on the mountain Psou on the western bank of the Nile near the present Schag. This monastery is known as the Der elahmar or Red Monastery, from the red bricks used in the enclosure wall, or Der Anba Bischai. We know little else of Pschai or his monastery[26].

---

22 Ladeuze 303 footnote 6.
23 Cfr. *Praec. S. Pachomii,* XLIX, Acta SS. Maii III 346.
24 *Vita Pachomii,* c. 22, Acta SS. Maii III 304-305; Ladeuze 176-177; Schiwietz 158; Zoeckler 207-208.
25 Schiwietz 217.
26 Leipoldt 36-37.

Better known is the White Monastery, so called because the outer wall is built of white limestone. It was founded by Pgol, but rose to the zenith of its glory under his nephew. Schenute was born in the village of Schenalolet in the nome of Schmin about 333 or 340. He entered the monastery of his uncle not later than 371, perhaps already at the age of nine years after the death of his parents. He succeeded Pgol as abbot not later than 385 and died July 1, 451 or 452, at the age of 118 years[27].

Connected with the White Monastery there was another for nuns. Besides these, two other monasteries for men and one for women were under Schenute's jurisdiction and several of those founded by Pachomius joined his community[28]. At Schenute's death it is estimated that he had 2,200 monks and 1,800 nuns under him[29].

In the monastery of Schenute two monks occupied a cell together[30], but their apartments were separated by some sort of corridor[31]. If, after a thorough training in the monastery, a monk felt drawn to the eremitic life, he might be permitted to take it up, but he always remained under the jurisdiction of the abbot and was obliged to appear four times a year at chapter[32]. Boys and, in the monasteries of the nuns, girls were admitted to be educated, but it is not stated how far their education extended[33].

Schenute enacted similar regulations for the relations of the monks of the White Monastery among themselves and with the nuns, as Pachomius had for the monks of Tabennisi. But in several respects they were by far stricter than the latter[34]. All communication with relatives seems to have been for-

---

27 Leipoldt 37-47, 158; Ladeuze 242-245.

28 Leipoldt 158.

29 Leipoldt 93.—All applicants for admission as monks were detained for examination and instruction in the porter-house for a month or longer; if they were found deserving, they then made their profession and were admitted to the monastery to continue their monastic training. This is perhaps the earliest mention of a novitiate. Leipoldt 112-113.

30 Leipoldt 98.

31 Ladeuze 311.

32 Leipoldt 104-106.

33 Leipoldt 113, 139; Ladeuze 313-314.

34 Ladeuze 320-321; Leipoldt 145-146.

bidden. A monk was not allowed to visit even his sister, if she were a nun at the same monastery; neither was she permitted to visit him, though he were at the point of death; nor was one monk allowed to visit another except with permission of the abbot. When they went out of the monastery, the first monk was not to lose sight of the last. If seculars or monks called at the nuns' convent, only the superioress was permitted to speak with them in the presence of two elderly nuns[35]. Like Pachomius, Schenute appointed an elderly monk to represent him and provide for the needs of the nuns. Leipoldt even conjectures that he and a few other monks may have resided in the nuns' convent[36].

Nevertheless, great hospitality was shown at the monastery. A guest might spend two consecutive nights in the guest-house[37]. But a woman was not allowed to spend the night at the porter-house except by special permission of the abbot[38]. The laity of the neighborhood enjoyed the privilege of attending the services in the monastery church[39]. Still Schenute was not inflexible, if necessity prompted an exception. On one occasion, when the Bedouins overran the country, he opened the monastery, whose massive walls of masonry offered a safe protection against the savage hordes, to about 20,000 refugees, whom he took care of at the expense of the monastery for three months. His successor showed a similar charity to about 5,000 during a famine six years after Schenute's death[40]. But on the whole he drew the lines of the cloister stricter than did Pachomius[41].

ST. BASIL THE GREAT.

While cenobitic monasticism in Egypt was in its most flourishing stage, the "Father of Eastern Monasticism" was putting forth his efforts to inaugurate his institution in Pontus. St. Basil[42] was born about 316 or 319. His enthusiasm for

---

[35] Leipoldt 145-146.
[36] Leipoldt 145-146.
[37] Leipoldt 146.
[38] Leipoldt 138.
[39] Leipoldt 132, 161, 186; Ladeuze 215 footnote 4.
[40] Leipoldt 171-174; Ladeuze 321.
[41] Leipoldt 145-146.
[42] Montalembert I 201-205.

the monastic life being aroused by his sister, St. Macrina, he visited several renowned monks of Syria, Mesopotamia, Palestine and Egypt. After a short absence he returned to Pontus and settled on the Iris at Annesi, opposite the convent of his sister.

At first Basil lived as a hermit in his mountain retreat, but soon his fame attracted other monks and he established them into a community and gave them his "Regulae Fusius Tractatae"[43] and "Regulae Brevius Tractatae"[44], two sets of questions and answers which form no corporate whole, but merely suggest ways and means to attain the perfection of the monastic ideal[45].

Basil chose the cenobitic form of monasticism for his monks as being superior to the eremitical, because the latter appeared egoistical, whereas the former more perfectly united the monks into one body and offered them occasion for mutual encouragement or correction, as the case might be[46]. Still he would not refuse his monks their choice of a solitary life, provided their superior approved of it[47].

Our saint sees the proper safeguard for the spiritual life in the retirement of the cell; a monk who leaves it does not return to it the same man, even though by the grace of God he escapes the snares set for him; if necessity compels him to come forth from his retreat, he must arm himself with the fear of God as with a breastplate and return as soon as his task is done[48]. No one is allowed to go out of the monastery except in case of necessity[49] and with permission of the superior[50]; and only to such should it be permitted, as can do so without danger to themselves and with benefit to others; they should not go singly, but several together for mutual protection and edification[51]. Even for speaking with visitors

[43] MPG XXXI 889-1052.
[44] MPG XXXI 1051-1306.
[45] Zoeckler 287; Morison 20; Montalembert I 204
[46] *Reg. fus. tract.* 7.
[47] *Reg. brev. tract.* 74.
[48] *De renuntiatione saeculi* 5, MPG XXXI 635-638.
[49] *Reg. brev. tract.* 120; *Poenae* 12, MPG XXXI 1307.
[50] *Poenae* 9, MPG XXXI 1307.
[51] *Reg. fus. tract.* 39, 44.

the permission of the superior was required[52]. He strongly objected to receiving visits from relatives or paying visits to them[53], unless it be for the "edification of the faith"[54]. Thus he sent Dionysius back to his mother to win her over to the monastic life[55]. But he was not as strict as Pachomius in cutting his monks off from all communications with the nuns. His monks might serve them in various capacities, but they must always shield themselves against temptation and evil tongues by the companionship of at least one and not more than two other monks and a like number of nuns[56]. Outsiders were not to be admitted into the inner apartments of the monastery except by the one charged with overseeing them[57]. St. Basil did not found a double monastery, neither did he forbid such, and in later times several grew up in communities following his rule[58].

Attached to his monastery there was a school. Some of the pupils were orphans; others were brought to the monastic school by their parents. He would not absolutely forbid accepting anything for their education, still he strongly advised against it. Nor was the school intended only for such children as should later make religious profession, though in time they might do so. Except regarding the common prayer, the pupils had a special program and separate buildings, in order that the quiet of the monastery might not be disturbed by them[59].

The rule of St. Basil, if rule it can be called, is followed by almost all the monks of the Orient. The most prominent legislator for Eastern Monasticism of a later date is Theodore Studite (759-826), abbot of the Studium in Constantinople. In his "Poenae Monasteriales"[60] and "Poenae Quotidianae"[61] he

---

[52] *Poenae* 48, 50, MPG XXXI 1311, 1314; *Epitimia in Canonicas* 10 17 MPG XXXI 1315.

[53] *Reg. fus. tract.* 32; *Reg. brev. tract.* 188, 189, 311, contra Heimbucher I 124.

[54] *Reg. brev. tract.* 189.

[55] Ep. X, MPG XXXII 271-274.

[56] *Reg. fus. tract.* 35; *Reg. brev. tract.* 108-111, 114.

[57] *Reg. brev. tract.* 141.

[58] Morison 98-99; Zoeckler 289-290.

[59] *Reg. fus. tract.* 15; *Reg. brev. tract.* 53, 292, 304, 305; Epp. CXCIX 18, CCX 2, MPG XXXII 717-720, 769-772; Morison 101-108; Heimbucher I 124.

[60] MPG XCIX 1733-1748.

[61] MPG XCIX 1747-1758.

supplies for the deficiencies of St. Basil's rules. He forbids the monks to go out without the superior's permission[62] or to spend the night in the village without leave[63]. Guilt fastens upon one who knows of a brother's secretly going out and does not report it[64], as upon the porter through whose carelessness a monk secretly goes out[65], or who loses the key[66]. In a letter to his disciple Nicholas he gives special instructions to avoid all unnecessary association with outsiders, especially with women; nevertheless he allows him to eat with his mother and sister. Neither should he admit any woman into his monastery, except in case of necessity and in such a way, if possible, that neither she see the monks nor the monks her; this precaution should not easily be neglected. He should not leave the monastery frequently nor without necessity[67].

Thus we see that St. Basil did not impose such strict rules regarding the cloister upon his monks as Pachomius and Schenute did. Nevertheless he held to the principle that the monk must remain in the monastery and under the obedience of his superior.

The rule of St. Basil was not restricted to the Eastern Church. Through the translation into Latin by Rufinus of Aquileja, about the year 400, it penetrated into Italy and later many of its regulations found their way into the rule of St. Benedict.

As Rufinus made the rule of St. Basil accessible to the West by his translation into Latin, so John Cassian (360-415) as abbot of a monastery near Marseilles transplanted the rule and life of the Egyptian monks into Gaul[68].

But long before Rufinus' translation of the rule of St. Basil into Latin there were hermits as well as cenobites in Italy. They date further back even than the visit of St. Athanasius to Rome at the time of his exile in 341; still it is true that monasticism gained a new impetus through the efforts of the saint

---

62 *Poenae Quotidianae* 19, 21.
63 *Poenae Quotidianae* 60.
64 *Poenae Monasteriales* 35.
65 *Poenae Monasteriales* 63.
66 *Poenoe Monasteriales* 66.
67 Theodorus Studita, lib. I ep. X, MPG XCIX 939-944.
68 Heimbucher I 175-176; Zoeckler 340-346; Montalembert I 279-280.

and his two companions Ammonius and Isidore who broke down the barriers that had held nobles from the monastic life[69].

St. Martin of Tours (†397) founded the monastery of Liguge, and, after his elevation to the bishopric of Tours in 372, the Marmoutier near Tours into which he transplanted the semi-eremitic life of the Egyptian lauras[70].

Similarly John Cassian adapted the manner of life of the Egyptian monks to the conditions of Gaul and introduced it into his monastery at Marseilles[71].

The first monastic legislator of the Western Church is Caesarius of Arles (470-542)[72]. In his "Regula ad monachos"[73] he prescribed that all who enter his community promise to remain in it until death—stabilitas loci—(c.1) and in chapter 11 he forbade that women be admitted into the convent[74]. More renowned is his "Regula ad Virgines"[75], composed for the nunnery founded at Arles in 512 over which he placed his sister as abbess. It is supplemented by a "Recapitulatio" of which only a few chapters are entirely new[76].

The "Regula ad Virgines" was the first to oblige nuns to observe strict cloister: they were not permitted to leave it (C. I, Recap. c. 1) except for unavoidable necessity[77]. Neither men (c. 33) nor women (c. 34) were allowed to enter the monastery, except the bishop, the procurator, the priest, deacon and subdeacon and one or two lectors of proven character for the celebration of Mass and other divine services, as well as workmen who might be required for necessary work (Cc. 33-35). In order to enforce these rules, the door of the monastery was opened only at certain hours, but at all other times it was to be locked and the key kept by the abbess[78]. The saint had all other doors walled up and forbade that they be opened again (Recap. c. 19). Visits from relatives were permitted,

---

69 Cfr. Spreitzenhofer 1-27; Montalembert I 222-223.
70 Heimbucher I 169-172; Montalembert I 265.
71 Heimbucher I 175-176; Montalembert I 279-280.
72 Montalembert I 277-278.
73 MPL LXVII 1099-1104.
74 Heimbucher I 178-179.
75 MPL LXVII 1103-1116.
76 MPL LXVII 1115-1122.
77 Caesarius Arelat., *Sermo ad Sanctimoniales,* MPL LXVII 1122-1123.
78 C. 35; Recap. c. 9. The janitress prescribed in c. 21 of the Recapitulatio is an addition of a later date drawn from the rule of St. Benedict.

but only in the presence of an elderly nun (C. 37; Recap. c. 3). In like manner the abbess was obliged to be attended by two or three other nuns as often as she went to the parlor (C. 35). The table might be spread for pious women who had shown great favors to the monastery or to others who came from a distance to visit a daughter or the convent, but for none others, not even for the bishop (C. 36; Recap. c. 5). If the monastery wished to give alms to the poor, they should not be distributed at the door of the monastery, but by the procurator, in order to avoid any disturbance of the monastic solitude (C. 39). Girls above six years could be received, if they were presented by their parents; but no school for children not destined for the religious life was allowed. The "Regula ad Virgines" was the first to enjoin perpetual enclosure upon nuns. In this respect it has remained the model for all rules intended for cloistered nuns, until after several centuries the legislation was completely evolved[79].

ST. BENEDICT.

It was reserved for Benedict of Nursia (485-543) to frame a rule that should preserve the high ideals of monastic life and yet temper the severity of the life which the monks of the East led, so as to adapt it to the conditions and requirements of Western life[80].

His rule is famous for its wise moderation and the efficient organization that it gave his order. It is, therefore, not to be wondered at, that it soon all but superseded the other monastic rules and maintained an almost exclusive position in Western monasticism until the coming of the Mendicant Friars.

In the first chapter of his rule[81] St. Benedict tells us that it is intended for the very courageous class of cenobites who would take up the hard battle under the guidance of a rule and an abbot. He acknowledges, indeed, the excellence and holiness of the anchorites who have been trained in the school of the monastery. But for two other classes of monks he has

---

79 Cfr. *Catholic Encyclopedia*, v. *Caesarius of Arles,* III 136.
80 Montalembert I 305-356.
81 *S. P. Benedicti Regula cum commentariis,* MPL LXVI 215-952.

only words of the strongest condemnation: the sarabaites and the gyrovagi, who pretended great sanctity, only to conceal under the habit of a monk a restless and even dissolute life. To remove all temptation to such a life from his monks, Benedict would bind them by the vow, to remain in the monastery in which they made profession—stabilitas loci (C. 58). They should dwell in monasteries under the direction of their abbot (C. 5) and, except by his leave or command, they must not go out of the manastery (C. 67). In order to reduce the necessity for leaving the monastery, there are to be artisans of every kind as far as possible (C. 66). On their journeys they must observe their rule of prayer, etc. (Cc. 50, 51).

To provide for the proper guarding of the cloister an elderly monk is to be appointed to act as porter who must answer all summons to the door and announce the arrival of guests (C. 66). For receiving the latter St. Benedict lays down special rules of hospitality (C. 56). As is fitting, visiting monks should enjoy greater hospitality: as long as their conduct warrants it, they may take part in the exercises of the community and even be received into the monastic body, if they so desire and are found fit (C. 61). In chapter 59 Benedict makes provision for the reception of boys into his community, but they are to be received as oblates and not merely as pupils.

In these chapters St. Benedict manifests a deep appreciation of the cloister. The monastery is a haven that shields the monks against the storms raging roundabout. In order to enjoy its protection, they must remain within its sheltering walls, unless obedience or necessity calls them forth from their quiet retreat[82]. One is struck, however, by the absence of any reference to communications with women and especially to their admission into the monastery. The story which Gregory the Great relates of the saint's going to a villa outside the monastery to meet his sister, St. Scholastica[83], seems to

---

82 Delatte 81-82, 322, 466-467, 471.

83 Gregorius M., *Dialogi,* I 33, MPL LXVI 193-196. Her convent was situated about five miles from Monte Cassino.—There is no mention of St. Benedict's having founded a monastery for nuns, but it is not unlikely that he did. In this case he may have given them a rule very similar to that of his own monastery. At all events this visit of St. Scholastica is proof that nuns did not yet observe the strict cloister of later days. Cfr. Montalembert I 325-327.

warrant the conclusion that Benedict did not admit women into his monastery, a custom which, he trusted, the zeal of the abbots would preserve.

Like all human undertakings, the Order founded by St. Benedict suffered from the ravages of time, without, however, succumbing to them. Within its own bosom it found men willing and able to stem the tide of worldliness and rekindle the waning religious fervor. The first of its great reformers was St. Benedict d'Aniane (c. 750-821). His influence extended over many monasteries of France and contributed very much to the success of the Council of Aachen in 817, to which there will be frequent occasion to refer later. However, his reform was neither universal nor permanent.

The tenth century saw the reform of Cluny, which was inaugurated in 910. By this time the claustral plan of monastic buildings was fully developed and quite generally adopted. This helped very much in carrying out the few regulations that were necessary to secure for the monks that seclusion which was necessary for the pursuit of their retired life of prayer and work. In the cloister most of the time left after the Divine Office was spent in reading and writing and in the education of the younger monks[84]. To leave the cloister was permitted only in certain cases, for work on the farm[85]; for the processions on rogation days[86]; likewise for the visits of the deans to villas and granges belonging to the monastery, of which they had charge[87]. To shield the monks against disturbance, persons that did not belong to the monastery were not allowed the freedom of entrance or roaming about in it; clerics and laymen were admitted at stated times to satisfy their devotion and to view the monastery; visiting monks were allowed to join the community in choir[88]. Only clerics and monks were admitted to the table of the monks[89]; all others were entertained in the guest-house[90]. To avoid even the sus-

[84] *Uldarici Consuetudines Cluniacenses,* lib. II, c. 24; lib. III, c. 110; MPL CXLIX 712, 749.
[85] *Petri Ven. Statuta Congreg. Cluniac.,* 39, MPL CLXXXIX 1037.
[86] *Uldarici Consuet. Cluniac.,* lib. I c. 21, MPL CXLIX 669-670.
[87] *Uldarici Consuet. Cluniac.,* lib. III c. 5, MPL CXLIX 738-740.
[88] *Petri Ven. Statuta Congreg. Cluniac.,* 53, MPL CLXXXIX 1040.
[89] *Uldarici Consuet. Cluniac.,* lib. III c. 3, MPL CXLIX 736.
[90] *Uldarici Consuet. Cluniac.,* lib. III cc. 22-24, MPL CXLIX 764-767.

picion of familiarity with nuns, it was ordained that no convent of women should be allowed within a radius of two miles[91].

About the same time that the reform of Cluny was at its height, a similar movement spread from the abbey of Citeaux. In regard to the cloister its customs (usus) differed little from the regulations of Cluny, except that they expressly excluded women from entering the monastery[92]. This, however, is not to be considered an innovation: the "Instituta Monachorum Cisterciensium" refer this exclusion of women from the monastery to St. Benedict himself: "Et quia nec in regula nec in vita Sancti Benedicti .... legebant .... nec etiam feminas monasterium ejus intrasse ...."[93]

CARTHUSIANS.

As was to be expected of an order that aimed to combine the rigor of the ancient anchorites and the perfection of cenobitic life, the rule of the Carthusians, founded by St. Bruno of Cologne, (c. 1084), regarding the cloister was very strict from the beginning. To the Carthusian monk his cell is his world; he must not leave it except for a good reason[94]. In order to reduce this necessity to a minimum, the equipment of the individual cell was such, that Guigo feared some might be surprised at the number and variety of utensils allowed; but he assured them that this concession was made only in order to relieve the monk of the necessity of quitting his cell, which, he says, is allowed only when the community assembles in the cloister or in church[95]. Nevertheless it seems that an occasional walk in the desert or even an excursion to the Grand Son, which required a somewhat longer time, was permitted[96]. The usual provisions for guests were made. Only bishops and monks were to be admitted into the choir and cloister (domus

---

91 *Petri Ven. Statuta Cong. Cluniac.*, c. 47, MPL CLXXXIX 1038.
92 *S. Stephani Usus Ord. Cist.*, c. 120, MPL CLXVI 1499.
93 *Exordium Coënobii et Ord. Cist.*, c. 15, MPL CLXVI 1507.
94 *Guigonis Consuetudines*, 21, MPL CLIII 703-704.
95 *Guigonis Consuetudines*, 28, MPL CLIII 693-696.
96 Cfr. *Commentarium in Guigonis Consuetudines*, 28 n. 6, MPL CLIII 696. In recent times such a walk, "spatiamentum", is allowed every week. Vide *Catholic Encyclopedia*, v. *Carthusians*, III 390.

superior); they might speak to the monks in common, but for a private conference the guest, not the monk, was to seek the necessary permission[97]. All other guests were committed to the care of the procurator and cook in the guest-house (domus inferior) and no other monk might speak to them except with leave; in case of necessity, however, a word or two of direction was permissible[98]. Women were not allowed to enter the confines of the convent[99].

MENDICANT FRIARS.

When the rule of Chrodegang, Bishop of Metz (742-766), for the Canons Regular and the statutes of the Council of Aachen for the same were found to be unsatisfactory, the so-called rule of St. Augustine was compiled from the writings of that great Father of the Church and prescribed for them. This rule was also adopted by a large number of religious orders that were founded in the next centuries, of which the Order of Preachers is the foremost. In this rule there is no mention of the cloister. Neither does the rule of the Friars Minor contain any reference to the enclosure they were to observe in their convents. The reason seems to be found in the departure of the Mendicants from the position of the older monastic orders. The latter did not restrict their energies to one definite object; but it must be of such a nature that it did not take them away from their monastery. The Mendicants, however, chose a different course. Their purpose was to bring the message of hope and love of the Redeemer to the lowly, the down-trodden, the outcast. This they did by the example of their life as well as by instructions and sermons, by becoming like to them in poverty and humility and by going among them as their own[100]. Franciscan convents were but homes and schools, where the friars were inspired with the ideals that guided them in their service of the poor and lowly, centers, from which they spread their missionary activities.

---

[97] *Guigonis Consuetudines,* 10, 36, MPL CLIII 655, 711.
[98] *Guigonis Consuetudines,* 18, 20, 30, 32, 46, MPL CLIII 669, 673, 701, 703, 727.
[99] *Guigonis Consuetudines,* 21, MPL CLIII 681.
[100] Testament of St. Francis.

In the matter of enclosure their convents conformed to the standard of monasteries, in as far as it was compatible with this purpose.

Whilst St. Francis did not extend the enclosure to the convents of the friars, he forbade his brethren to enter the monasteries of nuns, unless they should have obtained special permission of the Holy See[101]. This was interpreted by Gregory IX[102] and Nicholas III[103] to mean that the friars were not allowed to enter the enclosure of nuns, but that they were permitted to go with leave of their superiors for the purpose of preaching or begging alms to those parts which were open to the laity; that they were not, however, allowed even to *visit* (accedere) the convents of Clares without leave of the Holy See. After a short time Gregory IX relaxed this rule, leaving the matter to the discretion of the Minister General[104].

We now come to a time when we find perpetual cloister of nuns with most of its details clearly prescribed for the first time. Since then little has been added save to define a few minor points. We must not, however, suppose that it is entirely new. It bears the marks of too complete development to be considered original and spontaneous. In fact, it is not at all new. St. Caesarius of Arles enclosed the nuns that gathered around his sister as early as 512, without providing in a special manner for contingencies that must arise frequently. No doubt one safeguard after another was added, as time advanced, until by the end of the twelfth century it was quite fully developed and ready to be imposed by general law upon all nuns. At the beginning of the thirteenth century it is met with in the second Orders instituted by the two founders of Mendicant Friars.

Nine noble women who had been converted from the Albigensian heresy by St. Dominic, entrusted themselves to his guidance and retired to a convent at Prouille in the Diocese

---

101 Reg. O. F. M., c. 11, *Seraph. Legisl. Textus orig.* 12.

102 Gregorius IX, bulla *Quo elongati,* 28 Sept. 1230, *Bullarium Franc.* I 68-69.

103 Nicolaus III, const. *Exiit,* 14 Aug. 1279, art. XX, *Seraph. Legisl. Textus orig.* 23.

104 "Quod cum audiret Papa Gregorius statim prohibitum illud in generalis Ministri manibus relaxavit." Oliger in AFH V 422.

of Toulouse, which they were never to leave[105]. This was the first convent of what later developed into the Second Order of St. Dominic. Later the same saint established convents of cloistered nuns at Madrid[106] and Rome[107]. The bull "Ne hostis antiquus" of October 23, 1232[108], by which Gregory IX confirmed the rule of the Dominican Sisters, gave papal sanction to the perpetual enclosure which St. Dominic had introduced.

As St. Dominic had gained the first candidates for his order of sisters by his evangelical preaching, so a few years later St. Francis attracted Clare by his example of evangelical poverty. On Palm Sunday, March 18, 1212, she came to Portiuncula to be initiated in a similar course. It does not seem that St. Francis composed a definite rule for St. Clare. We are, however, informed that from the beginning Clare and her associates lived in strict enclosure at St. Damian[109]. Special female servants who lived in the convent, attended to all communications with the outside world; lay-brothers of the Friars begged alms for their sustenance, except for the short time in 1230 that St. Clare dismissed them, when the Friars were removed as chaplains in consequence of the interpretation which Gregory IX made regarding chapter XI of their rule[110] and to which probably more force than the Pope intended was at first attached, until he restored the friars as chaplains of the monastery[111].

Even before the death of St. Francis, in 1218 or 1219, Cardinal Hugolin gave four convents of nuns who wished to follow St. Clare a rule which prescribed the rule of St. Benedict[112] with special regulations particularly regarding fasting and enclosure. Later, as Gregory IX, he formally prescribed

---

105 Acta SS. Aug. I 401-402.

106 Acta SS. Aug. I 474.

107 Acta SS. Aug. I 376.

108 *Bullarium O. P.* VII 410-413.

109 Oliger in AFH V 188-189.

110 Vide supra p. 26.

111 Oliger in AFH V 186-193, 421-423.

112 Nominally only, for the Clares were at no time obliged to observe the rule of St. Benedict, as Innocent IV declared in his letter *In divini timore nominis* of Nov. 13, 1243, to Bl. Agnes of Bohemia. *Bullarium Franc.* I 316-317.

it for the convent of S. Angelo of Ascoli[113]. Innocent IV imposed it upon the monastery of St. Damian[114]. Four revisions of it were approved by the Holy See before the lapse of barely half a century after Clare's flight to Portiuncula[115]. Strict cloister which St. Francis enjoined upon her and the heroic band that gathered around her is fully developed and prescribed by these five rules and forms a considerable part of each of them. The detailed account of it must be pardoned because of the wide application of their cloistral regulations found in later legislation.

Once a woman had become a nun she was not allowed to leave the monastery at any time during her life except in case of grave danger arising from hostile invasion, floods, fire and the like, or to institute a new foundation or reform of a monastery, for which Urban IV required the permission of the Cardinal Protector. For all other cases leave of the Holy See, of the Cardinal Protector or of the General or Provincial of the Friars Minor was required. According to the rules approved by Urban IV the Clares bound themselves by express vow to observe the enclosure. The law of enclosure imposed a very heavy burden upon the nuns. Therefore, the abbess was obliged to explain to every aspirant, what a severe life she was taking upon herself by entering their convent, so that she neither lightly bound herself to it nor could claim her freedom, because she was ignorant of it. This was all the more necessary, since in the beginning the vows were taken shortly after one was admitted.

To enable the nuns to live in this strict seclusion, the monastery had to be constructed in a special manner. The nuns' choir was separated from the outer chapel by a lattice-work of iron with iron spikes protruding. In the middle of this screen there was a window closed with an iron door and lock; which served

---

113 Gregorius IX, bulla *Cum omnis vera Religio,* 24 Maii 1239, *Bullarium Franc.* I 263-267.

114 Innocentius IV, bulla *Solet annuere,* 13 Nov. 1245, *Bullarium Franc.* I 394-399.

115 Innocentius IV, bulla *Cum omnis vera Religio,* 6 Aug. 1247, *Bullarium Franc.* I 476-483; bulla *Solet annuere,* 9 Aug. 1253, ibid. 671-678; Urbanus IV, bulla *Religionis augmentum,* 27 Julii 1263, ibid. II 477-486; bulla *Beata Clara,* 18 Oct. 1263, ibid. 509-521.

primarily for the communion of the nuns. It was, therefore, to be large enough to admit the ciborium and to permit the priest to pass his hand through, when distributing Holy Communion. It was to be opened only for Communion and at the time of sermons and to permit someone to see one of the nuns related to him or for some other urgent reason: in these latter cases permission could be granted by the abbess only after consulting the community. The grille was covered on the inner side with a black curtain to close out all view. Wooden shutters with iron locks were hung on the inside and might be opened at the time of sermons and at other occasions by leave of the abbess. If the nuns conversed with visitors at this grille, they were to cover their faces with their veils.

Only one door was to lead into the enclosure, to be opened only for persons who had the necessary permission to enter or leave. It was not to contain a smaller door or window and had to be set as high as convenience permitted; the stair that led up to it was to be raised by means of a chain, during those hours when no one was allowed to enter. The door was always to be locked, at night with two different keys, the one of which was in charge of the portress, the other of the abbess. The janitress or her assistant had to guard the door closely and was not to open it, unless she was certain that those seeking entrance enjoyed the necessary permission. Whenever lay-persons were to be admitted for some necessary work, the abbess should entrust the custody of the door to some reliable person, in order that the nuns might not be seen by any outsiders. However, to admit articles of greater bulk, a second door, which also had to be locked securely at all times, was permitted. Since the door to the cloister ought not be opened except when absolutely necessary, a "rota," or revolving table, was employed to pass in and out of the enclosure whatever was necessary. It was constructed in such a manner, that it offered no view into or from the enclosure; neither might it be so large, that any person could enter or leave the cloister by means of it. On either side there was a door which was locked at night. The "rota" was guarded by a nun as janitress and another as her assistant; they alone were permitted to speak there on matters pertaining to their office. Others were allowed to use it for conversation with visitors, only when the parlor was occupied.

The nuns were not permitted to enter the parlor. To converse with visitors, the parlors were so constructed, that the nuns within could communicate with those in the outer parlor through an iron grille provided with spikes and a black curtain like the grille in the chapel. If the number of nuns was large, a second such parlor could be permitted. If any person desired to speak to a nun, it might be permitted by the abbess, except during the forty days' fast after the feast of St. Martin and before Easter. The conversation had to take place at the grille in the parlor or with special permission of the abbess at the "rota" or even at the window in the chapel; two discreets, as the counsellors of the abbess were called, had to be present so that they could hear the entire conversation. Even the abbess had to observe this rule.

Just as the nuns were not allowed to leave the enclosure, so, too, entrance was denied to everyone who did not belong to the community, no matter whether he was a religious, a cleric or a lay-person, unless he obtained permission from one authorized to grant it, the Pope, the Cardinal Protector, or the General or Provincial Minister of the Friars Minor, or he enjoyed a special privilege. Thus Cardinals were allowed to enter with a retinue limited to ten persons. The King of France obtained a similar privilege to enter the convent of Longchamp[116]. In cases of necessity all those whose assistance was required were permitted to enter. They were, first, the canonical visitor with two companions who must not lose sight of him; he could speak with individual nuns only in the presence, but out of the hearing, of these companions and at least two other discreet nuns; the bishop and as many ministers as were required were permitted to enter for the benediction of the abbess or the consecration of a nun or for the celebration of Mass, if special permission had been obtained; the chaplain or confessor to administer the sacraments and to assist the dying, always, however, in the presence of at least two nuns; even during the confession of the sick they must remain within

[116] *Bullarium Franc.* II 482

sight of the confessor and the sick nun, but out of earshot; finally the doctor or others whose help was required for a task that the nuns could not perform, e. g., for repairing the building, extinguishing a fire, burying a deceased nun. As long as any of these were within the enclosure, they must be accompanied by at least two nuns, who must not lose sight of them. No nun was allowed to speak with any person who had entered on such occasions, except by authority of the abbess, and no one of those persons was permitted to enter before sunrise or after sunset except in case of necessity; for instance, the doctor, if a nun was in immediate need of his care, or the confessor, if a nun was dying.

If friars did not act as chaplains and providers, a special arrangement was made whereby chaplains and conversi bound themselves to the convent by the vows of obedience to the abbess, of poverty and of chastity. They were bound to observe the fasts of the nuns, but lived outside the cloister.

From the beginning the Clares had Sister-servants who took vows, lived within the convent, but were not bound by the law of enclosure[117].

Substantially this is the form of cloister which has been observed by nuns with solemn vows since the thirteenth century. Later legislation has only defined a few points more clearly and imposed it as papal enclosure upon all nuns.

THE REFORM OF NICHOLAS OF CUSA.

In the preceding pages we have traced the early beginnings of the cloister, especially in the Benedictine Order. While mentioning a few of its branches, we have passed over the majority, since the cloister owes scarcely any characteristic to them. We must, however, make some reference to the great reform of monasticism in Germany and the Lowlands about the middle of the fifteenth century. It was authorized by Pope Nicholas V and carried out by Cardinal Nicholas of Cusa. It

---

117 Cfr. the five rules of the Clares: Gregorius IX, bulla *Cum omnis vera Religio,* 24 Maii 1239, *Bullarium Franc.* I 263-267; Innocentius IV, bulla *Solet annuere,* 13 Nov. 1245, ibid. 394-399; bulla *Cum omnis vera Religio,* 6 Aug. 1247, ibid. 476-483; bulla *Solet annuere,* 9 Aug. 1253, ibid. 671-678; Urbanus IV, bulla *Religionis augmentum,* 27 Julii 1263, ibid. II 477-486; bulla *Beata Clara,* 18 Oct. 1263, ibid. 509-521.

did not aim at a change of the rule, still less did it attempt to brance off from the old Order. It sought rather to correct violations of the rule and, by pointing out the time-proven standards, to forestall a new departure from the spirit of St. Benedict. In this reform the limits of the cloister were clearly defined. Thus in the Carta Reformationis monasterii Sti Mauritii Althe Inferioris (Niederaltaich) of February 1, 1451 (1452), the following is found: "We decree, that the 'septa' of this monastery shall be the church of the monastery, the entire building of the Lord Abbot and all the monastic places (regularia loca) and the whole curia within the inner door together with the cellars (officinis) and barns within the surrounding wall. . . ."[118] These places were reserved for the monks and they may not leave them except with permission of the abbot; neither may outsiders, especially women, enter them.

At St. Emmeran's, Ratisbon, processions were ordered limited to the highest feasts; even then women were not allowed to enter the cloister (n. 26); the singing-school for boys was removed outside the monastery (n. 18); public baths were to be avoided by abbot and monks and women were excluded from the monastery bath (n. 25)[119]. Other statutes, which reenacted previous legislation, were laid down at the visitation of this and other monasteries by the Cardinal or his delegates. These statutes served admirably to renew the spirit of the Order and soon monasteries in this country were in a flourishing condition again.

The regulations of the following century insisted principally on the observance of the law of cloister as prescribed by the Council of Trent.

When in later centuries congregations with only simple vows came into existence, there was no question of papal cloister, as was binding in religious orders. They are not orders in the strict sense and, therefore, are not bound by the same laws. Nevertheless, all have seen fit to enact statutes that

---

[118] Otto Grillenberger, *Zur Reformgeschichte des Benedictinerordens im XV. Jhrhdt.*, in *Studien und Mitteilungen* (1889) X 8.

[119] P. Benedict Braunmueller, *Zur Reformgeschichte der Klöster im XV. Jhrhdt.*, in *Studien und Mitteilungen* (1882) III Bd. I 315-319.

imposed the obligation of the enclosure, though these do not bind with the same severity. Some of these congregations have even obtained from the Holy See the privilege of papal enclosure as regulars observe. Such a privilege was granted by Alexander VII to the Fathers of the Christian Doctrine, December 8, 1660, and was extended by reason of a communication of privileges to the Congregation of the Most Holy Redeemer, and accepted by the General Chapters of 1764 and 1855[120]. By a privilege granted by Clement XIV in 1769, papal cloister has been introduced in retreats of the Passionists[121].

In all religious institutes, therefore, we find the enclosure observed from the beginning. Circumstances, especially the purpose of the order, introduced some modifications without touching its essentials. In the convents of nuns the seclusion is most complete, although this final development is quite late. Among the orders of men, those termed contemplative approached nearest to that, while among the so-called active orders those devoting themselves in a special manner to works of charity, were allowed greater freedom. Still all, even these latter, observed enclosure, at least in so far that they excluded persons of the opposite sex from those apartments which they reserved for themselves, and the religious were not permitted to leave their convent except with the consent of their superiors.

---

120 Cfr. Constitutions C. SS. R., n. 370.

121 Clemens XIV, litt. apost. *Supremi Apostolatus,* Nov. 16, 1769, s. 5, *Bullarii Romani Continuatio,* VII 73-79. Vide infra pp. 58-59, 105-106.

CHAPTER III.

Ecclesiastical Legislation on the Cloister

1. PRIOR TO THE COUNCIL OF TRENT.

a) *For Male Regulars.*

THE Church viewed the rise and spread of monasticism with satisfaction and hearty approval, for she beheld in the movement another bud springing from the seed sown by the Son of God. Monasticism was putting into practice the counsels of the Master to leave all and follow Him. Always a wise Mother, she let the various monastic founders develop their institutions according to their own character and, as long as their followers trod in their hallowed footsteps, she did not interfere. But, when laxity began to creep in, all her authority was put forth to crush abuses and by wise laws to lead the monks back to the observance of their proper mode of life. This she did also in regard to the rule of retirement from the world and from these laws there grew up in the course of time a complete legislation regarding the cloister.

From the beginning the monks enjoyed the highest esteem of the faithful, of the lowly as well as of those in high places. But some began early to abuse this regard and became a disturbing element at the court of Constantinople. Therefore, the Council of Chalcedon in 451 commanded that all monks who were in the capital without leave of their bishop be expelled from the city and forced to return to their monasteries[1]. This is probably the earliest legislation of the Church regarding the obligation of monks to reside in their monasteries. Similarly in 650 the Council of Chalonnais forbade abbots and monks, under pain of excommunication, to go to the court of the Frankish King[2]. When later, with the establishment of the Holy Roman Empire, the emperor gained an important position even in ecclesiastical affairs, the abuse of coming to

[1] C. Chalcedonense, can. 23 actionis XV, *Ss. Conc.* IV 765.
[2] C. Cabilonense (650), can. 15, *Ss. Conc.* VI 390.

the court had again to be condemned by the Council of Meaux in 845[3] and subsequently by the Council of Molfetta c. 1090[4].

The many incursions of the barbarians at the beginning of the sixth century compelled the monks to seek shelter within the city-walls and, therefore, the Council of St. Agatha in 506 permitted monasteries to provide a place of refuge within the city[5].

Although by this time the cenobitic form of ascetical life had definitely gained the preference over the eremitical form, still many who had begun their "conversion"—as taking up the ascetical life was frequently called—as cenobites felt attracted to the solitary life for the sake of greater seclusion and greater opportunity for contemplation and mortification. For such it was provided that they might build cells for themselves, but within the confines of the monastery, remaining under the obedience to their abbot. The abbot himself was not allowed to have such a cell[6].

Various councils inculcated anew, what was already laid down in the monastic rule: that monks might not leave their monastery except by leave of their superiors. As long as the monks were directly subject to the diocesan bishops, these latter must give the necessary permission[7]. Later, when monks had become exempt from the jurisdiction of bishops, this permission was to be granted by the abbot or other superior[8]. The Council of Autun in 670 prescribed that the abbot grant the permission by letters addressed to the archdeacon of the city[9].

---

[3] C. Meldense (845), can. 57, *Ss. Conc.* VII 1836-1837.

[4] C. Melphictense (c. 1090), can. 9, *Ss. Conc.* X 477.

[5] C. Agathense (506), can. 38, *Ss. Conc.* IV 1389.

[6] C. Agathense (506), can. 38, *Ss. Conc.* IV 1389. This permission to lead a form of eremitical life within the monastery and under the obedience of the abbot is repeated by several later councils.

[7] C. Venetense (461), can. 6, *Ss. Conc.* IV 1055. This canon seems to refer to permission for a protracted absence, as it stands to reason that the bishop could not be approached for permission for every short stay outside of the monastery; neither is it likely that the council meant to subject the monks so completely to the jurisdiction of the bishops.

[8] C. Aquisgranense (816), lib. I cap. 145, *Ss. Conc.* VII 1405; Synodus Augustana (952), cap. 5, ibid. IX 636; Synodus Coloniensis (1280), cap. III, ibid. XI 1110; C. Parisiense (1212), pars II, cap. XI, ibid. XI 66-67; C. apud Campinacum (Cognac) (1238), can. 22, ibid. XI 562; C. Coloniense (1260), cap. 9, ibid. XI 794.

[9] Canones Augustodunenses VI, *Ss. Conc.* VI 535.

Again and again the bishops directed that the permission must not be granted arbitrarily, but only for a good reason[10]. And the Council of Cologne of 1260 insisted that permission must not be granted too frequently, but not at all to leave the monastery from the time of Complin (which in those days was still chanted immediately before retiring), till Prime, for of all times night certainly was the most suspicious; "nisi causa valde rationabili et necessaria"[11].

Another source of abuses was the fact, that monks often went out alone without a companion of their order. Therefore, it was repeatedly enacted that, as often as a monk left his monastery, another monk should accompany him to be at once a guardian and a help for a faithful observance of their mode of life, as far as the journey permitted[12]. This matter was considered so important that Pope Gregory I already had refused his approval of one Constantius as abbot of St. Claude in the Province of Picenum, because he had made the journey to that abbey without a companion[13].

Worse even than this was the case of those monks who dwelt alone in priories, chaplaincies, villas and manors which belonged to the monastery, but were situated some distance from it. Repeated enactments required that two or three monks should reside in such places; if this were not possible, procurators should be authorized to look after such estates and secular priests provided as vicars in the chaplaincies[14].

---

10 "Urgente necessitate," C. Quinisextum (692), can. 46, *Ss. Conc.* VI 1165; "ut sine ratione decenti discurrere prohibeantur", C. Aquisgranense (836), cap. III can. 24, ibid. VII 1726; "omnes qui non habent officium speciale vel necessitatem aliam . . . sedeant in claustro", C. Biterense (1233), cap. 19, ibid. XI 458; "nisi primitus obtenta licentia . . .; quodque causam exitus veraciter et absque fictione exponat . . .", Constitutiones Benedicti XI pro reformatione Can. Reg. O. S. A. (1339), 20, ibid. XI 1822-1823; "nec sine certa et honesta causa", C. Oxoniense (1222), can. 44, ibid. XI 284-285; the Council of Cologne in 1536 renews the canon of the Council of Chalcedon requiring the bishop's permission to take up ecclesiastical or secular causes for "ingentes necessitates", pars X, cap. 15, ibid. XIV 554.

11 C. Coloniense (1260), cc. 9 et 16, *Ss. Conc.* XI 794-795.

12 C. Aquisgranense (817), cap. 15, *Ss. Conc.* VII 1508; C. Eboracense (1194), decr. 9, ibid. X 1794; C. apud Castrum Gonterii (1231), cap. 28, ibid. XI 443; C. Budense (Budapest) (1279), cap. 64, ibid. XI 1100.

13 Gregorius I, lib. X ep. 22 ad Joannem subdiac., *Ss. Conc.* V 1492-1493.

14 C. Parisiense (1212), p. II cap. 16, *Ss. Conc.* XI 68; C. apud Castrum Gonterii (1231), cap. 29, ibid. XI 443; C. Biterense (1233), cap. 25, ibid. XI 459; C. apud Campinacum (1238), cap. 30, ibid. XI 564; C. Albiense

From the beginning of monasticism convents conducted schools for the education of youth. A most worthy occupation of monks, it endangered the quiet and retirement of the monks, if the schools were situated within the cloister. The Council of Aachen in 817, therefore, forbade any schools within the enclosure except for the "oblati." The monasteries were not, however, compelled to discontinue their schools for others than candidates for the religious life, but placed them beyond the confines of the cloister. Thus that canon hastened the general introduction of the *scholae externae,* although before this time some monasteries already had such schools beside the *scholae internae*[15].

A council of Tours in 1163 forbade monks to live outside their monasteries in order to devote themselves to the study of law, medicine and other sciences and commanded those who were in attendance at universities at that time to return to their convents within two months; for it was recognized that such studies were sometimes mere pretense to withdraw from the obedience to the religious superiors and that such monks might easily fall a prey to the snares of the enemy of religious life[16]. It was decreed preferable that within the cloister monks should have every opportunity for the study of those sciences which might be of benefit to them. Such schools for the younger monks were prescribed for every monastery[17].

A good reason and permission to be outside of the monastery does not imply that a monk may make visits, as he pleases; a very special permission for making visits was required by the Council of Cologne in 1280[18]. In order to make his stay with

---

(1254), cap. 55, ibid. X 734; C. Londinense (1268), cap. 43, ibid. XI 901; C. Langesiense (1278), cap. 13, ibid. XI 1042; Synodus Eboracensis (1466), ibid. XIII 1430-1431; this synod inflicted a fine of 40 solidi · sterling upon any abbot who granted such permission; C. Senonense (1528), cap. 27, ibid. XIV 475; C. Coloniense (1536), pars X, cap. 13, ibid. XIV 554.

15 Conventus Aquisgranensis (817), cap. 45, *Ss. Conc.,* VII 1510; Hefele IV 25-26.

16 C. Turonense (1163), can. 8, *Ss. Conc.* X 1421; likewise C. Pariseense (1212), pars II, cap. 20, et pars III, cap. 20, ibid. XI 69, 75.

17 C. Biterrense (1233), cap. 21, *Ss. Conc.* XI 458.

18 C. Coloniense (1280), cap. III, *Ss. Conc.* XI 1110; the same was required by the constitutions of Benedict XI for the Reform of the Canons Regular of O. S. A. (1339), c. 13, ibid. XI 1818.

lay-people a monk needed the permission of the bishop, according to a decree of the Council of the Province of Rouen in 1279[19].

Just as monks were not free to go out as they pleased, so, too, the time for their return was not left to their choice, but was to be determined by their superior[20], with the proviso that they return in time to assist at Divine Office[21].

Discipline suffered, not only because the monks went abroad, but also because the proper safeguards, set up by the monastic founders, were not observed at the convent itself; nay, often the former condition was possible only because the latter were neglected. The Council of Mayence of 813 recognized that the canonical visitors had it in their power to prevent such neglect and commanded them to exert watchful care that the regulations regarding the cloister were faithfully observed[22]. It was further enacted that every monastery should have its cloister with all the arrangements for choir, chapter, refectory, dormitory, library, etc., necessary for the preservation of monastic discipline[23]. To insure the safety of the cloister, a porter had to be appointed, whose duty it was to see to it that no one went out without lawful permission and that visitors were received with due hospitality, yet so that their visits did not interfere with monastic observance. In order to avoid every violation of the cloister during the night, when neither monks were allowed to go out nor visitors to be received, the porter, upon having locked the door after Complin, was to bring the keys to the superior[24]. Secret doors and out-of-the-way nooks must of necessity fall under suspicion and one would hardly believe it necessary to issue a

---

19 C. apud Pontem Audomari (1279), cap. 14, *Ss. Conc.* XI 1047.

20 C. Oxoniense (1222), c. 44, *Ss. Conc.,* XI 284-285; Constitutiones Benedicti XI pro reformatione Can. Reg. O. S. A. (1339), 20, ibid. XI 1822-1823.

21 C. Coloniense (1260), cap. 17, *Ss. Conc.* XI 795.

22 C. Moguntiacum (813), can. 20, *Ss. Conc.* VII 1247-1248.

23 C. Turonense (813), can. 24, *Ss. Conc.* VII 1265; C. Aquisgranense (816), lib. I cap. 117, ibid. VII 1390; C. Meldense (845), can. 53, ibid. VII 1835-1836; C. Pontigonense (876), can. 8, ibid. IX 287; Alexandri II ep. fragmenta (c. 1060), ibid. IX 1153; C. apud Campinacum (1238), can. 21, ibid. XI 562.

24 Regula Canonicorum Chrodegaudi (Chrodegang) ep. Metensis (c. 800), *Ss. Conc.* VII 1457-1458; C. Aquisgranense (816), lib. I cap. 143, ibid. VII 1403-1404.

special prohibition of them, yet such is the tenor of a canon of the Council of Paris of 1212[25]. Hospitality and generosity towards the poor had been insisted upon by almost every founder of a monastic institution and had at all times been encouraged by ecclesiastical authority. But a pretense of hospitality might open the door to a spirit of worldliness, against which various synods protested vehemently and passed laws to eliminate that spirit and restore monastic quiet and discipline. Free access of lay-men to the monastery was forbidden, lest the monks be exposed to their insolence and the converting of monasteries into inns subordinate monastic discipline to temporal gain[26]. The Assembly of Aachen in 817 forbade the admittance of lay-men into the refectory of the monks. It also prohibited lay-men as well as secular priests to live within the monasteries[27]. The Council of Bexiers in 1233 forbade soldiers and other lay-people to be admitted to the cloister except for funerals, if there were a custom to that effect, or in case of necessity[28].

One danger above all others the Church endeavored to remove as far as possible from religious; it was that threatening the vow of chastity. She, therefore, sought to shield this virtue by insisting upon a faithful avoidance of the society of women and forbade abbot and monks to admit them into the monastery[29]. In a letter to the abbot Valentine, about 592, Pope Gregory I reproves him for allowing women to come into his monastery and, what is worse, for tolerating his monks to become godfathers and thus enter a spiritual relationship and often a dangerous association with the women who acted as godmothers, both of which he forbids under pain of the

[25] C. Parisiense (1212), pars II cap. III, *Ss. Conc.* XI 64.

[26] C. Caesaraugustanum (691), c. 3, *Ss. Conc.* VI 1313-1314; Monachorum Hydensium Leges (966), 13, ibid. IX 671; C. Parisiense (1212), p. I c. 16 et p. II c. 10, ibid. XI 62 et 66; C. Bitterense (1233), c. 23, ibid. XI 458-459; C. Burdigalense (1255), c. 12, ibid. XI 741; Roffiacense (1258), C. 10, ibid. XI 778; C. Coloniense (1536), p. X c. IX, ibid. XIV 553.

[27] Conventus Aquisgranensis (817), cc. 42, 52, *Ss. Conc.* VII 1510-1511.

[28] C. Bitterense (1233), c. 17, *Ss. Conc.* XI 457-458.

[29] C. Turonense (567), can. 16, *Ss. Conc.* V 856; C. Antisiodorense (578), can. 26, ibid. V 960; C. Augustodunense (670), can. 10, ibid. VI 535; Capitulum Provinciale monachorum nigrorum ad Westmonasterium (1422), ibid. XII 352.

severest penalties[30]. Even more severe is a letter of the same Pope to the subdeacon Authemius, wherein he condemns an abuse which at first appears to deserve to be judged less harshly. Because of a barbarian invasion many men with their wives had taken refuge in the monastery of St. Peter on the island of Orphiaria (Orphiana); nevertheless the Pope commands him to remove all these women from the monastery; but the command loses its harshness, when we note that the Pope calls attention to the fact that there were sufficient places of refuge otherwise on the island[31]. While some extenuation can be offered for the foregoing, there is no excuse for monks employing women as servants in their monasteries. Yet the Second Council of Nice in 797 was compelled to forbid such a practice[32]. Finally, Pope Leo VII in a letter addressed to Abbot Hugh of St. Martin of Tours acknowledged the difficulty encountered in the effort to keep women out of a certain corridor beside the church despite the building of a wall for that purpose and appreciates the good will of the monks; still he considers it his duty to oblige the abbot faithfully to observe the law of cloister[33].

b) *For Nuns.*

Previous to the time of Boniface VIII the Councils contain but a small number of canons that refer specially to the enclosure of nuns. Since the nuns were not generally obliged to a stricter cloister than monks, there was little reason to enact special laws for them: the regulations made for monks applied also to them. Perhaps, too, there was less cause for complaint against nuns. For custom, far from relaxing the religious observance, was gradually leading up to the strict enclosure prescribed for all nuns from the beginning of the fourteenth century. Still at various times councils took occasion to remind nuns that they were bound to remain within their cloister[34]. Since the abbess was appointed to enforce the

30 Gregorius I, lib. III ep. 40, *Ss. Conc.* V 1161—apud Gratianum: c. 20, C. XVIII, q. 2.

31 Gregorius I, lib. I ep. 48, *Ss. Conc.* V 1062.

32 Synodus Nicaena II (797), act. VII c. 18, *Ss. Conc.* VII 911.

33 Leo VII, ep. 1 ad Hugonem Francorum Principem et Monasterii Sti Martini Turonensis abbatem, *Ss. Conc.* IX 594-595.

34 C. Remense (1148), c. 4, *Ss. Conc.* X 1110.

religious observance, she had to reside in her convent and must not leave it except with permission of the bishop, unless it were to pay homage to her liege-lord[35]. The nuns were not permitted to leave their convent without a just reason and the permission of their abbess[36]. The abbess could not grant permission to her nuns to go out or to remain outside the convent over night, except on rare occasions and for weighty reasons; when she permitted them to leave the convent, she had to enjoin upon them to return without delay[37]. It was not at all lawful for nuns to make a pilgrimage to Rome or other holy places because of the dangers to which travelling in the company of men, which could not be avoided on such journeys, necessarily exposed them[38]. Neither were they permitted to stay with their relatives more than three days or, on account of sickness and the like, more than six days without special permission of the bishop[39].

Long before the twelfth and thirteenth centuries, when custom and the rules of some orders obliged nuns to remain in perpetual enclosure, particular laws as well as the rules of female orders forbade men to enter their convents. If necessity required that men be admitted into the enclosure, they must be of good character, some nuns must be appointed to receive them, but they were not permitted to speak with the visitors except what was necessary[40]. Bishops and priests who said Mass or attended the sick and the like within the enclosure, must be above reproach and advanced in years; they

---

[35] C. Vernense (755), c. 14, *Ss. Conc.* VI 1666; Capitulare Caroli M. (779), c. 3, ibid. VI 1824; Statuta Rhispacensia Frisingensia Salisburgensia (799-800), c. 27, *MGH LL II Capitul. Reg. Franc.* I 229; C. Moguntiacum (813), c. 13, *Ss. Conc.* VII 1245; C. Turonense III (813), c. 30, ibid. VII 1266; C. Cabilonense II (813), c. 57, ibid. VII 1284-1285.

[36] Caroli M. Capitula (789), c. 3, *Ss. Conc.* VII 989; C. Cabilonense II (813), c. 62, ibid. VII 1285; C. Londinense (1268), c. 53, ibid. XI 905-906.

[37] Constitutiones Galteri Archiep. Senonensis (†923), c. 5, *Ss. Conc.* IX 577.

[38] Ep. Sti Bonifacii ad Cuthbertum Archiep. Cantii (747), *Ss. Conc.* VI 1569; C. Foriorliense (791), c. 12, ibid. VII 1007.

[39] C. Lambethense (1281), c. 18, *Ss. Conc.* XI 1167-1168.

[40] C. Epaonense (517), c. 38, *Ss. Conc.* IV 1581; C. Matisconense (581), c. 2, ibid. V 967; C. Closheviae (747), c. 20, ibid. VI 1579; C. Foriorliense (791), c. 12, ibid. VII 1007; C. Arelatense (813), c. 7, ibid. VII 1236; C. Cabilonense II (813), c. 63, ibid. VII 1285; C. Aquisgranense (816), lib. II c. 20, ibid. VII 1433; C. Londinense (1268), c. 53, ibid. XI 905-906.

must not enter alone nor speak to any nun without witnesses and must leave the monastery as soon as their task was finished. They were not to speak with the nuns individually. If any nun wished to go to confession, it must be done in the church in the presence of the other nuns, except in case of sickness[41].

For the better direction of the nuns the Second Spanish Council of 619 ordained that monks be appointed to give them spiritual instruction and to provide for their spiritual and temporal needs; but they were not permitted to enter the nuns' convent or speak frequently or alone with any of the nuns[42].

Even regarding the admission of women employed as servants the greatest care was to be exercised; they were not permitted to roam about, dress unbecomingly or carry gossip into the convent nor might their number be greater than was necessary[43].

After the greatest dangers of scandal or suspicion had been met by the preceding regulations, such occasion for suspicion as might arise from visits received by the nuns was also put a stop to. All visitors were to be received in the parlor and even there a nun had to be attended by two or more elderly nuns[44]. This rule obliged even in case of a visit by parents[45]. Priests and monks needed the permission of the bishop to speak with nuns in the parlor of their convent[46]. Except for very urgent reasons, all visits in the evening after Complin until after Prime in the morning were strictly forbidden[47].

---

[41] Statuta S. Bonifacii Archiep. Mogunt., c.. 14, *Ss. Conc.* VI 1891; C. Foriorliense (791), c. 12, ibid. VII 1007; Statuta Rhispacensia Frisingensia Salisburgensia (799-800), *MGH LL II Capitul. Reg. Franc.* I 228; Caroli M. Capitulare (c. 804), *Ss. Conc.* VII 1182; Caroli M. Capitulare (813), c. 5, ibid. VII 1288 & 1290; C. Turonense III (813), c. 29, ibid. VII 1265-1266; C. Cabilonense II (813), c. 60, ibid. VII 1285; C. Aquisgranense (816), lib. II c. 27, ibid. VII 1436.

[42] C. Hispalense II (619), c. 11, *Ss. Conc.* V 1667.

[43] C. Aquisgranense (816), lib. II c. 21, *Ss. Conc.* VII 1433-1434.

[44] C. Matisconense (581), c. 2, *Ss. Conc.* V 967; C. Cabilonense II (813), cc. 55 and 61, ibid. VII 1284-1285; C. Parisiense (1212), p. II c. 1, ibid. XI 71; C. Herbipolense (1287), c. 3, ibid. XI 1321.

[45] C. Parisiense (1212), p. II c. 1, *Ss. Conc.* XI 71.

[46] C. Arelatense VI (813), c. 7, *Ss. Conc.* VII 1236; C. Parisiense (829), lib. I c. 46, ibid. VII 1627.

[47] C. Cabilonense II (813), c. 56, *Ss. Conc.* VII 1284.

Finally, even during the day, visits were not to be permitted except on rare occasions and for good reasons[48].

In the course of the twelfth and thirteenth centuries the enclosure of nuns became stricter. As we have seen, all the rigor of the cloister was prescribed in the statutes of the Cistercian Nuns and in the rules of the Dominican Nuns and the Clares; and we may justly conclude that the majority of nuns were observing an enclosure of a similar nature. But there were some who were exposing themselves to great dangers and laying themselves open to suspicion by reason of their too great liberty. We are not in a position to judge whether their rule or constitutions imposed an obligation of strict enclosure or not. Against those nuns Boniface VIII raises a solemn protest in his constitution "Periculoso," and with a view to putting an end to such disorders he commands all, who have made profession, to live in perpetual enclosure and forbids them to leave their monastery for any reason, unless one of them is an evident danger or scandal to the others. Neither should any persons not belonging to the community be permitted to enter the enclosure except for a manifest necessity and with the permission of the proper superior. Permission to leave is also granted for cases where the abbess is bound to appear personally at court to show homage to the liege-lord or in suits pending before his tribunals. Finally the Pope commands all ecclesiastical superiors to enforce his constitution. In convents subject to bishops they are to proceed in their own name; in convents immediately subject to the Holy See they are to act as its delegates; in convents subject to Regulars the superiors of the order are bound in holy obedience to build a suitable cloister and take steps to enclose the nuns as soon as possible; if the latter resist, they are to be compelled by ecclesiastical censures without appeal and, if necessary, the aid of the secular power is to be invoked[49].

This is the earliest general law of the Church that imposed the strict enclosure on all nuns and it has been the basis of all later legislation concerning the cloister of nuns. In the following century a number of Councils passed special canons

[48] C. Oxoniense (1212), c. 46, *Ss. Conc.* XI 286; Synodus Wigorniensis (1240), c. 36, ibid. XI 585.

[49] C. un., *de statu regularium,* III, 16, in VI⁰.

prescribing the observance of the law of the enclosure as ordained by Boniface VIII and inflicted penalties upon all who violated it, since the Pope had not fixed any. The penalty generally was excommunication[50].

So much for the ecclesiastical legislation regarding the cloister prior to the Council of Trent. It will be noticed that most of these enactments emanated from particular councils. While the sum total covers practically every phase of the enclosure, still only a small number have a wider application. The reason is, that in disciplinary matters councils generally restrict themselves to correcting abuses and it is not likely, that in the earlier ages of monasticism any one abuse was so widespread, as to merit condemnation by a majority of the councils. Nay, the councils themselves protested repeatedly, that only in rare instances did the abuses they censured exist. But the day came when the decline of monastic orders was more widely spread. The centuries immediately preceding the Council of Trent mark perhaps the lowest level which monastic discipline has reached in any age. Even the more recent orders did not entirely escape the prevailing tepidity and laxity. We must not, however, suppose that the decay of the religious life was complete and general. Amid the too frequent laxity there were in every age and country men who strove to realize the ideal of their state. Witness the many attempts at reforms. These did not proceed only from councils; more frequently the religious themselves endeavored to restore the observance of the rule in its purity. Then, too, when councils took the matter in hand, very frequently monks were the prime movers, as was the case at the Assembly of Aachen in 817, where St. Benedict d'Aniane sought and obtained the support of the bishops of the Frankish Empire, to carry out the reform he had already introduced into a number of monasteries. Again, when Cardinal Nicholas of Cusa at the command of Nicholas V undertook the monastic reform in Germany (c. 1450), monks were his ablest assistants. Neither can it be objected

---

[50] Synodus Baiocensis (1300), c. 92, *Ss. Conc.* XI 1463-1464; C. Coloniense (1310), c. 18, ibid. XI 1532; C. Ravennat. III (1314), rubr. 11, ibid. XI 1611-1612; C°. Ravennati IV (1317) rubr. 23 ab Archiep. adjecta, ibid. XI 1675-1676; C. Palentinum (1322) c. 12, ibid. XI 1694; C. Bituricense (1336), c. 6, ibid. XI 2524.

that these were abbots and priors, that the generality of the monks were not in sympathy with the movement; for usually we can judge the character of the monks by their abbots and priors. In fact abuses are almost invariably laid to the door of the religious superiors and, therefore, we conclude that there must have been a considerable number who strove zealously to live up to the ideal set up in their rule. A reform movement of so wide-spread an institution with such lasting effects could not have proceeded from a few scattered individuals[51].

The question forces itself upon us then, how it was possible for such abuses to arise. Three factors probably more than any others contributed to the collapse of monastic discipline in general and of the cloister in particular. By hard toil and careful management on the part of the monks and by frequent donations from lay-men many monasteries in the course of time amassed great wealth. This was employed in the interest of religion and works of charity. While these purposes were never entirely lost sight of[52], monastic wealth excited the covetousness of worldly-minded men and thus became the source of two other evils that gnawed at the vitals of monasticism. Frequently abbeys were bestowed "in commendam" upon seculars, both clerical and lay, whom persons in high places of Church or State desired to reward or favor. Nominally they were abbots; in reality their whole interest was centered on the revenues of their monasteries. Such "commendatory abbots" were not men who would hold their monks to monastic observance and keep out of the cloister worldly elements[53]. In the next place the younger sons of families, who could not succeed to their father's estates, were frequently shut up in monasteries, in order to provide a living for them, especially if the family enjoyed the right of patronage; thus hope for advancement was held out to them. This practice increased the number of monks, but they were not likely to be imbued with the true spirit and zeal of their institute and only too often went out to the world from which they had been thrust

---

51 Cfr. P. Benedict Braunmueller: ***Zur Reformgeschichte der Klöster im XV. Jhrhdt.*** in ***Studien u. Mitteilungen*** (1882), III Bd. I 311-321.
52 Montalembert I 59-73.
53 Montalembert I 80-84.

in many cases against their will and at the same time became a stumbling-block for many of their brethren[54].

Whenever a monastic reform was contemplated, one of the first steps was to drive out of the monasteries such persons as did not belong to the community, especially if they were women, and to insist more strictly that monks reside habitually in their monastery; that abbots and priors be less liberal in granting permission to go out, finally that the religious, when outside of the monastery, conduct themselves in a manner more befitting their state. In this way monasticism was prepared for the great reformation about to be inaugurated by the Council of Trent.

2. AFTER THE COUNCIL OF TRENT.

a) For Male Regulars.

The general law regulating the cloister in monasteries of men had its beginning in the Council of Trent. The reforms within the Benedictine Order, which had laid the axe to the root of most of the evils affecting discipline, demanded an almost entire exclusion of women from the monastery and a stricter residence of the monks. The more recent Orders do not seem to have suffered a serious relaxation of rule and discipline, but rather to have observed the enclosure as customary in the better disciplined monasteries of the older orders.

Even the Council of Trent did not enact any canons excluding women from the monasteries of men. Its regulations tended to restore a stricter residence of the regulars within their monasteries under the obedience to their superiors[55]. It is significant that the Council laid down no rules regarding the admission of those not of the community into the monastery.

Repeatedly the Holy See derogated from the obligation of the enclosure as contained in the rules or constitutions of various orders by granting certain women, especially those of the nobility, as a mark of favor, privileges by which they were allowed to enter the cloister of convents of male regulars. Far from serving any good purpose, such visits tended rather to

---

[54] Montalembert I 84-86, 432, 461 footnote 55.
[55] Conc. Trident., sess. XXV, *de regularibus,* c. 4.

distract the regulars from the service of God. Therefore, Pius V by his constitution "Regularium" of October 24, 1566, revoked all such favors and threatened women with excommunication reserved to the Holy See, if they entered the enclosure of male regulars on pretense of such a privilege, while regulars who admitted or introduced them lost all offices they held, were declared incapable of acquiring others and besides suspended.

But soon this same Pope made an exception. January 28, 1568, Cardinal Alexander Cribellus attested to a declaration of Pius V made by word of mouth, whereby on the one hand his constitution "Regularium" was extended, so that not only those women who pretended to have such a concession as was revoked by that constitution, but all were forbidden under the same penalties to enter the cloister of male regulars; on the other hand, the Pope permitted all women to enter the enclosure for the purpose of attending Mass or Divine Office and assisting at processions and funerals. Besides this, whenever the attendance at service in the monastery church was so great, that the faithful could not conveniently enter and leave by the main door of the church, women as well as others of the laity might use the door of the cloister, provided they entered and left the church directly and by the shortest way[56]. This declaration was embodied in the constitution "Decet" of July 16, 1570.

Starting from the premise that as soon as favors and indults granted by the Holy See become a source of inconvenience they ought to be revoked, Gregory XIII on June 24, 1575, issued his constitution "Ubi gratiae" in which he renewed the revocation of such privileges. Later the Congregation of the Council with the approval of Gregory XIII declared that privileges to queens and foundresses were not affected by this decree[57].

From two decisions of the same congregation of the year 1584 we learn, that there is no question of the cloister, while a monastery is in course of construction, as long as the community is not installed, even though a few regulars stay there

[56] Quaranta 404-405.
[57] Quaranta 405.

to supervise the work; nor in the case of a house which has neither church nor community[58].

In the constitutions "Cum de omnibus" of November 26, 1587, and "Ad Romanum spectat" of October 21, 1588, Sixtus V prescribed that no religious who was on a journey, even if it were to Rome to place an appeal before the Holy See, be received in any convent, unless he were well known or could present letters from his superiors establishing his standing. The reason for this law was that many criminals chose to conceal their identity under the guise of monks in order to prey upon the trust which the unsuspecting faithful placed in their supposed state or to escape the arms of justice. For it happened that even murderers were received under this disguise as guests by unwary religious.

In the constitution "Nullus omnino" of June 25, 1599, Clement VIII laid down in greater detail the conditions under which a regular might lawfully leave his convent. He also prescribed that no one be allowed to go to Rome, unless he had obtained permission in writing from the General or the Cardinal Protector of the Order. Reserving to the General or the Protector the power to grant permission to go to Rome might at times work a hardship; therefore, the Pope modified that law to the effect, that the provincial might grant the necessary permission for such a journey, but only for a matter that concerned the whole province[59].

Clement VIII in his decree "Sanctissimus Dominus" of May 26, 1593, § 1, n. 2, reckoned among those sins which superiors of religious orders might reserve to themselves, stealing out at night, which must of its very nature be suspicious.

Because in some places pretexts were invented to circumvent the laws of the Church forbidding women to enter the enclosure of male regulars, Benedict XIV on January 3, 1742, issued the constitution "Regularis disciplinae" in which he renewed all the previous papal laws, allowing an exception only in favor of those women who were considered foundresses or extraordinary benefactresses and of those who were related

[58] Quaranta 405.

[59] Clemens VIII, decr. *Decretum illud,* 10 Martii 1601, Vermeersch, *De Religiosis,* II 383.

by blood or marriage to reigning princes, provided they already enjoyed this exemption.

In some missions where but a small number of religious resided, women were admitted to all parts of the houses and their confessions were heard even in private rooms. By the decree "Cum deceat" of August 26, 1780, the Congregation of the Propaganda insisted on the observance of the enclosure wherever two or three religious habitually resided. By a declaration of March 5, 1787, this decree was restricted to houses that belonged to the mission and where two or three religious habitually resided.

The latest legislation regarding the enclosure of male regulars, previous to the new Code, was that contained in the constitution of Pius IX "Apostolicae Sedis" of October 12, 1869. According to § 2, n. 7, excommunication reserved to the Holy See was incurred by women who violated the enclosure of male regulars and by the superiors and others who admitted them.

For the Vatican Council the schema of a constitution "De Clausura" had been drafted and was to have been presented to the Fathers of the Council for consideration. But through the forced adjournment of the Council this, as so many other matters of great benefit to the Church, remained undone. In §§ 1 and 2 all the previous legislation regarding the cloister with but little change was concisely but clearly brought together to be re-enacted by the Council. In § 3 it was proposed that the law of enclosure be extended to congregations with only simple vows, unless some special reason of great weight should advise against its introduction; in this case special precautions against dangers and scandals were to be taken.

b) For Nuns.

In most convents of nuns the law of the enclosure that Boniface VIII had prescribed was faithfully observed. But at the time of the Council of Trent there was a small number that either refused to obey that law or had relapsed into their former disregard of it. The Council, therefore, renewed all the provisions of the constitution "Periculoso"[60] to which it

[60] C. un., *de statu regularium,* III, 16, in VI°; vide supra p. 43.

added that in cases of necessity the reason for the nuns' leaving their convent had to be approved by the bishop and permission for outsiders to enter had to be obtained in writing from him or another superior of the convent under pain of excommunication, if they entered without that written permission. Finally, the Council authorized bishops and other superiors to transfer the nuns to old or new convents within cities or towns; for in many instances their convents which were "established outside the walls of a city or town were exposed, often without any protection, to robberies and other crimes of wicked men."[61]

The mind of the Church was clear and it was the duty of the nuns to obey. However, they would not submit to the law of the enclosure and easily discovered obstacles in the way of its enforcement. On the one hand, they maintained that they were determined to observe their rule as it was observed when they made their profession, but that they would not tolerate new burdens to be imposed, since those they bore were already too heavy. On the other hand, some nuns were compelled, owing to their poverty, to go out begging for their sustenance[62]. Whilst providing for the latter, Pius V would not listen to the former. In his constitution "Circa pastoralis" of May 29, 1566, he commanded that the enclosure be observed in accordance with the laws of Boniface VIII and the Council of Trent in all convents of nuns; that all nuns who had made or should make profession be bound by those laws, even if these had not been observed before, or if they were not expressly bound to strict cloister by vow or rule; and that those who resisted were to be compelled by ecclesiastical penalties to observe it. Those who until then did not take solemn vows were to be persuaded to do so and to observe the strict enclosure; those that refused were barred from receiving candidates, so that their convent must become extinct. For the assistance of those in want, the Pope ordained that extern sisters, who were not, however, permitted to enter the cloister, be commissioned to beg alms for the nuns; if this means

[61] Conc. Trident., sess. XXV, *de regularibus*, c. 5.
[62] Pennacchi I 706.

did not suffice, the bishop and other superiors of the convents were to provide in any other suitable manner. Finally, the number of nuns in a convent should not be greater than could well be supported by its income or usual alms.

Clear and precise as this decree was, it did not obtain the desired effect. For still another loophole was found. The laws of Boniface VIII and the Council of Trent had allowed the nuns to leave their convent "for some lawful cause, which is to be approved of by the bishop," but neither had defined what constituted a lawful cause which the bishop could approve of. Bishops frequently yielded to the insistent requests of nuns and permitted them to leave their convents in order to visit their relatives or other convents subject to their own. If the purpose of the law was not to be frustrated, it was necessary that the causes which would justify a nun's leaving her convent be defined. This Pius V did in his constitution "Decori" of February 1, 1570. They were specified as fire, leprosy and epidemic. But the two latter causes had first to be approved in writing not only by the regular superior but also by the bishop, even if the convent were exempt from his jurisdiction.

Despite the efforts of Pius V to meet the needs of those nuns whose convents could not support them from their incomes, many convents still continued in extreme distress, so that some of the nuns were compelled to seek relief outside as best they could, while those who remained in their convents suffered direst want. In order to supply their needs the constitution "Deo sacris" of Gregory XIII (December 30, 1572) commanded that all those ecclesiastics whose office or benefice imposed upon them the obligation of distributing certain alms to the poor should devote half the amount to the needs of such nuns.

In the same constitution the Pope forbade that any door lead from the nuns' convent into the public church which was open to the laity and that the nuns leave the cloister door, even if it were only to close the outer door through which lay-persons were permitted to enter into the parlors, since these were located outside the enclosure.

In the papal constitutions up to this time it was ordained that, even in case of necessity, permission to enter nuns' cloister be obtained from the bishop or the regular superior. The question was, therefore, raised whether the latter themselves might enter at their pleasure or only in case of necessity. This question Gregory XIII decided in his constitution "Dubiis" of December 23, 1581, to the effect, that they were permitted to enter only for a real necessity and accompanied by a few elderly and religious persons. If bishops or even Cardinals acted contrary to this decree, they incurred interdict from entering the church for the first offense, suspension from pontificals and divine offices for the second, and excommunication for every further violation. Regulars incurred suspension and excommunication every time they entered unlawfully.

October 10, 1664, Alexander VII issued the constitution "Felici" for Italy and the adjacent islands, in which he prescribed the conditions under which regular superiors and confessors of nuns were permitted to enter their enclosure. (1) Regular superiors were permitted to enter the cloister for the canonical visitation not more than once a year, (2) unless they were accompanied by the bishop or some other secular ecclesiastic appointed by him; (3) they had to make the visitation personally and be accompanied by another member of their Order, the General being allowed two companions; (4) during the entire local visitation they had to be attended by four nuns, the personal visitation being made at the grille and outside the cloister. (5) Regular-confessors attended by a companion of their Order were permitted to enter the cloister to minister to the sick and the dying; (6) they were not, however, allowed to live near the nuns' convent, (7) unless the distance to their own was very great.

All these laws did not effect the observance of the enclosure by the nuns. Too frequently and for specious reasons they sought release from this burdensome seclusion to which they had bound themselves by their profession; besides indults were too readily granted to open the doors of the cloister to the nuns or to outsiders. It was against the former abuse that Benedict XIV directed his encyclical letter "Cum sacrarum" of June 1,

1741, to the bishops of Portugal. Some nuns of that country had invented specious pretexts, especially care for their health, to excuse their leaving the monastery and spent sometimes several years at a considerable distance from their convent to the detriment of religious modesty. He, therefore, commanded the bishops to oblige all such nuns to return at once to their convents under pain of the penalties for violation of the enclosure and, to forestall any recurrence of such conditions, he revoked the faculties of bishops to grant permission to nuns to leave the enclosure.

In the constitution "Salutare" of January 3, 1742, the same Pope renewed all the laws of his predecessors regarding the enclosure of nuns and revoked all permissions, privileges and indults granted by the Holy See to any persons whatsoever, including Cardinals, Papal Legates and Nuncios, by which they were permitted to enter the enclosure of nuns and, if any one dared to make use of such a faculty, he incurred the penalties inflicted for violation of the enclosure of nuns. January 24, 1747, Benedict XIV forbade that women be received as servents or as pupils into the enclosure without special permission of the Holy See[63].

Benedict XIV was earnestly endeavoring to bring about a strict and universal observance of the laws of the Church and enlisted the assistance of the bishops of the whole world. But he found that their efforts were frequently frustrated by endless recourses and appeals to higher authorities. In his zeal for the observance of the enclosure in nuns' convents he forbade any appeal from a decree or decision of a bishop regarding it[64].

At the Vatican Council no change in the existing laws was contemplated. In the schema of the constitution "De Clausura" it was proposed to renew the previous regulations. Neither did Pius IX introduce any change in the law itself. In part II, section 6 of his constitution "Apostolicae Sedis" of October 12, 1869, he inflicted excommunication upon all persons without distinction of class, condition, sex or age, who

[63] Benedictus XIV, ep. *Per binas,* 24 Jan. 1747.
[64] Benedictus XIV, ep. *Per binas,* 24 Jan. 1747.

entered nuns' enclosure unlawfully and upon all who admitted or introduced them; likewise upon all nuns who left the cloister in any other manner than permitted by the constitution "Decori" of Pius V. Henceforth this was the only censure incurred for the violation of the enclosure of nuns. It is the last papal law bearing upon the enclosure of nuns previous to the new Code of Canon Law and does not in any manner regulate the cloister itself. This has remained the same since the time of Boniface VIII. His successors contented themselves with renewing the existing legislation. At most they determined some points of that law to meet certain conditions that were threatening the enclosure.

c) *For Congregations with Simple Vows.*

We have seen that Pope Pius V had commanded all women who lived in community to take solemn vows and to observe the strict papal enclosure; if any refused, they were forbidden to receive candidates and any reception in opposition to his constitution was declared null and void[65]. Nevertheless some Tertiaries continued their community life after the manner of solemnly professed religious without taking solemn vows or living in strict enclosure. According to the law of Pius V their later receptions and professions ought to have been considered invalid. However, the Holy See tolerated them without giving canonical sanction to their institutes, even when it saw fit to approve their constitutions, and they were left entirely subject to the jurisdiction of the ordinary of the place[66]. Benedict XIV still adhered to this policy. For, when a question arose regarding the Institute of Mary or English Ladies, he would only acknowledge the sanction of their constitutions without the approval of their institute by Clement XI[67].

Even before the time of Benedict XIV a number of institutes had come into existence, whose avowed purpose was the care of the sick, infirm and orphans or the education of

---

[65] S. Pius V, const. *Circa pastoralis,* 29 Maii 1566; vide supra pp. 50-51.

[66] Benedictus XIV, *Institutiones eccl.,* XXIX 13, *Opera omnia* X 121-123; Lucidi II 245-247.

[67] Benedictus XIV, const. *Quamvis iusto,* 30 Aprilis 1749.

youth. The strict papal enclosure was out of question and, therefore, they had to forego the approval of the Holy See. However, the ravages wrought by the French Revolution were no mean factor in determining the Church to change her policy regarding such institutes. When peace was restored, the Church was compelled to yield to the intolerance of several European states which prevented nuns from taking solemn vows. She permitted these nuns to continue their religious life without papal enclosure[68].

With the passing of the strict enclosure from the convents of nuns who no longer made solemn vows there was removed the greatest obstacle that was seen to the approval of newer congregations whose chosen purpose could not be reconciled with it. In view of the many blessings that the latter were bringing to society to alleviate its suffering and to instruct the rising generation, the Church began to bestow the favor of her formal recognition upon them. In the matter of the enclosure no definite law was laid down. It was left to the bishop of the diocese[69] or to the constitutions of the various congregations[70] to determine whatever form of cloister they were to observe. In the draft of the constitution "De Clausura" (c. 6), it was proposed that the Vatican Council oblige bishops to impose episcopal enclosure by which sisters whose special purpose did not take them outside their convent should be forbidden to leave it as well as to admit outsiders; while those who were engaged with some extern occupation should be forbidden only to admit outsiders. But this constitution could not be presented to the Vatican Council before its forced prorogation.

The only general law of the Church obliging sisters with simple vows to observe enclosure was that contained in the constitution "Conditae a Christo" of December 8, 1900. In part II, § 4 Leo XIII entrusts the bishop with the care for

68 S. C. Ep. et Reg., in *Parisien.*, 1 Aug. 1839 ad 2 & 3, Bizzarri 86-87; Lucidi II 325.

69 Cfr. S. C. Ep. et Reg., in *Parisien.*, 1 Aug. 1839 ad 2 & 3, Bizzarri 86-87; in *Ravennaten.*, 18 Junii 1728, 23 Sept. 1757, et 10 Martii 1758, Lucidi II 325.

70 E. g. Filiae a S. Corde Jesu, who received the "decretum laudis" of the S. C. Ep. et Reg. May 14, 1841, Lucidi II 325-328.

the enclosure, episcopal or partial as the case may be, in houses of religious congregations of women, even if they are approved by the Holy See. In the "Normae" which the Congregation of Bishops and Regulars published June 28, 1901, as a guide for the framing of the constitutions for congregations that are desirous of obtaining the approval of the Holy See, numbers 170-177 suggest regulations for the enclosure[71]. They are fashioned after the enclosure of nuns with solemn vows, though not so strict as regards admission of outsiders and the sisters' leaving their convent.

---

[71] Vermeersch, *De Religiosis,* II 145-146.

CHAPTER IV.

Papal Cloister.

Canon 597, § 1.

What is known as the cloister dates back as far as monasticism itself. Before general or particular councils enacted any specific decrees, it was observed more strictly than now: men as well as women were barred from monasteries of either sex, nay, even from their churches[1]. In course of time this rule underwent considerable abatement, but to fresh pretexts for evading the obligation the Church by stringent laws opposed the minimum that must be expected. These laws, scattered over various papal constitutions with interpretations by the Roman Congregations, grew into a mass of legislation which became a source of obscurity. In many instances there was doubt whether a law was general or particular and how far the later law abrogated the earlier. This defect was recognized long ago; to correct it a draft of a constitution "De Clausura" precisely formulating the law of the enclosure was prepared for the consideration of the Vatican Council, but the untimely prorogation of this assembly stopped any action on the proposed legislation. It remained for the new Code of Canon Law to clear up the many difficulties.

The law of enclosure that is obligatory in houses of religious is contained in canons 597-607, 679, § 2, and the penalty for its violation in canon 2342.

Canon 597, § 1. In all the houses of Regulars, whether of men or women, canonically established, even though not formal, the papal enclosure must be observed.

In obliging regulars to observe papal enclosure this canon does not introduce a change in the laws enacted by the Popes, —especially those for male regulars by Clement VIII in the constitution "Nullus omnino"[2] and Benedict XIV in his con-

[1] Cfr. Benedictus XIV, const. *Regularis disciplinae,* n. 1.

[2] It is doubtful whether this constitution applied outside of Italy and the adjacent islands. Cfr. Vermeersch, *De Religiosis,* II 59-64.

stitution "Regularis disciplinae," and for nuns by Boniface VIII in the constitution "Periculoso" and by Pius V in the constitution "Decori."

By *regulars* are meant all those religious and those only who belong to a religious order strictly so called[3], by whatever name they may go, whether monks or friars or canons or clerks regular, whether nuns or canonesses[4]. At no time did the Church by general law oblige congregations with simple vows, whether approved by the Holy See or only by a bishop, to keep papal enclosure. A modified or disciplinary cloister was enjoined[5]. Nevertheless, as provided in the draft of the constitution "De Clausura" prepared for the Vatican Council, papal enclosure was extended to several congregations with simple vows upon application of the highest superiors. Such religious accept every obligation of the cloistral law and incur those penalties for their transgression that are contained in the papal grant. By a decree of Alexander VII of December 8, 1660, the Fathers of Christian Doctrine obtained the privilege of papal enclosure[6]. This was extended by reason of communication of privileges to the Congregation of the Most Holy Redeemer and accepted by its general chapters of 1764 and 1855. But the penalty for the violation of the cloister in Redemptorist convents is not the same as that contained in canon 2342 n. 2. Excommunication is incurred only by the Redemptorist who "dares," "audeat," to introduce a woman into the enclosure; a woman who enters does not incur any penalty[7]. Among the privileges which Clement XIV granted the Passionists by the apostolic letters "Supremi apostolatus" of November 16, 1769, papal enclosure is the fifth.

---

[3] Canon 488 n. 7.

[4] Ojetti, v. *Clausura*, n. 1163. Although the Jesuits do not for the most part take solemn vows, they are regulars (Paulus III, const. *Regimini*, 27 Sept. 1540, Wernz III n. 607) and are subject to the law of papal cloister. Hollweck 229 footnote 4. Those points contained in canon 597, which refer exclusively to nuns' cloister, will be discussed under canon 600. Vide infra pp. 104-107.

[5] Cfr. Leo XIII, const. *Conditae a Christo*, cap. 2, IV; Ojetti, v. *Clausura*, n. 1163; Pennacchi I 778-787; Mocchegiani I 199; Hollweck 229 footnote 4; Ayrinhac 267.

[6] *Brevia Apostolica Congregationi Patrum Doctrinae Christianae Concessa* (Romae 1749) 53.

[7] *Constitutiones C. SS. R.*, n. 370.

The penalty inflicted for the violation of the cloister in this concession approaches that of the Code. A woman who "dares or presumes," "audeat vel praesumat," to enter the cloister of a Passionist retreat or a person who introduces her incurs the same censures and punishments as are inflicted for the violation of the enclosure of male regulars[8].

If the law of the cloister is to be binding in a house of regulars, it must have been "canonically established," viz., erected with the approval of the Holy See and the written consent of the ordinary of the place. No house of regulars may be established in any other manner[9]. The name by which a house is known is of no consequence: monasteries, convents, hospices, residences or houses are all subject to the law of the enclosure, provided they are canonically erected and form the habitual residence of regulars[10]. It does not matter how many regulars thus dwell there; for it is expressly stated that the law of the enclosure binds even in houses not "formal." A religious house is "formal,"[11] if there dwell in it "at least six professed religious, four at least of whom must be priests if it is a house of a clerical institute"[12]. The law of enclosure continues, even if all the regulars are temporarily absent. For, once the cloister is established in a house by the habitual residence of regulars, it remains in force as long as the house continues to serve that purpose. True, when all the inmates are

---

[8] *Bullarii Romani Continuatio,* VII 73-79. Cfr. Praenotanda ad schema constitutionis *De Clausura;* Pennacchi I 778; Mocchegiani I 199; Hollweck 229 footnote 4; Ayrinhac 267.

[9] Canon 497 § 1. Cfr. Votum consultoris S. C. Ep. et Reg. in *Americana votorum,* 2 Sept. 1864, *Bizzarri,* 727-730.

[10] A decree of the Congregation of Bishops and Regulars approved by Pius VII Aug. 22, 1814, ordained: "Clausurae leges diligenter serventur in omnibus religiosis domibus, etiamsi hospitiorum vel domorum generalitiarum vel alio quovis nomine appellentur." Bizzarri 44; Pruemmer II 97.

[11] The term "domus formata", "formalis", was sometimes employed by authors to designate a house completed and permanently inhabited by a community to distinguish it from one in course of construction or from one that did not serve as an habitual, but only temporary, residence of religious, e. g., a grange, hospice, etc. Piatus, *Praelectiones,* I 351, cfr. 344; Hilarius a Sexten 192; Bachofen 159.

[12] Canon 488 n. 5. The term "domus formata" does not mean a "canonically" established house, as Charles Augustine, III 59, supposes. Cfr. canon 497 § 1.

absent, the purpose of the law ceases, but only by chance, a circumstance not recognized by the law[13].

While a dwelling is being erected for regulars, the law of enclosure need not be observed, even if one or the other regular stay continually on the grounds to supervise the work; for the building is not a "house of regulars," until the community is installed. Thus it was decided in 1584 by Cardinal Alexandrinus in the name of the other Cardinals of the Congregation of the Council[14]. Still, according to a declaration of the Congregation of Bishops and Regulars of October 4, 1588, while a convent is under construction, women may not be admitted to the actual living quarters of the few regulars who supervise the work, although the law of cloister is not yet in force. As soon, however, as the superior and his community take possession of the building, though it be not yet finished or inclosed by a wall, the law of enclosure goes into effect, and this applies to all parts of the adjoining forest, which the religious reserve for their own use[15].

A different condition arises if regulars reside in a rented building. This may happen, when they come to settle in a place and have not yet acquired permanent quarters, or in missionary countries on account of the poverty of the missionaries. In regard to the missions of China there is a declaration of the Congregation of the Propaganda of March 5, 1787, to its decree "Cum deceat" of August 26, 1780. By this decree

---

13 Cfr. S. C. de Religiosis, 29 Dec. 1909, ad V, where it was decided that women who enjoy a papal indult permitting them to enter hermitages of the Camaldolese Congregation of Monte Corona may not be admitted to the novitiate or the "professorium", even when the novices or the clerics are not present. A. A. S. II 62-63. Bonacina, *De Clausura etc.*, q. V p. II n. 7, whose argument against the cessation of the law, because per accidens the danger to be prevented ceases, is founded on the principle enunciated anew in canon 21; Hilarius a Sexten 195: "juxta plures"; Appeltern 248; Piatus, *Praelectiones,* I 358, where he quotes a number of authors holding the same view. As supporting the opposite opinion Piat cites: Pellizarius, *Manuale Regularium,* V, VI, 64, "ait id non esse omnino improbabile".

14 Quaranta 405.

15 Ferraris, v. *Conventus,* III 8. Appeltern, 241, footnote 6, says in this connection: "Cap. Gen. XLI, n. 10, Ordinis nostri, ad quaesitum: 'An monasterio nondum perfecto, introducto solum choro, et familia ibi constituta, debeat P. Provincialis curare, ut servetur clausura?'—Resp.: 'Affirmative. Nec differat illam declarare, licet differre possit clausuram horti dum iste nondum est circumdatus muro.'"

the Congregation had subjected missions where two or three religious habitually resided to the law of the cloister; by the later declaration this decree was restricted to houses owned by the mission; houses which are rented are free from the obligation of the enclosure. The same may be said of any house rented by regulars; such a house cannot be called the fixed residence of regulars and is, therefore, not subject to the law of the cloister[16].

Still less can there be question of the cloister in such houses as are not intended for *habitual* residence of regulars, in case they are outside the enclosure-wall of the monastery. Granges, villas and the like, which some orders maintain for special purposes, as for recreation or recuperation after an illness, do not fall within the law of enclosure, even when a number of regulars are staying there. For in no sense are they canonically erected houses of regulars: they have neither church nor community[17]. Notwithstanding which, regulars ought to be cautious in admitting women even into such houses[18]. Hence the General Constitutions of the Franciscan Order ordain: "He who permits women to enter our hospices should be severely punished by the Minister Provincial."[19] If, however, a regular community dwelt there, the law of the cloister would

---

16 Cfr. Vermeersch in *Catholic Encyclopedia,* v. *Cloister,* IV 60. This ought not to be applied to a religious house that has been "secularized" by an impious government and sold to some individual who rents it out to the regulars for their use. For, generally, the parties concerned hold such "renting" more specious than real. But if the government uses the greater part of the confiscated monastery for municipal purposes and allows a handful of religious to occupy a small wing, it can hardly be said that cloister must be observed even in the section left to the regulars, since the monastery is open to all and the regulars themselves are considered, not so much as religious, but rather as rectors of the church. Thus Pennacchi I 802; Mocchegiani I 203-204. On the other hand, Cappello asserts that the Congregation of Bishops and Regulars has more than once declared that in such cases male regulars are bound to observe partial enclosure as far as possible. Cappello, *De Visitatione,* II 441. Vermeersch is of the opinion that one or two regulars could very well keep up the enclosure, albeit the rest of the community had been expelled. Vermeersch, *De Religiosis,* I 179.

17 Quaranta 405; Vermeersch, *De Religiosis,* I 176; Appeltern 241; Charles Augustine III 311.

18 Bonacina, *De Clausura etc.,* q. V p. I n. 2.

19 "Gravi quoque poena a Ministro Provinciali plectatur qui mulieres in hospitia nostra ingredi permiserit." *Constitutiones Generales O. F. M.,* n. 213.

have to be observed, presuming, of course, canonical erection[20].

The test laid down by Pruemmer for Dominicans[21], whether there is an obligation of enclosure in a house: if there is obligation of choir, there is also an obligation of keeping enclosure, whereas, if there is, as a rule, no choral obligation, there is none of heeding the law of cloister, will not hold good as a general principle. According to canon 610 § 1 the obligation of *choir* begins, indeed, with the habitual residence of *four* regulars bound to recite the office in choir—and in this case usually one or two lay-brothers also reside in the house, bringing the number of regulars there up to five or six—nevertheless Pruemmer admits that the law of *enclosure* must be observed even in houses where only *three* regulars reside[22].

The question then arises whether there is an obligation of observing cloister in a house of fewer than three inmates. Mocchegiani inclines to the opinion that, with but one or two regulars living in a house, there can scarcely be any obligation of enclosure, since such a house cannot be called a monastery or convent[23]. Mocchegiani adds that Laymann, following Sanchez, restricts this freedom from enclosure to a place of temporary residence[24]. Alphonse of Liguori[25], Ojetti[26] and Koeck[27] accept this view. Appeltern, speaking of granges, hospices, etc., says in a footnote: "Authors more commonly except [i. e., admit an obligation of enclosure in] hospices in which some (at least three) permanently lead the life of regulars in common peculiar to convents, whether or not they have

---

20 Mocchegiani I 197; Appeltern 241.

21 " . . . (pro nobis Fratribus Praedicatoribus)." Pruemmer II 97, based on a statute of the chapter of 1640 which is still in force and obliges the chanting of the office in choir, if three friars who are obliged to choir are present.

22 Pruemmer II 97.

23 Mocchegiani I 203. Whatever its weight in the past (cfr. Bonacina, *De Clausura etc.*, q. V p. II n. 1), this point of name can no longer be pressed, for the Code speaks of *houses*. Perhaps the word "conventus" is to be taken in the sense of "community" and one or two can hardly be said to form a "community."

24 Laymann lib. IV tr. V c. 12 n. 5, quoted by Mocchegiani I 203.

25 S. Alphonsus de Ligorio lib. VII c. II n. 231.

26 Ojetti, v. *Clausura*, n. 1178.

27 Koeck 44, footnote 4.

a church with the Blessed Sacrament."[28] From this it follows that it is at least not certain that the law of enclosure binds in houses where not more than two habitually reside.

Canon 597, § 2.

The law of papal enclosure affects the whole house inhabited by the Regular community, including the orchards and gardens the access to which shall be reserved[29] to the religious, but excluding the public church with its[30] sacristy, the guest-house, if there be one, and the parlor, which last should, where possible, be situated near the entrance of the house.

In this paragraph is set forth which parts of regular houses are affected by the law of enclosure. First of all, the entire house inhabited by the regular community: the private cells or the dormitory, the refectory, kitchen, infirmary, the cloister in the architectural sense, the cellars, library, study and recreation rooms and other similar apartments[31].

Besides the house usually a plot of ground, a garden, grove or orchard is reserved to the regulars for the purpose of recreation, exercise and the like. This space immediately adjoins the house and usually a wall encloses both house and garden. All space thus reserved for the use of the regulars and surrounded by the enclosure-wall comes within the cloister. It does not matter that the garden have an entrance also from without, e. g., from the street: it still remains part of the monastery and

---

28 "Ad communius excipiunt hospitia, in quibus aliqui (saltem tres) semper permanent modo regulari et collegialiter ad instar aliorum conventuum, quamvis non habeant Ecclesiam cum Eucharistia." Appeltern 241, footnote 2, where he quotes Th. Fr. Rotario, *Theologia Moralis Regularium,* t. II l. II c. III p. I n. 8; Salmanticenses, *Cursus Theologiae Moralis,* tr. XV c. V n. 181; Antonius a Spiritu Sancto, *Directorium Regularium,* tr. III disp. VI n. 704; Hyac. Donatus, *Rerum Regularium Praxis Resolutoria,* t. I p. II tr. III q. VIII n. 1. Cfr. Sleutjes 283.

29 "Shall be reserved" ought to read "is reserved," "reservatis."

30 "Continente", "contiguous", of the Latin is omitted in the *Authorised English Translation* and must be supplied.

31 Ferraris, v. *Conventus,* III 9; Mocchegiani I 195; Ojetti, v. *Clausura,* n. 1178; Pennacchi I 775; Matthaeucci 102; Lucidi II 149; Hilarius a Sexten 193; Reiffenstuel lib. III tit. XXXV nn. 26 & 27; Bonacina, *De Clausura etc.,* q. V p. I n. 1; Piatus, *Praelectiones,* I 351; Leitner 410; Blat 585-586; Charles Augustine III 311-312.

is always considered such[32]. But, if the garden is entirely separated from the house, for instance, by a public thoroughfare, it is not subject to the law of enclosure[33].

Pruemmer goes too far, when he says: "Pariter sub clausura continentur hortus, sacristia et chorus religiosorum, si nonnisi transgrediendo clausuram ad ista loca perveniri potest; sin autem e loco clausurae non subiecto aditus patet, tunc hortus, sacristia et chorus iuxta probabilem et in praxi tutam sententiam non continentur in clausura."[34] It is true, the sacristy and choir in the latter hypothesis do not come within the cloister. But the garden reserved for the regulars lies within the enclosure, even when there is a way of entering it without passing through the cloister, provided the garden be immediately and directly accessible from the house. Neither will the authorities he quotes bear him out. Suarez, tr. VIII, lib. I, 7, 2, speaks only of the sacristy and the choir. Ferraris, under the word *Conventus,* art. III n. 13, refers only to the sacristy; in n. 10 under the same title he states: "The gardens and fields that are united with the convent, as also the cloister, come under the name of the enclosure, so that women who enter them incur excommunication."[35] As authorities he quotes S. C. Ep. et Reg., *in una Dominic.,* 24 Apr. 1582, *in Laudensi,* 13 Sept. 1583, in *Arben.,* 3 Junii 1606. In n. 11 Ferraris continues: "Otherwise [i. e., they are outside the cloister], if the same gardens and fields are separated from the enclosure by special [convenienti] key and wall."[36] Ferraris' view regarding the garden is adopted by Pennacchi[37] who (on page 776) treats only of the choir and sacristy[38]. Moreover, Matthaeucci, in

[32] S. C. Ep. et Reg., *Ordinis Praed.,* 24 Aprilis 1582, in *Laudensi,* 13 Sept. 1583, in *Arben.,* 3 Jan. 1606, Ferraris, v. *Conventus,* III 10; Bonacina, *De Clausura etc.,* q. V p. I n. 6; Mocchegiani I 195; Lucidi II 149-150; Piatus, *Praelectiones,* I 352, who adds in footnote 2; "S. Congr. Episc. et Regul., die 1 Junii 1685, declaravit poenas incurri, si mulieres adultae in ea (scil. hortos et viridaria) ingrediantur. (Bullarium Capucinorum I 131)."

[33] Ferraris, v. *Conventus,* III 11.

[34] Pruemmer II 98.

[35] "Viridaria, seu Horti, et Prata cum Conventu, et Claustra conjuncta veniunt nomine Clausurae, ita ut mulieres ipsa ingredientes excommunicationem incurrant." Ferraris, v. *Conventus,* III 10.

[36] Ferraris, v. *Conventus,* III 11.

[37] Pennacchi I 775.

[38] Passerini, *de stat.,* 189, 8, 375; S. C. Ep. et Reg., 1 Martii 1836, the other authorities quoted by Pruemmer, I have not been able to verify.

answer to the question about gardens accessible from the public highway, states that, if the regulars may enter them without asking leave of their superior, such gardens are part of the cloister and forbidden to women; but if regulars may not go into them without special permission, they are outside the enclosure; hence women are allowed to enter, even though the religious can enter by an entrance other than that from the street. His reason is that such gardens are considered to be outside the enclosure, a view confirmed by the practice and customs of regulars who need no permission of their superior to go about within the cloister[39]. Reiffenstuel mentions, as an example of a place that belongs to the "necessary cloister" or which is determined by law and which the superior can not remove from the enclosure, the gardens that are within the wall of the convent[40]. Most conclusive is the decision of the Congregation of the Council in *Ferentina* of April 5, 1794, confirmed February 20, 1796, which is cited in the footnotes of the Code among the documents bearing on this canon. In this case a "hortus frigidus" lay within the enclosure-wall, but was shut off by an inner door always kept locked from the remainder of the enclosure reserved for the religious. A special reason for excluding this "hortus frigidus" from the cloister seemed to be found in the fact that in it were the stables, barn, chicken-house and lodgings of the servants. Nevertheless the Congregation decided in both instances, that the "hortus frigidus" lying within the wall of the enclosure was comprised within the cloister, the old custom notwithstanding[41].

Therefore, the conclusion is (a) that gardens, etc., directly attached to the house and to which the regulars have free access, belong to the enclosure[42]; (b) that gardens are only

39 Matthaeucci 102.

40 Reiffenstuel lib. III tit. XXXV n. 27; Mocchegiani I 198.

41 Pallottini, v. *Regularium Monasterium,* II 15.

42 Pennacchi I 775; Ojetti, v. *Clausura,* n. 1178; Piatus, *Praelectiones,* I 352; Ballerini IV 94; Appeltern 246; Lucidi II 149-150; Hollweck 229, footnote 3; Hilarius a Sexten 193; D'Annibale, *Comment.,* 85; Blat 585; Biederlack 234, who states: "Ex can. 597. § 2. patet, quaenam conventuum aut domorum spatia clausurae subsint, ea scilicet spatia, quae ordinariae religiosorum commorationi inserviunt adeo ut quamdiu intra ea spatia commorantur, extra domum versari non dicantur. Hinc clausurae subest non tantum aedificium ad habitationem destinatum, sed etiam hortus, officinae, aliaeque attiguae domus, ad quae liber religiosis patet accessus; imo etiam silva attigua, si religiosis in ea libere commorari licet."

then outside the cloister, when they are separated in some manner from the enclosure, e. g., by a wall or street. With this solution the conclusion of Pruemmer, viz., that in determining the enclosure a distinction must be made between the egress of the regulars and the entrance of women, becomes untenable, except as it applies to the sacristy and choir[43].

From the law of enclosure the Code exempts the public church. In early monasticism the church was as a rule closed to the laity; it was only after the rise of the Mendicant Orders[44], that it was everywhere thrown open to men and women[45]. Since then the public church, that is, one that can be entered directly from the street without passing through the cloistered space of the monastery, was always judged outside the enclosure[46]. However, an inner church, i. e., a church or chapel accessible only by way of the enclosure, is subject to the law. In missionary countries greater freedom is allowed: women may go to the inner church or chapel to attend Mass and other services or to make their confession, but they must enter and leave by the shortest way through the enclosure, without loitering at the private apartments of the mission[47].

Where the sacristy had no ingress but by way of the cloister, such sacristy was part of the enclosure, hence forbidden to women[48]. This still holds good, for such a sacristy is not contiguous to the church. Again there can be no question of a sacristy being part of the enclosure, if the only approach to it is from the church[49]. But what if the sacristy has two entrances, one from the convent and the other from the church? Ferraris cites several rescripts of the Congregation of Bishops and Regulars, in which it declared that the sacristy was subject to

---

[43] Pruemmer II 98-99. In the second edition of his *Manuale* he does not repeat this contention. Pruemmer² 288-289.

[44] Sebastianelli, *Praelectiones J. C., De Personis*, Romae 1905², 408.

[45] Cfr. Pius V, const. *Decet;* Benedictus XIV, const. *Regularis disciplinae*, n. 1; Pennacchi I 776; Hollweck 229; Vermeersch, *De Religiosis*, I 176.

[46] Blat 586.

[47] S. C. de Prop. Fide, decr. *Cum Deceat*, 26 Aug. 1780.

[48] Bonacina, *De Clausura etc.*, q. V p. I n. 4; Ferraris, v. *Conventus*, III 12; Piatus, *Praelectiones*, I 352; Charles Augustine III 312.

[49] Bonacina, *De Clausura etc.*, q. V p. I n. 4; Ferraris, v. *Conventus*, III 12; Mocchegiani I 195; Piatus, *Praelectiones*, I 352.

the law of the enclosure. On April 28, 1605, the Congregation declared: "Sacristia comprehenditur sub clausura"; and August 10, 1615: "Sacristia choro contigua alicujus monasterii religiosorum sub clausura comprehensa."[50] A decree of the same Congregation on June 1, 1685, subjected the sacristies of Capuchin monasteries to the law of enclosure[51]. Nevertheless Ferraris states that almost universal custom is to the contrary[52], and Pennacchi acknowledges that custom has changed the previous law and that the sacristy need no longer be considered subject to the law of the enclosure[53].

This custom is now established as positive law by the Code. If the sacristy adjoins the public church, it must be considered as part of the church and, therefore, outside the enclosure[54]. Still regulars ought to limit the admission of women to cases of real need, especially while the clergy are vesting for service or when time and circumstances would lend color to suspicions.

The Code does not make mention of the choir. There never was any serious doubt that in monasteries of male regulars it was outside the enclosure. Bonacina voices as the common opinion that the choir is not subject to the law of cloister, because it is part of the church[55]. This holds, if the choir is accessible from the church. If, however, the only means of ingress is through the cloister, then the choir lies within

---

50 Ferraris, v. *Conventus,* III 14.

51 Bonacina, *De Clausura etc.,* q. V p. I n. 4; Matthaeucci 102-103; Mocchegiani I 196-197; Pennacchi I 777, who prints the decree in extenso. Appeltern 246, footnote 5, states that in answering the question whether sacristies of Capuchin monasteries having a door leading into the church and another into the cloister were included within the enclosure, the Congregation of Bishops and Regulars on March 1, 1836, approved of their observing enclosure in such sacristies; and that the Congregation commanded the Provincial to enforce the observance of enclosure in such sacristies.

52 Ferraris, v. *Conventus,* III 15.

53 Pennacchi I 777-778; Mocchegiani I 196; Ojetti, v. *Clausura,* n. 1178; Piatus, *Praelectiones,* I 352-353; Ballerini IV 94; Hollweck 229, footnote 3; Vermeersch, *De Religiosis,* I 176; Reiffenstuel lib. III tit. XXXV n. 27; D'Annibale, *Comment.,* 85. But Matthaeucci (102) and Bachofen (152) held the opinion that, if a door lead from the cloister into the sacristy, the latter was subject to the law of enclosure, even though another door opened into the church.

54 Charles Augustine III 312; Leitner 410; Blat 586; Cerato 121.

55 Bonacina, *De Clausura etc.,* q. V p. I n. 3; Pennacchi I 776; Mocchegiani I 197; D'Annibale, *Comment.,* 85; Cavigioli 106.

the enclosure[56]. The reason why sacristies and choirs are not necessarily embraced by the law of enclosure lies in the fact that there is, as a rule, little or none of that danger which the institution of the cloister is to guard against. Yet superiors would act quite within their rights, if they enclosed the sacristy or choir, the more so if conditions made it advisable.

If a monastery has a special house to shelter guests enjoying the hospitality of the regulars, this guest-house is not subject to the law of cloister; it is not at all intended for the regulars and is situated apart from the cloister[57].

Besides the porter-house every monastery needs a parlor to receive visitors calling on business or to see relatives among the regulars. Such parlors are the offspring of custom and, although within the monastic building, they were open to outsiders, which placed them legally beyond the cloister. Hence the regulars themselves did not have free access to them[58]. The Code recognizes this custom. For obvious reasons parlors should be near the entrance to the convent: the farther they are from the entrance, the more space of the monastery must be cut off from the cloister. As to the number of rooms to be set aside as parlors, no fixed rule can be laid down; the number of regulars in the convent as well as the frequency of visitors received must be decisive. The judgment is left to the prudence of the superiors, as provided in the following paragraph[59].

From the foregoing it will be seen that some places must be enclosed, while others must be outside the enclosure. As to these two classes superiors have no further liberty than to determine their extent. The refectory, for instance, must be inside the enclosure, and there can be no reason for placing it outside. The same is true of the kitchen[60]. This would not

---

[56] Bonacina, *De Clausura etc.*, q. V p. I n. 3; Mocchegiani I 197; Pennacchi I 776; Piatus, *Praelectiones,* I 353; Appeltern 246; Hollweck 229, footnote 3; Reiffenstuel lib. III tit. XXXV n. 27.

[57] Cerato 121; Leitner 410; Blat 586; Cavigioli 106.

[58] Ojetti, v. *Clausura,* n. 1178; Ballerini IV 94; Hilarius a Sexten 193; Vermeersch, *De Religiosis,* I 176.

[59] Cerato 121; Blat 586; Leitner 410.

[60] Reiffenstuel lib. III tit. XXXV n. 27; Mocchegiani I 198; Ojetti, v. *Clausura,* n. 1179.

apply, if through lack of competent cooks in the community laypersons were employed in this capacity. For then it would no longer be reserved for the exclusive use of the regulars, but would rather be governed by canon 599. The limits of some of these precincts are set up in the building itself; of others the boundaries must be specially defined. The garden adjoining the house must be enclosed: in this respect superiors have no choice; but how much is to be allowed for the use of the regulars, the superiors must decide, due regard being paid to the needs of the community. Likewise regarding the parlors.

One might ask how far the freedom of superiors extends, as to including within the cloister or excluding from it such parts of the monastic building, as are not directly touched by the Code. Ballerini[61] and Hilarius a Sexten[62] follow Sanchez[63] in acknowledging a custom which would permit superiors to exempt a vestibule from the enclosure, so that women might enter it. However, a decision to the contrary was given by the Congregation of the Council, April 18, 1750. Between the church and the convent of the Friars Minor Conventual at Urbania there was a vestibule (atrium) with four doors: one from the street, another into the church, a third into the chapel of the Poor Souls and the fourth into the monastery. This last had hitherto been considered the cloister door. Until the bishop of the diocese had forbidden women to enter this vestibule, it had been customary to conduct processions through it, in which men and women took part. The religious appealed from the decree of the bishop to the Congregation of the Council, which upheld the bishop in his contention that said vestibule was subject to the law and closed to women[64]. In view of this decision it would seem that superiors are not free to exempt any part of the monastery from the enclosure but those mentioned in canon 597 § 2 and those coming under canon 599 § 1. Under given conditions a vestibule might well be counted a part of the parlor and, therefore, placed outside the enclosure.

---

[61] Ballerini IV 94.
[62] Hilarius a Sexten 193.
[63] Sanchez L. VI c. 17 n. 18.
[64] Pallottini, v. *Regularium Monasterium,* II 16.

The same holds good for any part of the garden which is surrounded by the cloister-wall. The entire plot enclosed falls under the law of enclosure.

Canon 597, § 3.

The parts of the house subject to the law of enclosure must be clearly indicated; it pertains to the higher Superior or to the General Chapter according to the constitutions, or, in the case of a monastery of nuns, to the Bishop, to determine exactly the limits of the enclosure or to modify them for lawful reasons.

That both the regulars and those not belonging to the community may know where the cloister begins, signs must be posted to make it clear what parts beyond these limits are reserved exclusively for the regulars. Any sign that will safeguard the cloister and keep out women will fulfill the requirements of the law. Blat[65] considers the sign "CLOISTER," "CLAUSURA," sufficient. Charles Augustine[66] thinks such signs as "PRIVATE ENTRANCE" or "POSITIVELY NO ADMITTANCE" will do. Perhaps it would be better to unite the two suggestions and have the sign read: "CLOISTER: NO ADMITTANCE." Such a sign would express more clearly what this paragraph requires, for even those who are not aware of the strict law in the matter will readily understand that this sign has a very special purpose. A more explicit sign would be advisable at an entrance where a porter cannot constantly be stationed.

Here the question naturally arises whether it is necessary that a barrier shut off the parts protected by the law of enclosure. In other words, must a door separate the parlors from the cloister? Must a fence, wall or moat surround the garden, etc., reserved for regulars?

Custom as well as the respective rules of various orders have always surrounded the reserved space with a wall or other barrier and the decrees of the Popes always presuppose

---

[65] Blat 586.
[66] Charles Augustine III 313.

the existence of the "septa."[67] Matthaeucci interprets the meaning of "septa" so strictly, as to suggest his belief in the necessity of an enclosing wall[68]. Defining the word "enclosure" Pennacchi says: "By the name cloister (clausura) of convents . . . is understood the whole space contained within the walls (septa) of the monastery or convent."[69] In a footnote he quotes an almost identical definition by Bonacina[70], which in turn is accepted by Mocchegiani[71]. Therefore, Lehmkuhl holds that the reserved space must be enclosed by a wall or some similar barrier that will so effectively prevent unlawful entrance, as to necessitate the use of force, unless the porter open the door[72]. On the other hand Vermeersch favors the opinion of Passerini, that any visible sign which indicates the beginning of the cloister suffices[73]. This latter view gains weight, when it is remembered that the cloister does not cease, if by accident the wall has collapsed, "because the foundations always remain, which are the limits of the already established cloister."[74] Furthermore on October 4, 1588, the Congregation of Bishops and Regulars decided that the law of cloister goes into effect as soon as the regular community has entered the new convent, albeit the building is not yet finished or surrounded by a wall, moat or fence[75]. Finally, in the decree ordering Capuchins to enclose their sacristies, that Congregation takes exception to the view of many who "assert that the sacristy, gardens, orchards and woods contiguous to the monastery, both those that are *open* as well as those that are

---

67 Cfr. Benedictus XIV, const. *Regularis disciplinae;* Pius V, const. *Decet;* S. C. Ep. et Reg., 4 Oct. 1588, Ferraris, v. *Conventus,* III 8 (in Latin: Pennacchi I 768-769).

68 Matthaeucci 102.

69 Pennacchi I 775.

70 Bonacina, *De Clausura etc.,* q. V p. I n. 1.

71 Mocchegiani I 195. Cfr. Ojetti, v. *Clausura,* n. 1178; Bachofen 151-152; Hilarius a Sexten 193.

72 Lehmkuhl in *Kirchenlexikon,* v. *Clausur,* III 445.

73 Passerini, *De Hominum Statibus,* III 461, n. 376, quoted by Vermeersch in *Catholic Encyclopedia,* v. *Cloister,* IV 60. But cfr. Vermeersch, *De Religiosis,* I 176, where he adopts the common definition of the enclosure and seems to demand a surrounding wall.

74 Matthaeucci 102. In 1671 the General Chapter of the Capuchins (XXXVII n. 3) declared itself to that effect. Appeltern 248, footnote 3.

75 Ferraris, v. *Conventus,* III 8.

surrounded by a wall or fence, are not comprised in the cloister," and forbids the admittance of women to those places[76].

The opinion that a wall is not essential seems to be upheld by the Code which does not mention any further precaution than that the enclosure be "clearly indicated."[77] Still there can be no doubt that the rearing of a wall or fence is more in harmony with the purpose of the law, for thus the safeguarding of the cloister is rendered by far easier, while at the same time the desired privacy is secured.

If the constitutions of an order reserve the right of determining the limits of the cloister to the general chapter, not even the general superior can per se fix its boundaries[78]. Provision is then usually made that in cases of emergency arising between chapters one of the higher superiors is authorized to make changes with the consent or at least upon advice of his counsellors. Perhaps the general chapter will exercise its power, not by determining the limits of the cloister in the individual convents, but by ordering that some of the parts left open by the Code, e. g., the sacristy or the choir, be enclosed in all the monasteries of the order. In determining the cloistral limits such regulations of the general chapter must be held tantamount to those of the Code[79].

Where the constitutions do not reserve such right to the general chapter, it is wielded by the higher superiors of the order. They are: the abbot of an independent abbey, provincials of those orders which are divided into provinces and *their* superiors, the vicars of any of them, finally all who exercise authority similar to that of provincials. In other words, higher superiors are (besides abbots) those who have jurisdiction over *several* houses which are united to form a distinct subdivision of the order[80]. Only superiors such as these are

---

[76] S. C. Ep. et Reg., decr. 1 Junii 1685, Pennacchi I 777-778.

[77] Cfr. Blat 586; Charles Augustine III 312-313; Pruemmer[2] 288.

[78] It is not likely that this power will be reserved to the general chapter in any order. The length of time between chapters would seem to make such a reservation inadvisable. It may happen more easily in a congregation not widely spread.

[79] Blat 586.

[80] Cfr. canon 488 n. 8.

empowered to fix the boundaries of the enclosure[81]. In defining these limits they must be guided by the rules laid down in § 2 of this canon as well as by any that may have been passed by the general chapter.

In the exclusive right to define the limits of the enclosure there is implicitly included the right and the duty of determining the time when the obligation of observing cloister begins, which must, however, coincide as far as possible with the introduction of the religious community into a convent[82].

The same superiors who can lawfully define the limits of the cloister in the first place, can also change them[83]. Needless to say, in changing them they are bound by the same rules that governed them the first time: apartments that necessarily belong to the cloister may not be set apart from it and opened to women. This, of course, does not mean that a room once chosen to serve, for instance, as refectory could not be changed into a parlor. Such a change may be entirely justified, the room that is to take its place as refectory being now enclosed. Thus, too, the boundaries of the cloister may be moved, so that the parlors, garden, etc., would be enlarged, reduced or transferred; the sacristy and choir could be enclosed or, after having been enclosed, opened again. For any change, however, there must be "lawful reasons." The Code does not specify them; they are left to the discretion of the superior making the change. There would, for example, be sufficient reason to change the limits of the enclosure, if it were found that the rooms set aside as parlors are too small to satisfy the requirements of the regulars[84]. It goes without saying that the limits could not lawfully be altered merely for the purpose of evading the canonical penalties[85].

---

[81] Mocchegiani I 198; Reiffenstuel lib. III tit. XXXV n. 27; Pennacchi I 775-776; Ojetti, v. *Clausura*, n. 1179; Piatus, *Praelectiones*, I 345; Charles Augustine III 312; Blat 586; Leitner 410, Pruemmer[2] 288-289.

[82] Vermeersch, *De Religiosis*, I 176; Piatus, *Praelectiones*, I 345; Appeltern 241.

[83] Pennacchi I 776 and footnote 1; Piatus, *Praelectiones*, I 345; Bachofen 152; Pruemmer II 99; Charles Augustine III 312.

[84] Biederlack 235.

[85] Cfr. Charles Augustine III 312; Blat 586; Leitner 410; Pruemmer[2] 289.

In defining the limits of the cloister superiors should endeavor to guard the monastery as far as possible against all occasions of sin, all danger of scandal and even of suspicion as well as all distraction, in order that the aim of the Church in imposing the obligation of enclosure on regulars may be attained: to secure the quiet of the regulars and to remove from them all dangers and annoyances which may arise from needless contact with the world[86].

In assigning the power of fixing the boundaries of the enclosure in convents of male regulars to higher superiors and the general chapter, the Code denies to the local superior and to the provincial chapter every right to determine or to change them.

---

[86] Mocchegiani I 198.

CHAPTER V.

Papal Cloister of Male Regulars.

1. Total Cloister.

Canon 598, § 1.

At no time did the Church by general law prohibit male regulars to admit men into the enclosure of their convents. A particular law published by the Congregation of Bishops and Regulars, December 1, 1679, and confirmed by Innocent XI, September 20, 1685, forbade Friars Minor Observant to admit men into their cloister for the chase or for games or to lodge them more than three days; clerics as well as the syndic apostolic were not included in this prohibition[1].

Long before the Council of Trent canon law shows plainly that cloister of some kind was thought necessary for every convent[2]. But it remained for Pius V in his constitution "Regularium" of October 24, 1566, to establish the first general law imposing enclosure upon male regulars. He expressly forbade women, having or claiming a special papal indult, to enter the convents of male regulars. At once doubts arose as to the extent of this constitution, which prompted the Pontiff to publish another, "Decet," in which this prohibition was extended to all women, not only such as vaunted a special permission of the Holy See. Again special indults began to multiply. Then Gregory XIII in the constitution "Ubi gratiae" revoked them another time. January 3, 1742, Benedict XIV published the constitution "Regularis disciplinae" which denounces all who claim the permission or privilege to admit women into the enclosure even on the occasion of processions[3].

---

[1] S. C. Ep. et Reg., 1 Dec. 1679, 10 Maii 1680, 4 Dec. 1699, Ferraris, v. *Conventus,* III 33-35.

[2] C. 11, C. XVI, q. 1; c. 20-22, C. XVIII, q. 2.

[3] The exemption which Benedict XIV allowed in this constitution will be discussed under the next section. Vide infra pp. 81-82.

Canon 598, § 1. Within the enclosure of male Regulars, women of whatever age, class, or condition, must not under any pretext be admitted.

Having established in canon 597 the extent of the cloister of regulars, the Code in canon 598 § 1 forbids the admission of women into it. To meet all subterfuges on the term "women," the Code adds: "of whatever age, class or condition." This had already been forbidden by Eugene IV in the constitution "Regularium vitam" in regard to the monasteries of the Benedictine Congregation of St. Justina: "No one is allowed to admit (ducere) on any occasion any women whatever, lay or religious, of whatever age, station, rank, dignity or condition they may be, nor are the women themselves permitted to enter or remain within the enclosure of said Congregation."[4] Again, in the decree of the Congregation of Bishops and Regulars of June 1, 1685, ordering the sacristy of Capuchin monasteries enclosed, besides the penalty inflicted upon adult women trespassing the cloister, it was provided that girls who enter said places were liable to punishments at the discretion of the ordinary of the place[5]. Ferraris, too, proves that the enclosure of male regulars was shut to girls of any age[6]; he adds, however, that in many places the contrary practice was in vogue, the dangers parried by the exclusion of women being absent in the case of small girls[7]. Several authors excused regulars from the penalty of excommunication, but not from sin, if they admitted infant girls[8].

In this regard the Code is very explicit. Henceforth admittance to the cloister of male regulars is forbidden to females of whatever age, not even a girl-infant may be admitted. Neither will nobility of birth or social standing warrant an exception[9], nor can any reason whatever be urged as an ex-

---

[4] Mocchegiani I 201. However, Piat very justly remarks that this constitution of Eugene IV contained a special regulation for one Benedictine Congregation. Piatus, *Praelectiones,* I 354.

[5] Pennacchi I 778.

[6] Ferraris, v. *Conventus,* III 19.

[7] Ferraris, v. *Conventus,* III 20.

[8] Mocchegiani I 202; Piatus, *Comment.,* 181; *Praelectiones,* I 353-354; Pennacchi I 788-789; Hilarius a Sexten 195; Hollweck 229, footnote 6; D'Annibale, *Theologia Moralis,* III 205, footnote 3; Vermeersch, *De Religiosis,* I 178; Pruemmer II 101.

[9] Cfr. Blat 586; Charles Augustine III 313-314; Sole 291-292; Leitner 410.

cuse: no need of assistance, no service to be rendered, no exercise of piety will serve as a pretext[10].

Canon 598, § 2.

From this law are exempt the wives of rulers of states, with their retinue[11].

The exception which is made in this paragraph is taken over from the former legislation. Since it was held that ecclesiastical laws did not bind the highest civil rulers, unless they made express mention of them, it was the more common opinion among canonists that queens and empresses and their daughters were not prohibited from entering the enclosure of male regulars[12]. Reiffenstuel argues that empresses and queens

[10] Mocchegiani (I 200), citing St. Alphonse n. 231 and D'Annibale, n. 117, excuses women as well as those who admit them from all guilt of sin and from censure, if they take refuge in a convent of regulars, in order to escape being killed. On the supposition that the cloister of regulars were the only possible shelter, this exception would be entirely justified. In this case the positive law must yield to the higher law of self-preservation. A similar condition might arise in times of epidemic. If so many of the regulars fell victims to the disease, that there would not be a sufficient number of brethren left to nurse them, and if no other men could be found to take care of them, the regulars would be excused from all guilt in admitting women for that purpose. In such cases the conditions laid down in canon 81 would be verified and the ordinary, i. e., the major superior, could dispense; if he could not be reached, the local superior could proceed on the same principle. But only in case of very great necessity could such an exception be allowed. Bonacina, *De Clausura etc.*, q. V p. IV n. 4; Paschalis de Siena 122. Vide infra p. 88.

[11] Here again the *Authorised English Translation* fails to give the exact meaning of the original and omits the word "actu." This paragraph were more correctly rendered thus: "From this law are exempt with their retinue the wives of those who exercise supreme authority over peoples."

[12] Pennacchi I 787-788, who adds that, the entrance of queens being a rare and harmless occurrence, the purpose of the cloister is not foiled; Ferraris, v. *Conventus,* III, 22; Piatus, *Comment.*, 177; Mocchegiani I 199-200; Bonacina, *De Clausura etc.*, p. V p. II n. 5, who, however, demurs at granting this exemption to convents of nuns, though acknowledging its probability. Ibidem q. IV p. I n. 4; Pennacchi I 719-722; Lucidi II 160. Permission for the entire royal family together with their entourage to enter the enclosure of both men's and women's convents was among the privileges granted by Benedict XIV and Pius VII to the King of Saxony and renewed by Leo XII Dec. 11, 1827. By two grants of Alexander VII, *Singularis* and *Spirituali,* both of Dec. 24, 1655, (Bullarium Taur. XVI 102 seq.), Christine of Sweden obtained permission to enter all the convents of Rome. Scherer II 772, Anmerkung 77. A similar concession was granted by Pius IX Nov. 29, 1857, whereby the women of the Imperial and Royal Family, the Archdukes of Austria and their retinue were allowed to enter the Capuchin monasteries of the Tyrolese Province. Bullarium Ord. Cap. X 356 quoted by Hilarius a Sexten 194-195. Regarding the exception made in the constitution of Benedict XIV *Regularis disciplinae* vide infra pp. 81-82.

and their daughters deserve such special mention and are not included in *general* words of a law (*In generali,* 81 de Reg. Juris in 6); (2) "in odiosis" such persons are exempt unless explicitly included; (3) because Pius V in the constitution "Regularium," Gregory XIII in "Ubi gratiae" and Paul V in "Monialium" in revoking privileges to enter the enclosure of male regulars, enumerate countesses, marchionesses and duchesses, but do not speak of those of higher rank, he concludes that those Popes did not intend to revoke the privileges of such persons; lastly he appeals to a declaration of the Cardinals quoted by Hyacinth Donatus (t. IV tr. IV q. 12, t. I tr. IV q. 49) that the constitution of Gregory XIII did not derogate from the privileges of those of royal borth[13]. Nor did authorities narrow this exemption to empresses and queens and their daughters. Ferraris[14] already judged duchesses exempt, if their husbands were sovereign rulers. Later authors extended this to the wives of all sovereigns, no matter by what title they were known[15]. This opinion is "canonized" by the Code, which defines its scope as follows:

(1) Only the *wives* of rulers are exempt. It is not necessary that either wife or husband be Catholic[16]. They must, however, live in lawful wedlock; if, therefore, they had married after the civil divorce of either party, the exemption would not apply. The mother, daughters and other female relatives, whether by blood or by marriage, of the supreme ruler of a state, are not included in this exemption, even if they accompany him; but they may enter with his wife, as belonging to her entourage[17]. A fortiori: if a woman is the sovereign of a state, as were Empress Mary Theresa of Austria, Queen Victoria of England, or now Queen Wilhelmina of Holland, the recently resigned and the reigning Duchess of Luxemburg, she no doubt enjoys this privilege and, if married, her

---

13 Reiffenstuel lib. III tit. XXXV n. 42.

14 Ferraris, v. *Conventus,* III 21.

15 Ballerini IV 93; Hilarius a Sexten 194; Hollweck 223, footnote 4; Vermeersch, *De Religiosis,* I 178.

16 Cfr. Pruemmer II 101: " . . . (addit Ferrari, De stat. rel. 168; dummodo sint catholicae, sed non probat istam restrictionem)." Hollweck 229, footnote 2, also seems to restrict the exemption to Catholic empresses and queens.

17 Blat 587.

Prince Consort participates in it[18]. For on the principle: where there is the same reason, there is the same disposition of the law, what is said of a reigning prince is applicable to a reigning princess; and the latter's husband enjoys whatever privilege is granted the former's wife.

(2) Their husbands must hold supreme authority over a people (supremum populorum principatum). Charles Augustine in commenting on this paragraph says: "The president's wife, and the governor's wife, we are sorry to say, are not included in this privilege, because their husbands are not actual rulers in the commonly accepted sense of the word."[19] Is this interpretation correct? Whether or not our president and our governors must be classed with "rulers," is not to the point. Vermeersch held that even under the former legislation a president's wife was exempt: "The law makes exceptions for queens and women of like rank, as, for example, the wife of the president of a republic."[20] The canon under discussion has no other meaning. For the Latin phrase of the Code, "qui tenent supremum populorum principatum," has a wider scope than such civil authorities as are strictly called "rulers," i. e., monarchs; "principatus" means more than royal or imperial monarchical sovereignty. Its primary meaning is "the first place, preeminence, preference," its second "the chief place in the state,"[21] and it is just in this latter sense that it is employed in the Code. On comparing the text of the Code with the constitution "Regularis disciplinae" of Benedict XIV of January 3, 1742, § 8, which reads: ". . . . . eorum, qui sunt Domini in temporalibus locorum,"[22] it is found that the Church takes into consideration the changed constitutions of very many civil governments. At the time of Benedict XIV

[18] Fanfani 124; Leitner 411.

[19] Charles Augustine III 314. Hollweck, 223 footnote 4, expressed the same view.

[20] Vermeersch in *Catholic Encyclopedia*, v. *Cloister*, IV 61. *De Religiosis*, I 178, he says: "Excipiuntur Reginae (aut personae aequiparatae)."

[21] Forcellini, v. *Principatus*.. Cfr. Suetonius, *Caligula*, 22: ". . . nec multum afuit quin statim diadema sumeret speciemque *principatus* in *regni* formam conuerteret."

[22] It is true, Benedict XIV is not speaking of the same exemption as the Code is treating of; still the words he employed will serve to elucidate the meaning of the words of the Code.

only a small number of the old republics still existed and the newer ones had not yet arisen. Neither can it be objected that the word "principatus" was applied in post-Augustan times to the Empire. This very use militates in favor of this view rather than against it: it was employed in lieu of the hated "regnum," to designate the power of the Caesars who by a legal fiction received their authority from Senate and people. The inference, therefore, is that the Church advisedly chose the word "principatus" in order to include in this exemption the consorts of all bearers of the highest civil power. This is the interpretation of Blat: ". . . whether they are styled kings, emperors, princes, presidents of republics, or by any other name."[23] Cerato[24], Leitner[25], Fantani[26], Brandys[27] and Stadtmueller[28] accept the same view and Poeschl inclines to it when he asks: "Only monarchs?"[29] There can, then, be no doubt that our president's wife as well as the wives of the governors of the several states enjoy this exemption. For as long as one holds to state rather than federal sovereignty, he must admit that our governors "hold the supreme authority over the people" in the sense of the Code.

(3) The wife of such highest executive comes under this exemption only during her husband's administration (actu). Therefore, after the abdication or dethronement of a monarch, or after the expiration of the term of office of a president or governor this privilege of the wife ceases; neither does she retain it after her husband's death.

(4) The wife of such supreme executive may take with her a suitable retinue. Sometimes the number of these ladies is specified in papal indults by which entrance into the enclosure of a monastery is granted. In the present canon no limit is set. The number of persons in the retinue will depend to a great extent on the rank of the person. Reiffenstuel permits every member of the suite of the exempted person to enter

23 ". . . . sive reges, imperatroes, principes, reipublicae praesidentes, aliove nomine designentur." Blat 587.
24 Cerato 121-122.
25 Leitner 410-411.
26 Fanfani 124.
27 Brandys 67.
28 Stadtmueller 15.
29 "Bloss Monarchen?" Poeschl 297.

with her; nor does he recognize any obligation of confining it to a few elderly persons. No general rule can be laid down, unless it is established by the constitutions of an order or by lawful custom. In the absence of such statute or custom it must be left to the prudence of the superior[30].

Does this exemption hold only for the country which the husband of the privileged woman governs? In prior legislation no such restriction was placed on queens, empresses, and other sovereign ladies. The conclusion, then, is that the wives of supreme civil authorities may enter the enclosure in foreign countries as well as in those ruled by their husbands, "because," as Charles Augustine points out, "the text does not limit the privilege to their own country."[31]

The exemption spoken of by Benedict XIV in his constitution "Regularis disciplinae", § 8, to which reference was made above, differs from that of the Code in canon 598 § 2. That Pope did not grant the general exemption of this canon; he merely declared that he did not mean to revoke certain privileges granted to some ladies. They were of two kinds. The one recognized the claim of ancestors or heads of certain noble families who as founders or great benefactors of a monastery had reserved for the ladies of their families the right to enter its enclosure. This right, however, must be approved of by papal bull or brief, and then they are permitted to enter the enclosure usually but four times a year, outside the seasons of Lent or Advent, the great feasts of the year, the particular feasts of the monastery, holydays of obligation, the chanting of the Divine Office; nor may they partake of any refreshments in the monastery or remain after nightfall[32]. The other appertained to women related by blood

---

30 Reiffenstuel lib. III tit. XXXV nn. 44-49; Hilarius a Sexten 194; Leitner 411.

31 Charles Augustine III 314.

32 S. C. Ep. et Reg., in *Panormitana,* Junii 1723, Ojetti, v. *Clausura,* n. 1176. Cfr. S. C. de Relig., 29 Dec. 1909, ad I-V, A. A. S. II 62-63. Pruemmer II 106. Such privileges were granted to the Princess Stefania Branciforte as foundress June 1723 and to the Prince of Scilla June 22, 1725. Bizzarri 317-318. The Duchess Charlotte Colonna of the city of Caserta (Magdalunum) obtained a concession whereby she was allowed to enter a convent of nuns, founded by her, six times a year accompanied by six ladies; for her successors it was restricted to three times a year and a retinue of three. S. C. Conc., in *Magdalunen.,* 22 Aprilis 1719, Zamboni IV 432.

or marriage to dukes, counts, and others of similar rank; they could enter convents in the territory subject to those princes, provided said privilege was based on previous legitimate title or custom. Both these kinds of privileges Benedict XIV admitted, if they had been granted by papal brief or bull; the beneficiaries were, however, not allowed to wander through the cloister or offices, or to eat in the convent, but only to assist in the Church at Mass and other exercises of devotion[33]. These concessions are not abolished by the Code, since there is not embodied in the present canon an annulling clause, as would be necessary according to canon 4. Any woman who claims such a privilege must prove that it has not been revoked by the constitution of Benedict XIV or, if it is of a later date, that it was lawfully granted[34].

Are women still permitted to take part in processions through the cloister? In the constitution "Decet" which was directed to the Carthusians of the Monastery of Monte Vergine Pius V granted permission to women to enter the cloister to attend Mass and other Divine Offices, to take part in processions, to assist at funerals etc., and to enter and leave the church by direct way through the enclosure, as often as the concourse of people made entrance and leaving by the church door inconvenient. This faculty was not peculiar to the Carthusians, a) because in the introduction of that decree the Pope states that he is interpreting his earlier general constitution "Regularium"; b) by reason of communication of privileges; c) because according to Donatus[35] the Pope by oral declaration extended it to all regulars. Pennacchi is of the opinion that even after the constitution of Benedict XIV "Regularis disciplinae" and that of Pius IX "Apostolicae Sedis" the permission granted by Pius V remained in force[36].

---

[33] Pennacchi therefore concludes that, if the church of the monastery lies outside the enclosure, women enjoying such a privilege cannot make use of it, since Benedict XIV permitted their entrance into the enclosure to go to the church for Mass and other services and for no other purpose. Pennacchi I 773-774.

[34] Biederlack 234 and footnote 4.

[35] *In Praxi Regularium,* tom. I tr. IV q. 3 p. 161, quoted by Pennacchi I 797-798.

[36] Pennacchi I 797-801; cfr. Matthaeucci 103; Reiffenstuel lib. III tit. XXXV nn. 74-77; Bonacina, *De Clausura etc.,* q. V p. IV nn. 6-11.

On the other hand there can be no doubt that it was revoked by Gregory XIII in his constitution "Ubi gratiae." This is proven by several decrees of the Congregation of Sacred Rites, all of which are printed in the *Decreta Authentica Sacrorum Rituum Congregationis* published under the auspices of Leo XIII and enumerated in the footnotes of the Code among the documents bearing upon this canon. The decrees:

For the Diocese of Orihuela (Alicante): The Bishop of Orihuela at the instance of the Fisc of his Cathedral has asked for a declaration: Whether the decree published by this S. C. Sept. 30, 1628, prohibiting women to enter the enclosure (septa) of monasteries of regulars on occasions of processions of the Rosary and the like, must be observed, notwithstanding the bull of Pius V permitting women to enter the enclosure of monasteries during similar processions. The S. C. answered: "That the decree published Sept. 30, 1628, from which [it appears that there] is a revocatory bull of Gregory XIII, being of a later date, must be observed." June 11, 1629.

The decree of Sept. 30, 1628, is as follows:

For the Diocese of Orihuela: The Archdeacon of Orihuela has stated that in [that] city there was a custom that women took part in private processions of regulars . . . through their cloister (claustrum) contrary to the enactment of Gregory XIII, and asked that it be declared: whether this was lawful and was to be permitted? And the S. C. replied: that "it was not lawful nor to be permitted, except by express leave of the Holy See."[37]

For Regulars of the Whole World: Their Eminences, the Cardinals ordered: "After consulting His Holiness, that a prohibitory decree be published, by virtue of which women may no longer enter the enclosure (septa) on occasion of any processions whatsoever and that regulars who permit women to enter the cloister be liable to the same penalty [as they]." July 5, 1631[38].

---

[37] *Decreta Auth. C. S. R.*, n. 506. What is contained in [ ] is supplied in English.

[38] *Decreta Auth. C. S. R.*, n. 564.

For the Diocese of Sulmo: To the question: whether women were allowed on occasion of processions to enter the enclosure (septa) of monasteries of regulars, especially if there is a custom, the S. C. replied: "that it was by no means lawful for women to enter the enclosure of monasteries of regulars on occasion of any processions, notwithstanding any contrary custom." Nov. 24, 1635[39].

For the Diocese of Cosenza: At the request of the Dominican Fathers of the city of Terra Mendicini in the Diocese of Cosenza that it be decided: whether they could conduct a procession around their convent, carrying the Blessed Sacrament; and whether women were allowed to enter the first enclosure of the convent at the time, when the same Fathers held the procession of the Most Holy Rosary. And the S. C. replied, as to the first: "The custom may be retained;" as to the enclosure: "It is not allowed." Dec. 10, 1667[40].

These decrees of the Congregation of Sacred Rites prove conclusively that the exception permitted by Pius V was revoked by Gregory XIII[41]. Since it is not renewed in the Code, women are not allowed to enter the enclosure of male regulars to take part in religious processions and the like, except by express leave of the Holy See[42]. Yet Pruemmer excepts an immemorial custom which the ordinary, i. e., the

---

[39] *Decreta Auth. C. S. R.*, n. 627.

[40] *Decreta Auth. C. S. R.*, n. 1364.

[41] Mocchegiani I 205-206; Piatus, *Praelectiones,* I 355; Hilarius a Sexten 195; Ballerini IV 93; Bachofen 158; Appeltern 248, who, however, in footnote 6 cites a decree of the Congregation of Bishops and Regulars of Aug. 18, 1713, (An. J. P. XIV 345 n. 1163 ad 4) permitting women to enter the enclosure of male regulars on occasions of processions. Again as late as Dec. 10, 1852, the Holy See granted a special indult to the Capuchins of the Province of Linden in Poland. Bullarium Capuc. X 280 n. CXXXVII quoted by Appeltern 248 footnote 9. On the other hand, about twenty-five years ago the Cardinal Prefect of the Congregation characterized a petition for a similar indult: "Scandalosum."

[42] Biederlack, page 235, takes the same view, but for reasons which are not conclusive. He holds that the concession of Pius V to the Carthusians of Monte Vergine was extended to other orders only by communication of privileges (which is not admitted; vide supra p. 82), which he maintains is revoked—but is it certain that canon 613 § 1 has retroactive force? In the second place he bases his view on the words of canon 598 § 1 "sub quovis praetextu"—these words, however, scarcely suffice to revoke a privilege.

higher superior, may tolerate, if in his prudence he judges that it cannot be abolished[43].

Canon 2342, N. 2.

Canon 598 § 1 contains the whole law regarding the enclosure of male regulars, for violation of which a penalty is inflicted in the Code. The discussion of this penalty is, therefore, in order.

Pius V already in the constitution "Regularium", as interpreted by his constitution "Decet," excommunicated all women who unlawfully entered the cloister of male regulars, and suspended and deprived of office the regulars who admitted them. To the latter penalty Gregory XIII in his constitution "Ubi gratiae" added excommunication. All these penalties were renewed by Benedict XIV in his constitution "Regularis disciplinae." Since Pius IX published his constitution "Apostolicae Sedis," the only penalty incurred ipso facto was excommunication reserved to the Pope, which women who entered the cloister of men's convents brought upon themselves as well as regulars who admitted them[44]. The Code renews this censure, but with important changes.

Canon 2342. The following incur ipso facto excommunication reserved simpliciter to the Holy See:

2. Women who violate the enclosure of male regulars, and Superiors and others, whoever they may be, who introduce or admit women of any age whatsoever; besides, religious who introduce or admit them should be deprived of their office, if they hold any, and of the active and passive voice.

The first penalty inflicted by the Code for violation of the enclosure of male regulars is excommunication which is incurred ipso facto, i. e., by the very act of unlawfully entering the cloister. No trial, no sentence, not even a declaration that this penalty has been incurred is necessary[45]. However, before

[43] Cfr. can. 5. Pruemmer2 289. In the 1. ed. of his *Manuale* he considered it more probable that such entrance on the occasion of processions was forbidden. II 102.
[44] Pius IX, const. *Apostolicae Sedis,* II 7.
[45] Canon 2217 § 1 n. 2. Sole 51-52.

a judicial declaration that the penalty has been incurred one is excused from observing the censure, if by observing it he would betray his guilt; before such a declaratory sentence he cannot even be compelled in the external forum to observe it, unless the crime be notorius[46].

This excommunication is reserved simpliciter to the Holy See. A person who has incurred it can ordinarily be absolved only by the Pope or by one who has received the needed faculty. If, however, it is a burden for the person to wait, until faculties can be received from the Holy See or other competent authority, on account of scandal, danger to one's good name and the like, any confessor can absolve him from the censure; in this case, however, application for the "mandata" must be made to the Holy See or other superior authorized to absolve from the censure either personally or through the confessor within a month; if this is neglected, the excommunication revives[47]. If, however, the penitent is absolved in danger of death, he has no further obligation of applying for the "mandata," even if he recovers[48].

Before as well as after the constitution of Pius IX "Apostolicae Sedis" it was disputed among canonists whether girls above the age of reason and below twelve years incurred excommunication in entering the enclosure. Bonacina[49], Pennacchi[50], Hilarius a Sexten[51], Appeltern[52], Ballerini[53], Vermeersch[54], and Mocchegiani[55] held the affirmative, Piat[56], Ojetti[57], Hollweck[58], Pruemmer[59], and Paschalis de Siena[60] the negative view.

---

[46] Canon 2232 § 1. Sole 86-88.
[47] Canon 2254. Cerato 34-36; Sole 136-138.
[48] Canon 2252. Cerato 31-33; Sole 133-134.
[49] Bonacina, *De Clausura etc.*, q. V p. II n. 2.
[50] Pennacchi I 788-789.
[51] Hilarius a Sexten 195.
[52] Appeltern 247.
[53] Ballerini IV 93.
[54] Vermeersch, *De Religiosis,* I 178.
[55] Mocchegiani I 221.
[56] Piatus, *Praelectiones,* I 353.
[57] Ojetti, v. *Clausura,* n. 1186.
[58] Hollweck 229 footnote 6.
[59] Pruemmer II 101.
[60] Paschalis de Siena 121

While by canon 598 § 1 it is forbidden to admit females of any age, only those that have attained the age of puberty, i. e., are twelve years old[61], are excommunicated, if they violate the enclosure of male regulars. Girls below twelve years do not incur this censure, since, according to canon 2230, such as have not yet reached the age of puberty are not liable to penalties "latae sententiae"; they are to be corrected by punishments of an educational character, provided they are baptized and have completed their seventh year, since such are bound by the "merely ecclesiastical law" contained in canon 598 § 1[62]. If not through ignorance, it will usually be through levity, that such girls transgress the law, and the correction should tend to impress upon them its importance[63].

Excommunication is incurred only by those who "violate" the enclosure of male regulars, not by such as enter with lawful exemption mentioned in canon 598 § 2[64] or with papal dispensation. Again, women may be ignorant of the law of the enclosure and by the constitutions of Pius V "Regularium" and Gregory XIII "Ubi gratiae" only those women incurred excommunication, who *presumed* to enter the enclosure of male regulars; therefore, ignorance of the law excused them from the censure, not only if their ignorance were "crassa et supina," but even if it were "affected," i. e., if on set purpose they made no effort to inform themselves on the matter[65].

---

61 Canon 88 § 2. Cfr. Cappello, *De Censuris,* 110; Sole 291-292; Cerato 123; Blat 696.

62 Cfr. canon 12. Leitner 410; Ayrinhac 267; Cappello, *De Censuris,* 108; Sole 83-84. An application of this will be found in the decree of the Bishops and Regulars of June 1, 1685, ordaining that girls not yet of the age of puberty (mulieres vero adhuc non adultae aetatis), who enter the cloister of Capuchin monasteries, be punished at the discretion of the ordinary of the place.

63 Blat 696; Cerato 123; Sole 83-84; Ayrinhac 267; Biederlack 235.—Cerato, page 123, says: "'Mulieres violantes'; ergo censurae non subjiciuntur *religiosae.* C. 2219 § 3, 2246 § 2." and again: "'Introducentes vel admittentes eas': . . . Non tamen videtur comprehendi introductio *religiosae* . . ." Now canon 2219 § 3 says that a penalty may not be extended from one person to another, and canon 2246 § 2, that a reservation receives strict interpretation. How these two canons bear out the exemption of religious women from the censure is unintelligible. If Cerato's interpretation were correct, one might say with as much logic that canon 598 does not forbid the admission of female religious into the cloister of male regulars; for in both cases the text reads "women." But who would dare say this?

64 Vide supra pp. 77-81.

65 Bonacina, *De Clausura etc.,* q. V p. III n. 1.

Even after the constitution of Pius IX "Apostolicae Sedis" some authors postulated this presumption as a condition for incurring excommunication[66]. Hilarius a Sexten on the other hand concluded that, since the constitution of Pius IX says simply: "violantes," vincible ignorance no longer excused from the censure[67].

Women may not know that they are forbidden to enter the cloister of male regulars, or, if they do, they may not be aware of the penalty of excommunication for entering unlawfully or that the place they are entering lies within the enclosure. Under the present legislation ignorance of any of these points, provided it is not "crassa et supina," excuses them from incurring this censure[68]. Women of unsound mind and therefore not capable of moral guilt, cannot be punished[69].

There can be no question of violation of the cloister on the part of one who is physically forced to enter, e. g., by being dragged in[70]. Not only physical force, but also grave fear, even if only relatively so, or a serious burden will excuse from the observance of this law and from the censure. For this reason a woman whose life is threatened may take refuge in a monastery of regulars. The evil that threatens need not be as serious as this, provided it is the true motive of the person affected[71].

Does the word "violate" include every entrance of a woman not exempt or dispensed, or does it imply an express evil intention? Although the law of the cloister, as far as it forbids the entrance of women, is primarily intended to shield regulars against all danger of violating their vow of chastity, still it has also the purpose of protecting their good name as

66 Piatus, *Praelectiones,* I 357-358; Appeltern 248.

67 Hilarius a Sexten 195-196.

68 Canons 2202, 2229 § 3 n. 1; cfr. Cappello, *De Censuris,* 20; Ayrinhac 68-69; Sole 79-82; Cerato 40-43.

69 Canon 2201. Bonacina, *De Clausura etc.,* q. V p. II n. 2; Pennacchi I 787; Hilarius a Sexten 195; Piatus, *Praelectiones,* I 355; Appeltern 247; Bachofen 158. Since excommunication is inflicted only on baptized persons (canon 2241 § 1), an unbaptized woman who enters the enclosure of male regulars is not liable to this censure; but those admitting an unbaptized woman would be excommunicated, if they were baptized.

70 Canon 2205 § 1.

71 Cfr. canons 2205, 2218 § 2, and 2229, § 3 n. 3; vide supra p. 77, footnote 10. Sole 26-28, 55, 82; Ayrinhac 37-38, 51; Cerato 39-43.

well as to spare them unnecessary distractions. The law, therefore, makes no distinction and any woman not lawfully excused is excommunicated, regardless of her intention[72].

Formerly there was a discussion, whether the censure affected only such women as entered or were admitted into the cloister under pretext of some faculty, because Pius V in the constitution "Regularium" and Gregory XIII in the constitution "Ubi gratiae" mentioned only such as claimed to enjoy a special indult. But the upholders of the affirmative overlooked the fact that Pius V first orally, as attested by Cardinal Cribellus January 28, 1568[73], and later by the constitution "Decet" of July 16, 1570, declared that it had been the intention of his letters of October 24, 1566, to "include not only women having and pretending (to have) permission and indults to enter monasteries, but all and whatsoever other women." According to Navarrus[74] the Congregation of Bishops and Regulars attested that the bull of Gregory XIII was to be interpreted in the same manner, and Reiffenstuel cites Navarrus as authority that Gregory XIII published a declaration to that effect[75]. Since Pius IX in his constitution "Apostolicae Sedis" mentioned "violantes" without any restriction, it was commonly accepted that neither an "evil intention" nor a "pretext of a faculty or indult" was required for incurring this censure[76]. Neither does the Code contain any phrase modifying "violantes" and, therefore, all offending women incur this excommunication[77].

---

72 Pruemmer II 104; Hilarius a Sexten 195; Piatus, *Praelectiones,* I 357; Appeltern 247-248; Cappello, *De Censuris,* 107. A decree of the Congregation of the Council of March 10, 1602, reserved to the Holy See the excommunication incurred by those who violate the enclosure of nuns "ob malum finem," whereas the penalties previously inflicted were not reserved. St. Alphonsus lib. VII 221. No other ecclesiastical legislation regarding the cloister carries that phrase.

73 Matthaeucci 103-104.

74 Navarrus, *De Regularibus Commentarii quattuor,* IV 62 nota 4, and *Enchiridion seu Manuale Confessariorum,* XXVII, 150, Excom. 61, adde 2[0], quoted by Piatus, *Praelectiones,* I 357.

75 Reiffenstuel lib. III tit. XXXV n. 74.

76 Pennacchi I 768; Piatus, *Praelectiones,* I 357; Appeltern 247. Before the constitution *Apostolicae Sedis* this view was held by Bonacina, *De Clausura etc.,* q. V p. II n. 1; Matthaeucci 103-104; Reiffenstuel lib. III tit. XXXV n. 71-74.

77 Cappello, *De Censuris,* 107; Ayrinhac 267.

In determining when a woman has entered the enclosure, all canonists are very severe and almost all agree that, as soon as the threshold is passed, so that her entire body is within the limits of the enclosure, the woman has entered, is guilty of grievous sin and excommunicated[78]. Vermeersch is a trifle more lenient: he would excuse one who has, indeed, entered as explained above, but immediately withdraws from the cloister. And justly so; for a step or two within the enclosure can hardly be considered a grave matter. In the absence of a wall, door or other material barrier, "somewhat more latitude may be allowed."[79]

If a woman has entered the enclosure through no fault of hers, because she was ignorant of the law or because necessity excused her, she is bound to leave as soon as the cause of her entrance ceases. If she tarries or goes to places to which she has no right to go, she sins grievously, but does she incur the censure? By no means, for the word "violate" signifies an *unlawful entrance*[80]. Now a woman who is already within the enclosure no longer *enters* it; she is innocent of precisely that offence which is visited with excommunication[81].

Besides the women who enter the enclosure of male regulars, the Code excommunicates the superiors and all other persons who introduce or admit females of any age. Superiors are those, and their vicars, who exercise jurisdiction over regulars, not only the higher, but also the local superiors, whether they be known as abbots, priors, presidents, guardians or by any other name. Moreover, all other persons guilty of the same crime incur the censure. In this the Code is more severe than the constitution of Pius IX, in which besides the superiors only the *regulars* who introduced or admitted women incurred this penalty[82]. As appears from the constitution of Gregory

---

[78] Canons 2242 § 1, 2213; Pennacchi I 723; Hilarius a Sexten 195; Cappello, *De Censuris,* 107-108, cfr. 111; Cerato 122; Sole 289.

[79] Vermeersch in *Catholic Encyclopedia,* v. *Cloister,* IV 61. Cfr. Biederlack 239.

[80] Cfr. n. 1 of this canon.

[81] Cfr. canons 2219 § 3, 2228, 2242, § 1; Bonacina, *De Clausura etc.,* q. V p. IV nn. 15-16, q. IV p. IV n. 22; D'Annibale, *Comment.,* 86, footnote 11; Hilarius a Sexten 183; Cerato 122; Cavigioli 103. Regarding those who in such cases cause or permit a woman to tarry within the enclosure vide infra pp. 95-97.

[82] Pennacchi I 791; Mocchegiani I 202; Piatus, *Comment.,* 181.

XIII "Ubi gratiae" § 3, regulars fell under this ban, who admitted women into their *own,* not, however, who introduced them into *another* convent[83]. Not even lay-brothers were subject to this censure under the previous legislation, if they did not take solemn vows, inasmuch as only regulars were mentioned in the former laws[84]. For the same reason lay-servants of the monastery were free from it[85].

At present all persons (Superiores aliique, quicumque ii sint), whether professed or not, whether lay-brothers or novices or postulants or oblati, clerics or lay, men or women, whether in any way connected with the convent or not, one and all[86] are liable to the same penalty as the regular superior[87]. All doubt as to the meaning of that phrase is dispelled by reference to the last clause of this section of canon 2342, where another penalty is inflicted only on religious.

The next question turns around the signification of the words "admit" and "introduce." Matthaeucci defines them thus: "Let it be noted that those words . . . have not the same import; 'introducere' comprehends every actual help given towards the entrance of women into the convent, as to invite, counsel, approve, encourage, show the way, remove obstacles, open the door and such like; 'admittere,' however, means to receive, to grant entrance, and authoritatively to permit women to enter; he only can do this, who is bound by his office to prevent it, viz., the superior and the janitor or the sacristan who must guard the doors of the convent or church respectively. Such fail against their official duty, if they do not close the door, do not resist and do not expel [women] as soon as they enter by intimating to them the censures and impressing upon them the offence of God and

83 Hilarius a Sexten 196; Piatus, *Praelectiones,* I 360.

84 Piatus, *Praelectiones,* I 360; Bachofen 158.

85 Pennacchi I 790-791; Hilarius a Sexten 196; Appeltern 249; Vermeersch, *De Religiosis,* I 178; Hollweck 229, footnote 5.

86 Except Cardinals. Cfr. Canon 2227 § 2.—Neither are minors below the age of puberty, boys below fourteen and girls below twelve, subject to this censure, but they may be punished in other ways. Canon 2230. Cfr. what has been said above regarding girls below the age of puberty, p. 87.

87 Cappello, *De Censuris,* 110; Blat 696; Ayrinhac 267; Sole 292; Biederlack 235; Cavigioli 106.

the contempt for the Apostolic Constitutions."[88] This definition is in substance accepted by Ferraris[89], Ojetti[90], and Mocchegiani[91], while others are at variance with it[92]. It would lead through a labyrinth of sharp distinctions to enumerate all their different opinions. Suffice it to sum up their general conclusions. "Introducing" required some positive co-operation, but canonists disagreed as to which co-operation entailed the censure. The more common opinion mantained that only superiors, janitors, and the like could "admit" women either positively, by granting them entrance, or negatively, by not preventing their entrance when they could and must. In determining wherein such co-operation consisted both as regards "introducing" and "admitting," most authors went too far[93].

Without entering further into the argument about the mooted distinction between "admit" and "introduce," a solution of the real question: Which co-operation entails excommunication? must be sought through canons 2231 and 2209 with due reference to the interpretation of the previous law.

Canon 2231 divides co-operators into two classes: those mentioned in canon 2209 §§ 1-3 are considered equally guilty and suffer the same penalty as the principal agent, unless the law provides otherwise; those enumerated in §§ 4-7 of that canon do not contract the same degree of guilt as the principal culprit, hence are not liable to the same penalty[94]. These canons lead to the following conclusion: a) all those *in collusion* with the intruder[95] incur excommunication; b) likewise those who render her such assistance as is *indispensable* to

---

88 Matthaeucci 103.
89 Ferraris, v. *Conventus,* III 30; v. *Moniales,* III 59.
90 Ojetti, v. *Clausura,* n. 1187.
91 Mocchegiani I 202, 222.
92 Pennacchi I 791-796; Hilarius a Sexten 187-188, 196.
93 Matthaeucci 103; see his definition of "introducere" and "admittere" above p. 91; Ferraris, v. *Conventus,* III 30; v. *Moniales,* III 59; Ojetti, v. *Clausura,* n. 1187; Mocchegiani I 202, 222; Hilarius a Sexten 187; Piatus, *Praelectiones,* I 358-359, 379; Appeltern 249; D'Annibale, *Comment.,* 127; Hollweck 225, footnote 12; Ayrinhac 266-267; Blat 696; Cappello, *De Visitatione,* II 439; *De Censuris,* 109; Lehmkuhl II 706; Sole 292.
94 Ayrinhac 70-71; Sole 84-85, 32-36.
95 Canon 2209 § 1.

her purpose[96]; aid given to render the violation merely *easier* does not involve the censure, provided there is no collusion with the culprit[97]; c) excommunication is incurred by him who commands or commissions another to enter unlawfully or to admit or introduce an unauthorized person, since he is the principal cause of the crime[98]. To the last there are two exceptions: 1) if even without his action the violation of the cloister would have taken place[99]; in this case his command has no efficacious effect upon the transgression; 2) if his command or commission had, indeed, been the cause of the entrance or admission of an unauthorized person, but had been retracted, before the crime was committed, even though the other parties persist in their purpose[100]. Those who advise, invite or urge an unauthorized person to enter or to admit or introduce such a person are excommunicated, only if they are the cause of the violation of the cloister[101].

Besides the preceding cases all authors agreed that superiors and others specially charged with the care of the enclosure were liable to excommunication, even if their co-operation were only negative, i. e., if they did not prevent the violation of the cloister, when they were obliged and able. Notwithstanding that this opinion was unanimous, it must not be accepted in its entirety. For, in the first place, canon 2342 does not offer any ground for a distinction between those entrusted with the care of the cloister and those not so charged. Then, in view of the principles laid down in the Code regarding penalties it is necessary to distinguish such *negative* co-operation. Should anyone who is able, not prevent the unlawful entrance or admission of a woman, and his neglect amount to *tacit or express permission* to enter and be intended as such, his co-operation must be judged the same as *positive*

[96] Canon 2209 § 2.

[97] Canon 2209 § 4. Whether opening the door, removing obstacles, showing the way into the cloister, will render one liable to the censure, must be decided according to these two distinctions.

[98] Canon 2209 § 3.

[99] Canon 2209 §§ 3 and 4. Cfr. Sole 34; Cappello, *De Censuris,* 14.

[100] Canon 2209 § 5. Cfr. Sole 35-36; Ayrinhac 45-46.

[101] Canon 2209 §§ 3 and 4. But a timely retractation will free them from the censure as was said regarding the "mandans" under c) 2). Canon 2209 § 5; cfr. Sole 34-36.

co-operation by common consent[102], with the result that everyone so guilty, whether charged with the custody of the cloister or not, is excommunicated.

But what, if the neglect must not be construed and is not intended as consent or approval or permission? Suppose a religious while engaged in conversation with a visitor in the parlor notices a woman about to enter, but neglects to hinder her although he could easily do so: is he excommunicated? By no means; and this again applies to superiors and all others alike[103]. In such a case collusion, complicity, and moral influence by command, counsel, and the like are out of the question. Paragraph 6 of canon 2209 defines the guilt of those neglecting their office and canon 2231 states that such co-operation does not entail penalties decreed by law, unless the contrary is expressly stated[104], which is not the case in canon 2342 n. 2. But it might be objected that the Code does not consider "admitting" or "introducing" mere co-operation, but distinct crimes and that, therefore, the solution of the question is not to be made according to canons 2209 and 2231, but on its own merits. The assumption is denied. For the entrance of women is prohibited and their "admission" or "introduction" is ordinarily the means of their entrance, and therefore co-operation. There are two reasons why co-operators are mentioned in canon 2342 n. 2. First, this canon repeats the old law and retains mention of them, lest the conclusion be drawn that, owing to the omission of reference to them, they are no longer liable to censure. Secondly, it extends the subject of this censure beyond the ordinary rules of co-operation[105]. But granted that those "admitting" or "introducing" can not be classed as mere co-operators, still the case under discussion will not entail excommunication. For the "malice" required for a crime by canon 2200 is wanting. It is rather the case defined in canon 2203: such persons fore-

---

102 Canon 2209 § 1.

103 Superiors, janitors, and the like sin grivously in such cases and are liable to severe punishment by the proper superior. Others have *per se* no obligation of preventing the violation of the cloister, though an obligation may arise from other heads, e. g., charity. But at present we are concerned only with the question of the censure.

104 Sole 34-35, 84.

105 Vide infra pp. 97-100.

see the violation of the law and do not employ those means which a prudent man would: their guilt is very nearly, but not quite "malice" in the sence of the Code[106]. They do not "admit" or "introduce" in the commonly accepted meaning of the word[107], but merely connive at the unlawful entrance. Therefore, whether one considers "admitting" and "introducing" as forms of co-operation or as distinct crimes, he is forced to the conclusion that one who is guilty of *merely negative co-operation* with a woman's unlawful entrance does not incur the censure[108].

Still less reason is there to conclude that the censure is incurred if owing to the negligence of a superior or porter a woman enters unlawfully[109].

Again, suppose a woman has entered the cloister, no matter whether she was aware of the law or not, whether she was admitted or not. There is no difficulty, if those who see her and have it in their power immediately make an effort to have her leave and escort her out. If, however, the superior or janitor or even others in whose power it lies, do not forthwith take the necessary steps or if anyone detained her by engaging her in conversation, by showing her through the convent and the like, there can be no doubt that they sin grievously, but do they incur the censure? Some authors held that in such a case *superiors* and *janitors* who *tolerate,* and *others* who *cause* her to tarry within the cloister, must be reckoned among those "admitting or introducing," and, therefore, subject to excommunication. They argued either from the spirit and intention of the law[110], or from a wider meaning of "admittere" in the sense of "receiving, approving, as-

---

106 Cfr. Sole 13-16.

107 Cfr. canon 2228.

108 This conclusion was universally admitted in regard to those who were not specially entrusted with guarding the enclosure. Matthaeucci 103; Ferraris, v. *Conventus,* III 30; v. *Moniales,* III 59; Ojetti, v. *Clausura,* n. 1184; Mocchegiani I 202; Hilarius a Sexten 187; Piatus, *Praelectiones,* I 358-359, 379; Appeltern 249; D'Annibale, *Comment.,* 127; Hollweck 225, footnote 12; Pennacchi I 792; Lehmkuhl II 706; Cappello, *De Visitatione,* II 439; *De Censuris,* 109; Blat 696; Ayrinhac 266-267.

109 Cfr. canons 2231 and 2209 § 6; Hollweck 229, footnote 5.

110 Matthaeucci 103; Bonacina, *De Clausura etc.,* q. V p. IV n. 16; Ferraris, v. *Conventus,* III 31; Hollweck 229, footnote 5.

sociating."[111] Reiffenstuel, whose view was adopted by most recent authors objected to this, except in as far as it referred to superiors and other custodians of the enclosure[112]. If one adheres closely to the words of the Code, it appears that neither superiors nor any others incur excommunication in such a case. This view is based on the argument formulated by Pennacchi[113]. Though "admittere" may at times mean to "receive, approve, associate," this cannot be the sense of the word here. It is an old principle of law repeated in the Code, that "a penalty established by law is not incurred, unless the crime is complete in its kind according to the proper sense of the words of the law."[114] "Admittere" means to bid or permit a person to approach another or to enter a place[115]. Now, if an intruder is already within the enclosure, those that tolerate or even cause her to *delay* within the cloister do not "permit her to *enter*," nor do they "grant her *entrance*"; they do not "admit or introduce" her and, therefore, do not incur excommunication. Neither can the objection be raised, that this conclusion opposes the end and purpose of the law. It is true, if a woman is permitted to tarry within the cloister, the very dangers which the law of enclosure seeks to avert from regulars are increased; nevertheless that is not the crime which is visited with excommunication and the words of the law may not be stretched to include it. For according to canon 2219 § 3 a penalty may not be extended from one case to another, although the same or even a weightier reason exists for the latter. The direct and immediate purpose of the law of enclosure, however, is to prohibit the *entrance*, the *introduction* or the *admission* of unauthorized women into the enclosure and only these crimes are punished with excommunication. If superiors do not expel an intruder, they are

---

[111] Donatus, *Praxis Regularis*, tr. IV tom. I q. 6 n. 2 quoted by Pennacchi I 792.

[112] Reiffenstuel lib. III tit. XXXV n. 79; Piatus, *Praelectiones*, I 359; Appeltern, 249; Hilarius a Sexten 196; Mocchegiani I 202-203; Bachofen 158; Vermeersch, *De Religiosis*, I 178; Lehmkuhl II 706; D'Annibale, *Comment.*, 86, footnote 11.

[113] Pennacchi I 791-795.

[114] Canon 2228; Ayrinhac 65; Sole 77-79.

[115] Forcellini, v. *Admitto*.

neglectful of their duty, or, if others cause her to tarry, or do not escort her out, when they easily can, they are more or less guilty of co-operating with the material or formal sin of the intruder. Such cases can and should be severely dealt with by the superiors, but they do not constitute the precise crime for which the Code inflicts excommunication[116].

Not only in regard to the persons who incur excommunication for introducing or admitting women into the enclosure of male regulars, but also in regard to the age of the woman who is admitted is the present legislation more severe than the former law. All the papal constitutions used the word, "women," "mulieres," in this connection. Quite early the question arose as to how old a girl one might admit or introduce without incurring excommunication. Some took the view that, should one admit even an infant girl, he incurred the censure[117]. Others taught that the girl must have attained the use of reason, before one incurred excommunication for admitting her into the enclosure[118]. Still others maintained that, unless the girl had reached the age of puberty or twelve years, those who admitted her into the cloister did not incur excommunication. The reason assigned in support of this view was that the law rendered no one under the age of puberty liable to censure; since the regulars were excommunicated only for admitting "them," i. e., "women violating the enclosure," the conclusion, therefore, was that they incurred this censure, only if they admitted a woman above twelve years[119]. At the same time nearly all who accepted this view held that it was not lawful to admit girls under twelve years or even infants.

While the Code excommunicates only "women" (above twelve years of age) who enter the enclosure of male regulars unlawfully, it inflicts the same penalty on all who introduce or admit "women of any age whatsoever" (eas cuiuscumque

---

116 Canon 2231. Cfr. Cerato 122.

117 Lehmkuhl II 706; cfr. Ferraris, v. *Conventus,* III 18-19.

118 Bonacina, *De Clausura etc.,* q. V p. II n. 2; q. V p. III n. 2; Pennacchi I 796-797; Hilarius a Sexten 195; D'Annibale, *Theologia Moralis,* III 205; Ojetti, v. *Clausura,* n. 1187; Mocchegiani I 201; Vermeersch, *De Religiosis,* I 178; Paschalis de Siena 121.

119 Piatus, *Praelectiones,* I 354; Hollweck 229; Pruemmer II 102.

aetatis). Blat says that those incur this censure who admit or introduce ". . . *them,* i. e., women *of any age whatsoever,* therefore, also those below the age of puberty, yes, even if they are not yet seven years old, provided they do not lack the use of reason, because the word, 'women,' denotes the sex and all mentioned above violate the enclosure as was explained in canon 598, § 1,"[120] whereas in his explanation of canon 598, § 1 he states that girls may not be admitted, "even if they lack the use of reason, because the law does not directly affect them, but those admitting them."[121] If this is the case, why should those who admit or introduce infant girls be exempt from the censure, especially since the phrase of canon 2342 n. 2 "cuiuscumque aetatis" is, if anything, more forcible than that of canon 598 § 1 "cuiusvis aetatis"? Ferreres, too, thinks that probably excommunication is incurred, only if the girl admitted is above seven years[122].

On the other hand, Cappelo maintains that this censure is incurred by those who admit or introduce females of any age whatsoever, including infants (quin et nondum septennes). In the words of canon 2342 n. 2 "cuiuscumque aetatis" he sees the definite purpose to settle the controversy among canonists and to reject the opinion which held that the censure was not incurred for admitting girls below seven years[123]. This explanation is the only one that can be accepted. For a comparison of the words of the Code with those of Pius IX shows a striking difference. The constitution "Apostolicae Sedis" inflicted excommunication upon "women violating the enclosure of male regulars and upon superiors and others admitting *them.*"[124] According to the Code "women violating the enclosure of male regulars, and superiors and others, whoever they may be, introducing or admitting *them of any age*

---

[120] ". . . *eas* h. e. mulieres *cuiuscumque aetatis,* ergo etiam impuberes, imo etsi non septennes ast rationis usu non carentes, quia verbum mulieres sexum designat, et praedictae omnes violantes sunt clausurae ut explicatum est in can. 598, § 1." Blat 696-697.

[121] ". . . etsi usum rationes expertes, quia lex non ipsas sed admittentes directe prohibet." Blat 586.

[122] Ferreres II 128.

[123] Cappello, *De Censuris,* 110-111; cfr. 109-110.

[124] "Mulieres violantes Regularium virorum clausuram, et Superiores aliosve eas admittentes." Pius IX, const. *Apostolicae Sedis,* II 7.

whatsoever"[125] incur excommunication. Attention has already been called to two phrases of this canon differing from the law of Pius IX, viz., that not only *regulars* but *all persons* introducing or admitting women into the cloister are liable to this censure, and that not only *admitting* but also *introducing* women into the enclosure is punished with excommunication. Now we find a third distinctive phrase. Pius IX excommunicated regulars who admitted *women* (eas, i. e., mulieres), canon 2342 n. 2 excommunicates all who introduce or admit *women of any age whatsoever* (eas, i. e., mulieres cuiuscumque aetatis). Why interpret these words which do not "restate the old law without change" upon the authority of the former law and "in the light of the teaching of approved authors" of that law?[126] If the phrase "aliique quicumque ii sint" changes the limitation of this canon in regard to the subject of the penalty, the phrase "eas cuiuscumque aetatis" does the same in regard to the crime. Under the old legislation the more probable opinion held that excommunication was incurred for admitting girls below the age of puberty but above seven years; this on the strength of the word, "eas," i. e., "mulieres."[127] In adding to "eas" the words "cuiuscumque aetatis" the lawgiver could have had but one intention: that of making a change in the law. Since the present canon does not agree with the former law, it must be interpreted, "in so far as it differs from it, in the light of its own wording."[128] Therefore, by virtue of canon 598 § 1 no "woman of whatever age," and by this it means not even an infant girl, may be admitted into the cloister of male regulars; if it is nevertheless done, then by virtue of canon 2342 n. 2 all who introduce or admit a woman or even an infant girl incur excommunication[129].

A woman of unsound mind would not incur excommunication, if she entered the enclosure of male regulars, because she

125 "Plectuntur ipso facto excommunicatione etc.: 2. Mulieres violantes regularium virorum clausuram et Superiores aliique, quicumque ii sint, eas cujuscumque aetatis introducentes vel admittentes." Canon 2342 n. 2.

126 Cfr. canon 6 n. 2.

127 Piatus, *Comment.*, 181; Mocchegiani I 201-202; Pennacchi I 797.

128 Canon 6 n. 3. Cappello, *De Censuris*, 141; Sole 292-293.

129 Sole, 293, says: "etiam impuberes, etiam nondum septennes"; Cavigioli, 106: "Introducta, admissa adolescentula impubere vel infantula"; Ayrinhac, 267: "under twelve years of age"; Cerato 124.

is subjectively incapable of crime. But are those introducing or admitting such a woman also free from the censure? The almost general opinion was that regulars incurred excommunication in such a case[130]. Pennacchi, however, would excuse regulars who admitted such women from the censure, for the same reason as for admitting girls below the age of seven years[131]. In his commentary on this canon Cappello very correctly says: "We add that excommunication is incurred, even if weak-minded women are introduced or admitted, since the law makes no distinction and the same reason militates against it."[132]

Another penalty is decreed for *religious* alone, who introduce or admit women into the cloister of male regulars. If "religiosi," that is, not only regulars, but all who have made religious profession in any order or congregation, are found guilty of the offense under discussion, they are, besides incurring excommunication, to be deprived of any office they might hold and of both active and passive voice at elections. This penalty is not incurred *ipso facto,* but is to be adjudged by the lawful superior after trial and conviction[133]. It is not new, but was already contained in the constitution of Pius V "Regularium," nor was it revoked by the constitution of Pius IX "Apostolicae Sedis," as was the suspension that regulars incurred under the former constitution[134].

Before closing this chapter on the penalty inflicted for the violation of the enclosure of male regulars one point remains to be discussed. Does the cloister of male regulars come in any way under the jurisdiction of ordinaries of places? By the privilege of exemption which all regulars enjoy[135] they

---

130 Bonacina, *De Clausura etc.,* q. V p. II n. 2; Piatus, *Praelectiones,* I 355; Appeltern 247; Hilarius a Sexten 195; Bachofen 158; Paschalis de Siena 121.

131 Pennacchi I 789.

132 "Addimus, excommunicationem incurri etiamsi introducantur seu admittantur mulieres fatuae et mentis inopes, cum lex non distinguat ac eadem profecto militet ratio, nempe castitatis tuendae causa." Cappello, *De Censuris,* 111. Cfr. D'Annibale, *Comment.,* 85 footnote 9; Cerato 124; Ayrinhac 267; Sole 292.

133 Blat 697; Sole 293; Leitner 412.

134 Pennacchi I 802-804; Piatus, *Praelectiones,* I 359; Appeltern 249; Hilarius a Sexten 197; Hollweck 230; Ojetti, v. *Clausura,* n. 1188; Bachofen 157; Vermeersch, *De Religiosis,* I 178.

135 Canon 615.

are withdrawn from the jurisdiction of bishops in all matters except those that are expressly mentioned in the Code. As the Code does not commit the enclosure of male regulars to the care of bishops, they have no power to regulate or to guard it. Still canon 617 imposes a duty upon bishops that has a bearing upon the enclosure. If the regulars are remiss in the observance of the law of cloister, the ordinary of the place is bound to call the attention of the regular superior to its violation and admonish him to put an end to the abuse; if the regular superior does not heed his admonition, the ordinary cannot personally take any further measures to enforce the law, but is obliged to report the matter at once to Rome. Here all his duties in the matter end, unless the Holy See delegates him to act in its name and by its authority[136].

If the regular house in which enclosure is not observed is not formal, it remains under the vigilance of the ordinary of the place: if despite his remonstrance the regulars persist in their violation of the cloister, he must still refer the matter to the Holy See as above; but in the meantime, *if the abuse is a scandal to the people,* he can immediately take such steps as he deems necessary to check the abuse[137].

2. Partial Cloister.

Canon 599, § 1.

At an early date the education of children became a special avocation of monks. St. Basil in several of his "Regulae" treats of the schools. St. Benedict had a school for boys at his retreat at Subiaco, but it is not certain whether this was for "oblati" only, or also for children not destined for the order. At what time schools for any and all children were generally attached to monasteries, cannot be established with certainty. At the time of Charlemagne they received a new impetus and from then on most monasteries had schools, not only for the young religious but also for the children of the neighbors, both rich and poor[138].

---

136 Canon 617 § 1.
137 Canon 617 § 2.
138 Cfr. Turner, *Schools, Monastic,* in *Catholic Encyclopedia,* XIII 555-557.

Canon 599, § 1. When the house of male Regulars has annexed to it a house for boarding pupils, or for other works proper to the Institute, a separate part at least of the house should, if possible, be reserved for the habitation of the religious, and subject to the law of enclosure.

From these words it is manifest that, if male regulars conduct a boarding-school, it is desirable that there be individual buildings for the monastery and for the school[139]; if this is not feasible, at least a part of the religious house should be set aside for the living quarters of the regulars. Yet neither the one nor the other is strictly commanded; if either division is impracticable, the Code does not urge the observance and the decision on this point is left to the superior[140]. Implicitly it follows from this canon, that a day-school must always be situated outside the enclosure.

The same rules apply to a house of regulars destined for some work proper to the institute, e. g., hospitals, asylums, etc.[141]

Wherever this division of the living quarters from the school, hospital and the like is made, the law of enclosure must be observed in the part reserved for the regulars[142]. But what if the division is not possible? Blat is of the opinion that in this case the whole house is free from the law of enclosure[143].

Canon 599, § 2.

Even to places outside the enclosure reserved for extern or intern pupils or for works proper to the Institute, persons of the other sex must not be admitted except for a just reason, and with the permission of the Superior.

This paragraph shows how carefully the Church would shield regulars from danger and suspicion. Checks are therefore placed on the admission of women to places in charge of regulars, if these are not open to the general public, though not within the enclosure. All schools for day-scholars as well

139 Blat 587.
140 Leitner 411; Blat 587; Pruemmer² 289; Charles Augustine III 315.
141 Blat 587; Leitner 411; Pruemmer² 289.
142 Blat 587; Leitner 411; Pruemmer² 289.
143 Blat 587.

as for boarders fall under this prohibition. For a good reason, not necessarily a grave one, the superior of the house, but only he, may permit exceptions; thus the mother of a prospective pupil wishing to see the equipment of the school might be admitted. Prudence must direct one in the choice of time and other circumstances. The Code does not fix any penalty in case a woman is admitted without a good reason or by one other than the superior[144].

---

[144] Leitner 411; Blat 587-588; Pruemmer[2] 289; Charles Augustine III 315.

CHAPTER VI.

Papal Cloister of Nuns.

1. Exclusion of Outsiders.

Canon 600, N. 1.

Stricter by far than the enclosure of male regulars is that of nuns. Since the constitution of Boniface VIII "Periculoso"[1] nuns were not allowed to leave their convents except in extreme necessity, neither was anyone to be admitted into their cloister except to render some necessary service. This law was re-enacted by the Council of Trent[2] as well as by decrees of several later Popes[3]. The Code renews these laws with several modifications that are made necessary by the change of conditions.

Before proceeding to the consideration of the canons dealing specially with the enclosure of nuns, it will be advisable to call attention to a few points concerning canon 597. The enclosure of nuns is papal and is binding only on nuns properly so called, i. e., those female religious who take solemn vows[4]. This enclosure the Church considers so intimately allied to solemn vows that, as the Congregation of Bishops and Regulars replied: "especially since the Council of Trent the Holy See does not permit solemn vows to be taken in

---

[1] C. un., *de statu regularium,* III, 16, in VI°.

[2] Conc. Trident., sess. XXV, *de regularibus,* c. 5.

[3] Vide supra pp. 49-54.

[4] Cfr. canon 488 n. 7. Members of a religious order that normally take solemn vows, but owing to circumstances are allowed to make only simple profession, e. g., the Clares and Ursulines in this country, are still called nuns. In the United States there are at present four convents of Visitation Nuns where solemn vows are taken and papal enclosure is observed (with some modifications; vide infra p. 128, footnote 159): at Georgetown, Mobile, St. Louis, and Baltimore. S. C. Ep. et Reg., in *Americana votorum,* 30 Sept. 1864, Bizzarri 735-736. The fifth that existed at Kaskaskia, Ill., is dissolved. All other nuns in this country take only simple vows.

societies or communities of women, unless they live perpetually in inviolate enclosure."[5]

On the other hand, if for any reason the observance of papal cloister becomes impossible, the Holy See not only relieves the nuns of this obligation, but also reduces their profession to simple vows[6]. Likewise, if conditions do not permit solemn profession, the obligation of papal enclosure ceases; there remains only episcopal enclosure, as was declared regarding the vows of nuns in France after the French Revolution[7]. In one of its recent pronouncements the Pontifical Commission for the Authentic Interpretation of the Canons of the Code declared that all such indults remain in force[8].

As in the case of male religious, so, too, several convents of sisters with simple vows have by special concession of the Holy See introduced papal enclosure which then has the same obligation as the cloister of nuns, the penalties for its violation being determined in the individual grants. Such an indult was granted to a convent of St. Francis de Sales at Rhegium in Sicily, February 22, 1839[9], and to a convent of Sisters of the Most Holy Redeemer in Diocese of Catanzaro, December 6, 1839[10]. Before this concession is granted, it is necessary that the construction of the buildings with the gardens, etc., be adapted to the observance of enclosure; besides this the condition is generally made that all the sisters entitled to a vote give their consent by secret ballot, as in the case of the indults mentioned above[11]. The obligation of cloister in such convents does not arise from the general law, but from the particular indult; neither

---

[5] S. C. Ep. et Reg., in *Gandaven.*, 24 Sept. 1816, Bizzarri 411-412; in *Ravennaten.*, 6 Dec. 1839, ibid. 90-91; in *Januen.*, 15 Jan. 1841; *Reg.*, 13 Jan. 1843, Lucidi II 148; Ojetti, v. *Clausura,* n. 1177; Cappello, *De Visitatione,* II 436; Cavigioli 101.

[6] Cfr. S. C. Ep. et Reg., 17 Martii 1848, Bizzarri 732; Pennacchi I 718.

[7] S. C. Ep. et Reg., in *Parisien.*, 1 Aug. 1839, Bizzarri 86-87; D'Annibale, *Comment.*, 83 footnote 3; Cavigioli 102. Vide infra pp. 154-159.

[8] Pontif. Commissio ad C. C. authentice Interpret., 1 Martii 1921, III 2, A. A. S. XIII 178.

[9] Pennacchi I 717; Cavigioli 101-102.

[10] Bizzarri 88-89; D'Annibale, *Comment.*, 83 footnote 3.

[11] Cfr. Pennacchi I 718; Cappello, *De Visitatione,* II 436; Ojetti, v. *Clausura,* n. 1177.

does this indult change the nature of the sisters' vows which remain simple[12].

An enclosure imposed only by a precept of the rule, as is contained in the rules of the Clares approved by Gregory IX and Innocent IV[13], or one arising from a special vow such as is made by the Clares (Urbanists[14] and Colettines[15]), does not of itself become papal enclosure, unless the nuns take solemn vows or have obtained a special grant of the Holy See. The rule or vow, as the case may be, only imposes an obligation to observe enclosure in the same manner as papal enclosure, without the censures and other penalties for its violation, unless these are expressly added by the proper authorities[16].

In the monasteries of nuns there are no "neutral" places to which both nuns and outsiders have access. What are such in monasteries of male regulars, e. g., the public church and its contiguous sacristy, are outside the enclosure of nuns and, as we shall see below, no nun is allowed to go to these places except in the cases specified by law or by papal dispensation. The nuns' choir lies within the cloister and is closed to outsiders. It must be separated from the church by a screen. In this screen there is a small window which the nuns approach for communion, investiture, profession and the like[17]. This window is fitted with two doors; the key to the outer one is in the keeping of the confessor, that to the inner one is in the keeping of the abbess[18]. The roof also lies outside the cloister,

---

[12] S. C. Ep. et Reg., in *Rhegien.*, 22 Feb. 1839, in *Policastren.*, 6 Dec. 1839, Bizzarri 88-89; Ojetti, v. *Clausura*, n. 1177; Cappello, *De Visitatione*, II 436; Lucidi II 148-149.

[13] Gregorius IX, bulla *Cum omnis vera Religio*, 24 Maii 1239, *Bullarium Franc.*, I 264; Innocentius IV, bulla *Cum omnis vera Religio*, 6 Aug. 1247, ibid. 477; bulla *Solet annuere*, 9 Aug. 1253, *Seraph. Legisl. Textus Orig.* 32 and 37.

[14] Urbanus IV, bulla *Religionis augmentum*, 27 Julii 1263, *Bullarium Franc.*, II 479; bulla *Beata Clara*, 18 Oct. 1263, ibid. 511.

[15] Constitutiones S. Colettae approb. a Pio II, bulla *Etsi ex suscepti*, 18 Oct. 1458, *Seraph. Legisl. Textus Orig.* 42. Cfr. Appeltern 199.

[16] Pennacchi I 716; Hollwerk 224 footnote 9 c) and d).

[17] Gregorius IX, bulla *Cum omnis vera Religio*, 24 Maii 1239, *Bull. Franc.*, I 266; Innocentius IV, bulla *Solet annuere*, 13 Nov. 1245, ibid. 398; Urbanus IV, bulla *Religionis augmentum*, 27 Julii 1263, ibid. II 481-482; bulla *Beata Clara*, 18 Oct. 1263, ibid. 515-516.

[18] S. C. Ep. et Reg., 15 Sept. 1617; S. C. Conc., in *Janzen.*, 14 Apr. 1725, Pallottini, v. *Fenestra*, n. 6. Cfr. C. Mediolan. I Prov. (1565), Constitutiones p. III c. IX, *Ss. Conc.* XV 325; C. Toletanum Prov. (1590), p. I c. VII n. 10, ibid. XV, 1391.

as we shall see in the discussion of canon 601; so, too, the parlor to which visitors have access[19].

Finally, canon 597 § 3 states that the limits of the enclosure in convents of nuns are to be defined by the "bishop"[20] whose place is supplied during a vacancy by the vicar capitular or, in this country, by the administrator[21]; therefore, neither the superioress nor the regular superior to whom the nuns are subject have any authority in the matter; nor the vicar general, unless he be specially empowered by the bishop[22].

Canon 600. Within the enclosure of nuns no one, of whatever class, condition, sex or age may be admitted without the permission of the Holy See, except the following persons:

1. The local Ordinary or the Regular Superior canonically visiting the monastery of nuns, or other Visitators delegated by them may enter the enclosure, but only for the purpose of inspection, and on condition that they be accompanied by at least one cleric or male religious of mature age;

2. The confessor or his substitute can, with the due precautions, enter the enclosure to administer the sacraments to the sick or to assist the dying;

3. Rulers of states, with their wives and retinue; and also Cardinals;

4. The Superioress, after taking the due precautions, can permit the doctor, the surgeon and others, whose work is necessary, to enter the enclosure, having previously obtained at least the habitual approval of the local Ordinary; but if urgent necessity does not allow time to seek his approval, she may presume permission.

In keeping with the law of the Church since the constitution of Boniface VIII "Periculoso," every person without distinction of class (whether of the nobility or not), condition (social standing), sex or age is excluded from the enclosure of nuns. The word "age" settles a controversy that existed under the former legislation. Some canonists drew the conclusion that, since the entire purpose of the law ceased in the case of chil-

---

19 Vide infra p. 137.
20 Charles Augustine III 312; Blat 586; Fanfani 126.
21 Cfr. Canon 435 § 1.
22 Cfr. Canon 368 § 1.

dren who had not yet attained the use of reason, the law itself ceased in their regard[23]. Others correctly maintained the opposite view[24]. There can no longer be any doubt that children, even infants, may not be admitted within the enclosure[25].

Still conditions may arise that justify an exception. Before speaking of the special permission obtained from the Holy See, the cases will be considered, in which the Code itself establishes exceptions.

Boniface VIII permitted the admission of outsiders, "if there existed a reasonable and manifest cause"[26]; the Council of Trent, "in cases of necessity."[27] In his constitution "Dubiis" § 1 Gregory XIII ordained that bishops and regular superiors, too, could enter only in cases of necessity. In view of the purpose of the enclosure it is evident that the necessity which justifies the entrance of outsiders must exist on the part of the monastery, the community or some individual nun and that it cannot well be met by the nuns[28]. But what constituted a case of necessity was not defined. Authors, therefore, distinguished three classes of necessity for which admission into

---

[23] Reiffenstuel lib. III tit. XXXV nn. 39 and 40; Hilarius a Sexten 182. Nevertheless in the next sentence they advised against admitting infants for the very reason that in some cases at least it might become a source of danger.

[24] Ferraris, v. *Moniales,* III 58, who quotes several decisions of S. C. Ep. et Reg., *in Tudertina,* 7 Apr. 1579; in *Neapolitan.,* 22 Martii 1580; in *Cremonen.,* 12 Feb. 1585; in *Taurinen.,* 10 Jun. 1650; in *Pistorien.,* 24 Feb. 1579; in *S. Sever.,* 8 Maii 1595. Pennacchi I 718; Hollweck 225, footnote 11; Piatus, *Praelectiones,* I 379-380; Pruemmer II 106.

[25] Charles Augustine III 315; Blat 588; Ayrinhac 266; Biederlack 239.

[26] C. un., *de statu regularium,* III, 16, in VI°.

[27] "in casibus necessariis," Conc. Trident., sess. XXV, *de regularibus,* c. 5.

[28] S. C. Conc., 11 Sept. 1610, Piatus, *Praelectiones,* I 366; S. C. Conc., 9 Sept. 1611, Pignatelli VI, LXXXV, 114; Reiffenstuel lib. III tit. XXXV, n. 52; Bonacina, *De Clausura* etc., q. IV p. IV n. 1; Pennacchi I 724; Appeltern 252-253; Ojetti, v. *Clausura,* n. 1172; Lucidi II 152; Hilarius a Sexten 182. Still authors cite cases in which an exception may be made, even though the necessity affects only the persons that enter, but it must be an extraordinary and unforeseen necessity, for instance, if it were the only means of saving one's life. S. C. Conc., in *Limana,* Feb. 1586, Bonacina, *De Clausura etc.,* q. IV p. IV n. 13; Piatus, *Praelectiones,* I 366, 371. It would not, however, be allowed to receive women in a monastery to remove them from the occasion of sin, to protect a wife in the quarrels with her husband, much less to admit women to entertainments arranged by the nuns. Cfr. Pignatelli VI 85 and VIII 47 cited by Lucidi II 152-153.

the enclosure could be granted: (1) the bodily welfare of the nuns; (2) their spiritual needs; (3) the material needs of the convent[29]. The Code does not follow this division, but distinguishes rather according to the classes of persons to be admitted.

In the first place the superiors of the convent are allowed to enter the enclosure for the purpose of visitation. The Council of Trent granted bishops the right to visit the convents of nuns situated in their diocese, even if they were exempt from episcopal jurisdiction[30]. Alexander VII in his constitution "Felici" established special regulations for the visitation by regular superiors. Though his constitution was originally published only for Italy and adjacent islands, still not a few held it to be common law[31]. In view of the doubt that still remained, we are referred to the constitution "Dubiis" of Gregory XIII, whereby all prelates, secular as well as regular, were prohibited from using their right to enter the enclosure of nuns, except in cases of necessity, and accompanied only by a few elderly and religious persons.

A convent of nuns may be immediately subject to the Holy See or to the bishop in whose diocese it is situated or to regulars. Accordingly a different superior is entrusted with the visitation. Canon 512 § 1 n. 1 empowers the ordinary of the place to conduct the entire visitation, both personal and local, of all those convents of nuns situated within his diocese, which are immediately subject to himself or to the Holy See[32]. If the nuns are subject to regulars, the major superior is charged with the canonical visitation both local and personal[33]; and the bishop cannot hinder him in making the visitation of the cloister[34]. But even in this case the cloister is under

---

29 Pennacchi I 726.

30 Conc. Trident., sess. XXV, *de regularibus*, c. 5; Matthaeucci 78.

31 Matthaeucci 78; Ferraris, v. *Moniales*, III 74-78; Benedictus XIV, *De Synodo Dioecesana*, lib. IX c. XV n. 6.

32 Formerly the bishop acted as delegate of the Pope, when he visited convents immediately subject to the Holy See. Cfr. Pallottini, v. *Monasteria Monialium*, II 61, 63, 64; Matthaeucci 77; Mocchegiani I 230.

33 Canon 511; cfr. canon 603 § 2; Ojetti, v. *Clausura*, n. 1175; Mocchegiani I 230.

34 Formerly the bishop had to be informed of the time of the visitation. S. C. Conc., in *Lycien.*, 22 Sept. 1742 ad IV and V, Pallottini, v. *Monasteria Monialium*, II 103; Ojetti, v. *Clausura*, n. 1175.

the vigilance of the local ordinary[35] and by virtue of canon 512 § 2 n. 1 the bishop is authorized to visit the convent, but only regarding the enclosure[36]. Though the bishop is not authorized to make the personal visitation of the nuns, he may question them regarding matters pertaining to the enclosure[37]. In regard to the visitation of the enclosure the bishop does not merely supply for the neglect of the regular superior, as he does regarding the entire visitation of nuns according to canon 512 § 2 n. 1, but enjoys this right equally with[38] and independently of the regular superior[39]. Therefore, the latter may not pretend that he visit the monastery together with the bishop or assist at his visitation[40].

Since the constitution of Gregory XIII "Dubiis" permitted both secular and regular superiors to enter the enclosure only "in cases of necessity" and the Congregation of Bishops and Regulars repeated this as applying to the bishop in a decision of May 22, 1615[41], the conclusion was drawn that a bishop could not lawfully visit nuns' cloister, unless there were suspicion that it was violated[42]. At first sight this appears to have been renewed by the constitution of Benedict XIV "Salutare," which also permits the local ordinary and the regular superior to enter only "in cases of necessity,"[43] but in view of several decisions given by the Congregation of the Council it would seem that any just and reasonable cause may be understood[44]. The Sacred Congregation declared that the Bishop of Colimbria could visit the enclosure of nuns subject to the Cistercians

[35] Canon 603 § 1.

[36] S. C. Conc., in *Cathacen.*, 17 Nov. 1629, Pallottini, v. *Monasteria Monialium*, II 65; in *Basileen*, 9 Feb. 1574, ibid., 68; in *Ariminen.*, 27 Jan. 1748, ad I, II, III, ibid. 59; cfr. ibid., 49-51; Reiffenstuel lib. III tit. XXXV n. 67; Lucidi II 218-221; Matthaeucci 77; Mocchegiani I 230-231.

[37] Canon 513; Pontif. Commissio ad C. C. authentice Interpret., 24 Nov., 1920, *de religiosis*, ad II, A. A. S., XII 575; cfr. S. C. Conc., in *Regien.*, Martii 1608, Pallottini, v. *Monasteria Monialium*, II 80; S. C. Ep. et Reg., in *Nucerina Paganorum*, 8 Sept. 1725 ad VII, Bizzarri 319-320.

[38] Reiffenstuel lib. III tit. XXXV n. 67; Lucidi II 220.

[39] S. C. Ep. et Reg., in *Fossanen.*, 31 Aug. 1658, Lucidi II 220.

[40] S. C. Ep. et Reg., in *Fulginaten.*, 10 Jan. 1648, Lucidi II 220.

[41] Ferraris, v. *Episcopus*, VI 98.

[42] Mocchegiani I 234.

[43] Mocchegiani I 236.

[44] Mocchegiani I 236.

"even in the absence of any suspicion that the enclosure had been violated, or of any negligence of the regular superiors and without consulting them or asking their permission."[45] Matthaeucci[46] adduces two additional decisions of the same Congregation; one of September 24, 1622, according to which the bishop is allowed to visit monasteries subject to regulars and to speak to the individual nuns regarding the cloister without the intervention of the regulars; the other of the year 1638[47], which stated in a general way "that the bishop may enter the cloister accompanied by two respectable men." Therefrom he concludes that the bishop may, as often as he sees fit, visit the cloister of nuns subject to regulars, even though the regular superior perform his duty in the matter and there is no reason to suspect that enclosure is not observed[48]. Other decisions prove that the bishop could hold the visitation in such convents without the presence of the regular superior[49].

The Code prescribes the visitation of nuns' enclosure by the bishop every five years without any reference to neglect by the regular superior or suspicion that the cloister is violated. The same power is granted the vicar capitular or the administrator during a vacancy of the diocese[50].

Formerly the vicar general could not visit the enclosure of nuns, unless he had been specially authorized by the bishop[51]. Neither canon 512 § 2 n. 1 nor canon 600 n. 1 contain any such restriction. Hence the vicar general may, by virtue of his office and for the purpose of visitation, enter the enclosure of nuns who are subject to regulars with the same right as of all others.

---

45 S. C. Conc., in *Colimbricn.*, 26 Maii 1640, Benedictus XIV, *Op. Omnia*, XII 440.

46 Matthaeucci 79.

47 S. C. Conc., in *Recinen.*, 1638, ad VII, Matthaeucci 79.

48 Matthaeucci 79; Benedictus XIV, *Op. Omnia*, XII 440; Mocchegiani I 234-235; Ferraris, v. *Moniales*, III 95; Reiffenstuel lib. III tit. XXXV n. 67.

49 S. C. Conc., 22 Apr. 1617, Mocchegiani I 235; S. C. Ep. et Reg., in *Nucerina Paganorum*, 8 Sept. 1725, ad I, Bizzarri 319-320.

50 Mocchegiani I 231.

51 S. C. Conc., in *Regin.*, 1624, in *Gienn.*, 1625, Pallottini, v. *Monasteria Monialium*, II 74; Mocchegiani I 230-231; Matthaeucci 79.

Under the former legislation the bishop could delegate any ecclesiastic to conduct the visitation incumbent upon him; not so the regular superior. The Constitution of Alexander VII "Felici" bound the latter to make it personally: even if he were lawfully hindered, he could not have it conducted by another, but had to postpone it to another time[52]. Now the Code authorizes the regular superior as well as the bishop to entrust the visitation of nuns to another. However, the regular superior may delegate another, only if he is *lawfully prevented* from conducting the visitation in person[53], whereas the bishop is entirely free to conduct it personally or by a delegate[54].

Whether he acts in his own name or as delegate, the canonical visitor is permitted to enter the enclosure "only for the purpose of inspection." This inspection will differ materially, when made by a bishop in a convent subject to regulars from that made in a convent subject to himself or the Holy See or by a regular superior in a convent under his jurisdiction. In the latter case the bishop or the regular superior conducts the entire visitation; therefore, either may visit the entire monastery, not merely as far as the enclosure is concerned, but also regarding all matters of discipline and administration. But in a convent subject to regulars the bishop is restricted to the visitation of the cloister and, therefore, can visit all parts of the house as far as necessary: he may examine the communion-window, the confession-window, the inner and outer walls of the cloister, the windows, the inner choir and all rooms that lie within the enclosure as well as the parlors[55]. This visitation must not extend to matters that pertain exclusively to discipline[56]. The bishop may also inquire as to

[52] Mocchegiani I 232; Ojetti, v. *Clausura*, n. 1175.

[53] Canon 511; Blat 489; Charles Augustine III 135.

[54] Canon 512 § 1; Blat 489; Charles Augustine III 136.

[55] S. C. Conc., in *Florentina*, 29 Julii 1684, ad I; in *Aquilana*, 31 Julii 1723, ad II et IV, Benedictus XIV, *Op. Omnia*, XII 439-441; in *Ariminen.*, 27 Jan. 1748, ad I-IV, Ferraris, *App.*, n. 283; in *Hieracen.*, 26 Jan. 1692, ad I, ibid. n. 348bis; in *Olomucen.*, 11 Julii 1665, ad X, Zamboni IV 430; S. C. Ep. et Reg., in *Nucerina Paganorum*, 8 Sept. 1725, ad I, II, III, VI, VII, Bizzarri 319-320; Mocchegiani I 235-236; Charles Augustine III 136-137.

[56] S. C. Conc., in *Florentina*, 29 Julii 1684, ad I; *Ord. Minorum*, 19 Jan. 1686 ad II-IV; in *Aquilana*, 31 Julii 1723, ad II et VI, Benedictus XIV, *Op. Omnia*, XII 439-441; Mocchegiani I 238-243.

whether the enclosure is observed or whether abuses have crept in[57], but this investigation must be conducted at the parlor-grille[58], where the visitator must always hold the personal visitation.

Finally, the Code prescribes that the visitator "be accompanied by at least one cleric or male religious of mature age." Alexander VII in his constitution "Felici" ordained that the general of a religious order be accompanied during the inspection of the cloister by two members of his order of mature age and exemplary life, other superiors of lower rank by one. These companions were never to be out of sight of the visitator. Gregory XIII in "Dubiis" forbade visitors, both secular and regular, to enter the enclosure, unless attended by a few elderly and religious persons[59]. Although this constitution seemed to permit a bishop to take lay-persons as companions, the Congregation of Bishops and Regulars repeatedly declared that only ecclesiastics might accompany the visitator[60], unless the expert advice of laymen were required[61]. The word "few," "paucis," left a wide scope to the bishop as to the number of attendants[62]. Canonists sought to determine it by appealing to the decree of Clement V at the Council of Vienne, which fixed the number at eight[63], a restriction that is denied by Pennacchi, who bases his argument upon the constitution "Dubiis" itself as well as upon a decision of the Congregation of the Council

---

[57] Canon 513; Pontif. Commissio ad C. C. authentice Interpret., 24 Nov. 1920, *de religiosis,* ad II, A. A. S. XII 575; S. C. Ep. et Reg., in *Nucerina Paganorum,* 8 Sept. 1725, Bizzarri 319-320; Mocchegiani I 235; Charles Augustine III 136-137.

[58] S. C. Conc., in *Aquilana,* 31 Julii 1723, ad II, Benedictus XIV, *Op. Omnia,* XII 441; in *Ariminen.,* 27 Jan. 1748, ad II, Ferraris, *App.,* n. 283.

[59] S. C. Conc., *Ord. Minorum,* 19 Jan. 1686, ad V, Benedictus XIV, *Op. Omnia,* XII 441; 13 Maii 1582, Ojetti, v. *Clausura,* n. 1174.

[60] S. C. Ep. et Reg., in *Gallipolitana,* 22 Maii 1615, in *Tarvisina,* 20 Nov. 1601; in *Genuen.,* 16 Jan. 1607; in *Lucana,* 22 Jan. 1616, Ferraris, v. *Episcopus,* VI 98-101; Monacelli p. III form. XL nn. 12-14.

[61] S. C. Ep. et Reg., 18 Feb. 1593, Ferraris, v. *Episcopus,* VI 101; Monacelli p. III form. XL n. 12-14.

[62] Lucidi II 154.

[63] ". . . . Ipsos autem visitatores notariis duobus, et personis duabus suae ecclesiae, quattuorque viris aliis honestis utique et maturis praecipimus in ea, quam visitando facient, inquisitione fore contentos." C. 2, *de statu monachorum,* III, 10, in Clem.; Fagnani quoted by Pennacchi I 733-734; Monacelli p. III form. XL nn. 15, 16; Ferraris, v. *Episcopus,* VI 103; Mocchegiani I 237.

which would not settle the question, but merely replied that the apostolic constitutions were to be observed[64].

The Code does not limit the number of attendants, but leaves it to the judgment of the visitator: they ought to be few. Whether one or more, these companions must be chosen from the secular clergy or from some religious community of men. Note the word "religioso": he need not be a member of a religious order or even a cleric; a lay-brother in a religious congregation is eligible[65]. Whoever is chosen must be "of mature age." Blat thinks forty years will certainly satisfy[66]. The number of years alone will not be decisive, rather the character that usually attends years.

How often must or may the visitation of nuns' cloister be held? Formerly regular superiors were not permitted to enter the enclosure more than once a year, so that if one had canonically visited a convent, neither he nor any other regular superior was allowed to visit it again during that year[67]. If they deemed it necessary, they must first obtain leave from the local ordinary and be accompanied by him or some other secular cleric appointed by him[68]. Bishops, on the other hand, could conduct the entire or the cloistral visitation as often as they saw fit[69].

The Code is not explicit. Regular superiors are referred to their statutes: they must visit all the monasteries under their jurisdiction as often as these require[70], which must be at least every five years[71]. The bishop must conduct the visitation every five years[72]. May the regular superior enter the enclosure of nuns for the purpose of visitation oftener than is prescribed by the constitutions or the bishop more than once every five years? If one may draw a conclusion from the

---

64 S. C. Conc., *Ord. Minorum,* 19 Jan. 1686, ad V, Pennacchi I 733-735.

65 Blat 588; Charles Augustine III 316.

66 Blat 588.

67 Matthaeucci 81; Ojetti, v. *Clausura,* n. 1175.

68 Alexander VII, const. *Felici,* § 2; Mocchegiani I 232-233.

69 S. C. Conc., in *Colimbrien.,* 26 Maii 1640, Benedictus XIV, *Op. Omnia,* XII 440; 24 Sept. 1622; in *Recinen.,* 1638, Matthaeucci 79.

70 Canon 511; Charles Augustine III 135; Blat 489.

71 Cfr. canon 512 § 2 n. 1.

72 Canon 512 § 2 n. 1; Charles Augustine III 136; Blat 489.

previous legislation, the bishop could lawfully do so[73], but not the regular superior on his own authority.

The manner in which the bishop must conduct the visitation of the cloister of nuns subject to regulars pertains to liturgy rather than to Canon Law. It may be well to recall the following: he is not obliged to announce the day and hour to the nuns beforehand[74]. He may not visit the Blessed Sacrament, the Oleum Infirmorum, the confessionals, the cemetery and relics except in matters pertaining to the enclosure[75]. Neither may he visit the cells of the nuns regarding matters not pertaining to the cloister[76]. The superioress is obliged to deliver to the bishop a list of all the nuns, pupils and servants at the time of the visitation[77]. The bishop may not, however, enter the enclosure to make the prescribed investigation regarding an aspirant's or a novice's intention and her freedom from coercion[78], to invest a postulant, to admit a novice to profession, to solemnly give the veil to a nun, to administer the Sacrament of Confirmation unless the confirmand were in danger of death[79], to consecrate the abbess, or to assist at the election of the abbess[80], which must be held at the parlor-grille, unless he prudently fears that otherwise the freedom and the validity of the election might be imperiled[81]. But he may enter to bestow the blessing upon a nun or other inmate

---

73 ". . . . hodie eum posse non immerito Pighi affirmat." Cavigioli 104, footnote 1.

74 S. C. Conc., *Ord. Minorum,* 19 Jan. 1686, ad I, Benedictus XIV, *Op. Omnia,* XII 440.

75 S. C. Conc., *Ord. Minorum,* 19 Jan. 1686, ad II; in *Florentina,* 29 Julii 1684, ad I; in *Aquilana,* 31 Julii 1723, ad VI, Benedictus XIV, *Op. Omnia,* XII 440-441.

76 S. C. Conc., *Ord. Minorum,* 19 Jan. 1686, ad IX, Benedictus XIV, *Op. Omnia,* XII 441.

77 S. C. Ep. et Reg., in *Nucerina Paganorum,* 8 Sept. 1725, ad VI, Bizzarri 319-320.

78 Canon 552 § 2.

79 S. C. Ep. et Reg., in *Neapolitana,* 6 Jan. 1601, Lucidi II 153-154.

80 Canon 506 § 2. Cfr. Conc. Trident., sess. XXV, *de regularibus,* c. 7; S. C. Ep. et Reg., in *Syracusana,* 16 Oct. 1600, Lucidi II 153.

81 Cfr. Lucidi II 153-154; Pennacchi I 735.

82 Under the former legislation the bishop had to be attended on such occasions by the nuns' confessor and another priest. S. C. Conc., in *Mazarien.,* 10 Maii 1727, ad I et II, Benedictus XIV, *Op. Omnia,* XIII 263-265; Ojetti, v. *Clausura,* n. 1174.

in the hour of death[82] or to hear the confession of a sick nun who asks for him[83].

In the constitution "Felici" Alexander VII prescribed that the *regular superior* conduct the visitation quickly and in one day, but with due care; he must not begin it before sunrise nor protract it beyond sunset; neither he nor his companions were allowed to eat in the convent. Besides the companions of his own order he was to be attended by four of the older nuns of the convent who were not to leave him as long as the visitation lasted; all other nuns and all secular women and girls who were staying in the convent and were not prevented by necessary work had to assemble in the choir, before the visitator entered the cloister, and remain there until he and his companions had left the convent. For this reason the visitator was bound to inform the superioress in due season of the day and hour of the visitation.

Both Boniface VIII[84] and the Council of Trent[85] authorized bishops and regular superiors to appeal to the civil power for assistance in enforcing the law of enclosure. This was renewed by Pius IX in the constitution "Apostolicae Sedis."[86] The Code does not refer to this, since the appeal would be useless, owing to the so-called separation of Church and State in almost every country. At most the aid of the state could be invoked only on the score of housebreaking in case the intruders would endeavor to gain entrance by force[87].

Canon 600, N. 2.

Ever solicitous that her children, saint as well as sinner, should at all times, but especially in the hour of sickness, enjoy the benefits of her sacraments and sacramentals, the Church granted nuns whom bodily infirmity would not permit to come to the chapel the privilege of receiving the ministrations of their confessor within the enclosure. The right of the *regular* confessor to enter the enclosure was first clearly

---

[83] S. C. Conc., in *Mazarien.*, 10 Maii 1727, ad III, Benedictus XIV, *Op. Omnia*, XIII 263-265

[84] C. un., *de statu regularium*, III, 16, in VI°.

[85] Conc. Trident., sess. XXV, *de regularibus*, c. 5.

[86] Pius IX, const. *Apostolicae Sedis*, IV 6.

[87] Cfr. Hollweck 201, footnote 1, 226, footnote 17.

defined by Alexander VII in his constitution "Felici" § 5: "Furthermore the confessor of nuns, both ordinary and extraordinary, shall by no means enter the enclosure of the monastery except to administer the Sacraments of Penance, Eucharist and Extreme Unction to the nuns or other sick persons dwelling there, and to assist the dying; nor shall he enter at all except with a companion, who must be of exemplary life and mature age and who must remain in such a part of the monastery where he can always see the confessor and be seen by him." Decrees of the Congregation of Bishops and Regulars allowed confessors other than regulars to enter on the *principal feasts of the year* to administer the Sacraments of Penance and Eucharists to those nuns who were so sick that they could not either alone or with the help of other nuns approach the confessional and the communion-window; but they must enter alone and be received by elderly nuns who must conduct them by direct way to the infirmary and, during the confession of the nun, the cell was to be left open, so that the two accompanying nuns (comitatrices) who must remain near the door of the cell could readily see the confessor and the sick nun, but not hear them[88]. The Congregation of the Council also declared that the bishop and both the ordinary and the extraordinary confessor were permitted to enter the monastery without restriction, as often as they were called by a sick nun who desired to make her confession out of mere devotion[89].

The second section of canon 600 permits the nuns' "confessor or his substitute" to enter their enclosure. By the "confessor" is meant first and above all the ordinary confessor who is to be appointed for each convent of nuns according to canon 520 § 1. The "substitute" is the priest appointed in the same manner to supply for him during an absence, illness and the like. But those words must be taken in a wider sense. Whenever a sick nun desires to go to confession, the following may enter the enclosure: (a) the special confessor appointed by the local ordinary for an individual nun at her request, as

---

[88] Cfr. Benedictus XIV, *Op. Omnia,* XIII 264.

[89] S. C. Conc., in *Mazariensi,* 10 Maii 1727, Benedictus XIV, *Op. Omnia,* XIII 263-265.

permitted according to canon 520 § 2; (b) the extraordinary confessor prescribed in canon 521 § 1; (c) the special confessors mentioned in canon 521 § 2; (d) any confessor approved to hear women's confessions whom a sick nun, *even though not in danger of death,* requests according to canon 523[90]; (e) *in danger of death* any priest whosoever, even one who otherwise has no faculties to hear confessions, in conformity with canon 882[91]. Any one of these may enter the enclosure to hear the confession of a sick nun, even if the ordinary confessor or his substitute is at hand. The administration of Communion, both as Viaticum and out of devotion, and of Extreme Unction and assisting the dying is reserved by canon 514 § 2 to the ordinary confessor or his substitute. They may enter for this purpose, even if one of those mentioned above hear the confession of the sick person. In this case, however, they may permit him to administer the other sacraments and to assist her in her last moments, if these ministrations are to be tendered at the same time. And it would seem to be advisable to do so. Still the ordinary confessor would act within his rights, if he insisted on attending to these duties personally. If, however, neither the ordinary confessor nor his substitute is present, any of the priests enumerated above, after hearing the sick nun's confession, may administer the other sacraments and assist a dying nun in her agony. Moreover, if a nun were dying and the ordinary confessor or his substitute were not at hand, any priest might enter the enclosure to administer Viaticum or Extreme Unction or to assist her in her last moments, even though her confession were not to be heard[92].

But who is to bring Holy Communion to a sick nun who wishes to receive out of devotion in the absence of the ordinary confessor or his substitute? For just such cases the Congregation of Religious, September 1, 1912, published a rule that

---

[90] Charles Augustine III 163-164; Blat 504; cfr. 501; Leitner 337; Biederlack 89.

[91] Cfr. canon 514 § 2; Leitner 337; Blat 588 and *Commentarium libri III* p. I 234-235; S. C. Conc., in *Mazarien.*, 10 Maii 1727, Benedictus XIV, *Op. Omnia,* XIII 263-265; S. C. Ep. et Reg., in *Fossanen.*, Feb., 1734, Bizzarri 329-330; Ferraris, v. *Moniales,* V 82.

[92] Cfr. canons 864 § 1, 938, 939; Pennacchi I 732.

can be safely followed. Although it is not expressly taken up into the Code, it corresponds very nearly with the provisions of n. 4 of the present canon. In the first place it will be the chaplain who has been appointed as required by canon 529; if he, too, were absent, any priest may be called with the permission of the bishop. The latter can once for always authorize the superioress to designate the priest and grant him permission in his name. That decree prescribed that, from the time he enters until he leaves, the priest thus summoned be attended, if possible, by four nuns of mature age, and that a regular need not be accompanied by another member of his order[93].

As often as the confessor or any other priest taking his place enters nuns' enclosure, he must observe "the due precautions." What they are, the Code does not define; they must be gathered from the former legislation[94]. Still it cannot be said that each and every precaution of the previous law remains in force, since the general phrase "the due precautions" is scarcely sufficient to renew them. They must, however, serve as a guide.

According to the constitution of Alexander VII "Felici," §§ 5 and 7, whenever the confessor, if a *regular,* enters the enclosure to administer the Sacraments of Penance, Eucharist and Extreme Unction and to assist the dying, he must be accompanied by another regular of good character and mature age, who must always be able to see the confessor and to be seen by him[95]; he may not remain habitually in or near the nuns' convent, unless the distance between his monastery and that of the nuns is great: in this case the regular confessor and his companion, and no one else, may live under a separate roof removed from the nuns' convent at a distance to be

---

93 S. C. de Religiosis, 1 Sept. 1912, A. A. S. IV 625-626; cfr. Blat 588; Leitner 344-345.

94 Charles Augustine III 316; Blat 588-589; Leitner 344.

95 S. C. Ep. et Reg., in *Nolana,* 21 Feb. 1617, Ferraris, v. *Moniales,* V 65. Nevertheless the same Congregation declared a bishop might tolerate that a regular-confessor entered without a companion in view of a long-standing custom and of the difficulty of having an attendant. S. C. Ep. et Reg., in *Aesina,* 29 Maii 1846, ad II, Bizzarri 546-548; Pennacchi I 730-731. Cfr. S. C. de Religiosis, 1 Sept. 1912, A. A. S. IV 625-626.

approved by the bishop[96]. The Congregation of Bishops and Regulars permitted a bishop to tolerate a custom whereby confessors, both secular and regular, spent the night within the enclosure, if in the opinion of the physician a nun were at the point of death[97]. A confessor of nuns, even a regular, does not need special permission to enter the enclosure for the requirements of his office, provided he does not tarry in the convent, but leaves as soon as his task is done[98]. Without leave of the Congregation of Bishops and Regulars (now the Congregation of Religious) a regular confessor of nuns and his associate may not speak to them except as regards the administration of the sacraments[99].

If a *secular priest* acts as confessor, he must enter alone, go to the infirmary and leave by the shortest way; nor may he tarry even to visit other sick who are not in need of his ministrations at this time. He must be accompanied by two nuns who during the confession will remain out of ear-shot, yet so near the open door of the cell, that they can easily see the confessor and the sick nun[100]. The confessor may also enter the enclosure to assist a dying nun, after he has administered the last sacraments[101]. In some convents it had become customary that the confessor be relieved by the chaplain and he in turn by a third priest, in case the agony of the dying nun was very protracted. The Congregation left it to the prudent judgment of the bishop to tolerate or to forbid that practice[102]. It was likewise declared that the confessor might assist dying nuns

---

[96] S. C. Ep. et Reg., in *Ariminen.*, 22 Jan. 1576, 19 Aug. 1578, 2 Jan. 1579, et 22 Jan. 1593; in *Bononien.*, 3 Maii 1593; in *Januen.*, 14 Nov. 1603; in *Mantuana*, 22 Nov. 1604; in *Ulixbonen. Occidentalis*, 10 Sept. 1722; 22 Dec. 1592, Ferraris, v. *Moniales*, V 68 and 55; Lucidi II 158.

[97] S. C. Ep. et Reg., in *Aesina*, 29 Maii 1846, ad I, Bizzarri 546-548; Lucidi II 158. In commenting upon this decision Pennacchi calls attention to the conditions of this custom and remarks that such a custom could not be tolerated, unless 1) it were of long standing, 2) there were no scandal, 3) abolishing the custom would give rise to suspicions. Pennacchi I 730-731.

[98] S. C. Ep. et Reg., in *Comen.*, 9 Martii 1609, Ferraris, v. *Moniales*, V 64.

[99] S. C. Ep. et Reg., in *Nolana*, 21 Feb. 1617, Ferraris, v. *Moniales*, V 66.

[100] S. C. Ep. et Reg., 13 Sept. 1583, Ferraris, v. *Moniales*, V 65, 54; ejusd. Congr. litt. encycl. 21 Martii 1682, ibid. 56.

[101] S. C. Conc., in *Tranen.*, Jan. 1714, Bizzarri 301-302.

[102] S. C. Ep. et Reg., in *Fossanen.*, Feb. 1734, Bizzarri 329-330; Pennacchi I 729; Lucidi II 159.

also at night and that the bishop could grant permission for that purpose to the extraordinary confessor[103]. The declarations of the Congregation of Bishops and Regulars given in 1582 and 1590, that confessors of nuns were not under any circumstances permitted to eat in their convents[104], were later mitigated in case of a long stay and necessity[105]. As often as the confessor enters the enclosure, he must be vested in surplice and stole[106].

The Code states the full reason for which a confessor may enter the enclosure: to administer the sacraments to the sick and to assist the dying. This was always the extent of this permission, as can be seen from the constitution of Alexander VII "Felici" and a decision of the Congregation of the Council in a cause of the Diocese of Mazzara of May 10, 1727[107]. By "sick," "infirmis," are meant not only those in danger of death, but also those unable to come to the confessional and the communion-window[108]. Furthermore, that word includes besides the nuns postulants, novices and all other persons who lawfully reside within the convent, e. g., pupils[109].

In particular the Congregation of Bishops and Regulars declared that the confessor of nuns was not allowed to enter the enclosure for the burial of a nun[110]. This decision was confirmed in 1855 with the addition "that, if there were a custom to the contrary, it must not be tolerated except by leave of the ordinary in individual cases."[111] Finally, it was declared

---

[103] S. C. Ep. et Reg., in *Algaren.*, Julii 1736, Bizzarri 347-348; 13 Sept. 1583, Ferraris, v. *Moniales,* V 57; Lucidi II 159.

[104] S. C. Ep. et Reg., 13 Sept. 1582; Nonis Maii 1590, Lucidi II 160.

[105] S. C. Ep. et Reg., in *Pistorien. et Praten.,* 2 Martii 1855, Lucidi II 160; Pennacchi I 732.

[106] S. C. Ep. et Reg., in *Caietana,* 29 Jan. 1627, Ferraris, v. *Moniales,* V 64; Lucidi II 159.

[107] Benedictus XIV, *Op. Omnia,* XIII 263-265.

[108] Cfr. S. C. de Religiosis, 1 Sept. 1912, A. A. S. IV 625-626; S. C. Ep. et Reg., 13 Sept. 1583, Ferraris, v. *Moniales,* V 58.

[109] Cfr. canon 514 §§ 1 and 2; Alexander VII, const. *Felici,* § 5; Charles Augustine III 141-145; Biederlack 90; Fanfani 53-54.

[110] S. C. Ep. et Reg., in *Reatina,* 10 Martii 1577, A. S. S. XXXVII 441 ad calcem; in *una Dominican.*, 30 Junii 1582, *Ulissiponen.*, 11 Aug. 1610, Lucidi II 158.

[111] S. C. Ep. et Reg., in *Pistorien. et Praten.*, 2 Martii 1855, A. S. S. XXXVII 441; in *Bononien.*, 20 Aug. 1599, Ferraris, v. *Moniales,* V 52-53; Lucidi II 158; Pennacchi I 732.

that a custom whereby not only the confessor but also several other priests, regular as well as secular, entered the enclosure on these occasions could be tolerated[112]. The confessor may not enter the cloister to bless the cells of the nuns[113]; a custom to the contrary could be tolerated, but the permission of the bishop must be asked each time[114]. He may not enter to exorcise a nun[115]; nor to celebrate Mass[116]; but certainly may enter to pick up a consecrated host that has fallen within the enclosure, since the law of enclosure must yield to the reverence due to the Blessed Sacrament[117]. The confessor may not enter the enclosure to hear the confession of a nun who can come to the confessional or on the pretext of accompanying the doctor, laborers, etc.[118]

Canon 600, N. 3.

The first concession contained in the third section of canon 600 corresponds to that contained in canon 598 § 2. Note that canon 600 grants this exemption to the ruler as well as to his wife and retinue which may include men and women. The reason lies in the difference between canon 600, whereby men and women are barred from the enclosure of nuns, and canon 598 § 1, which forbids only women to enter the cloister of male regulars[119]. For the rest see the interpretation of canon 598 § 2[120]. What was said there concerning foundresses

---

112 S. C. Ep. et Reg., in *Zamoren.*, 24 Apr. 1903, A. S. S. XXXVI 203-205; *Ursulinarum,* 12 Nov. 1904, A. S. S. XXXVII 441-442. In the former of these decisions it was forbidden that the priests partake of any refreshments within the cloister, a circumstance that did not occur in the latter case. Pennachi I 732.

113 S. C. Ep. et Reg., 4 Sept. 1596, Ferraris, v. *Moniales,* V 60.

114 Pennacchi I 732; Lucidi II 159.

115 S. C. Ep. et Reg., 1 Julii 1606, Ferraris, v. *Moniales,* V 61; Pennacchi I 732; Lucidi II 159.

116 S. C. Ep. et Reg., in *Lancianen.,* et in *Pistor.,* 16 Julii 1685; in *Mantuana* 13 Junii 1591; in *Bononien.,* 2 Jan. 1601, Ferraris, v. *Moniales,* V 62; Lucidi II 159; Pennacchi I 732. Bl. Agnes of Bohemia obtained permission for her convent at Prague to have Mass celebrated five times a year in the choir, so that all could see the priest at the altar. Gregorius IX, bulla *Cum saeculi vanitate relicta,* 4 Apr. 1237, *Bullarium Franc.,* I 213.

117 Ferraris, v. *Moniales,* V 63; Pennacchi I 732; Lucidi II 159.

118 S. C. Ep. et Reg., 13 Sept. 1583, Ferraris, v. *Moniales,* V 59; Lucidi II 159.

119 Ferraris, v. *Moniales,* III 53-54; Lucidi II 160; Pennacchi I 718-722; Blat 590; Leitner 441.

120 Pages 77-81.

and others enjoying special privileges applies also in regard to the cloister of nuns[121].

The privilege accorded Cardinals to enter the enclosure of nuns is entirely new. In the constitution "Dubiis" Gregory XIII among others expressly forbade Cardinals to enter nuns' enclosure except in case of necessity, and Benedict XIV revoked all indults granted also to Cardinals both individually and collectively[122]. By virtue of the present canon Cardinals enjoy this privilege from the day of their promotion in consistory[123]. The Code does not state whether they may take their suite with them. Therefore, Blat says: "It appears that a suite even of one person is prohibited"; but he would permit a person to enter the enclosure to assist at the Cardinal's Mass, if he celebrated within the enclosure[124].

Canon 600, N. 4.

Besides the spiritual needs of the nuns, for which provision is made by the visitation and the administration of the sacraments in nn. 1 and 2 of this canon, the bodily welfare of the nuns and the maintenance of the conventual building will frequently require the entrance of others. Boniface VIII already permitted the entrance of honest persons into the enclosure of nuns for a reasonable and manifest cause and with the permission of the proper superior[125]. This was renewed by the Council of Trent[126]. Because leave to enter was granted without sufficient cause, Gregory XIII revoked all privileges and forbade bishops and regular superiors to give permission except in cases of urgent necessity[127]. The same Pope declared that the superiors themselves, even bishops and Cardinals, were allowed to enter only in such cases[128]. The permission to enter the cloister of nuns immediately subject to the Holy See or to the bishop always depended on the bishop; vicars general could not grant it unless specially authorized. The vicar

---

121 Ferraris, v. *Moniales,* III 55; Lucidi II 160.
122 Benedictus XIV, const. *Salutare,* Lucidi II 154.
123 Cfr. canon 239 § 1.
124 Blat 590.
125 C. un., *de statu regularium,* III, 16, in VI°.
126 Conc. Trident., sess. XXV, *de regularibus,* c. 5.
127 Gregorius XIII, const. *Ubi gratiae.*
128 Gregorius XIII, const. *Dubiis;* cfr. Pennacchi I 711-712.

capitular enjoyed the same right as the bishop[129]. In regard to convents of nuns subject to regulars there was much discussion and the Congregation of the Council gave different decisions in several cases. In 1597, and again as late as 1692, it declared that to grant this permission belonged exclusively to the regular superior[130]. Yet November 13, 1620, it declared that, any contrary law, statute or custom notwithstanding, the permission was to be sought not only from the regular superiors, but also from the local ordinaries. Moreover, when the matter was submitted another time to the Congregation, this decision was upheld with the extension that, where such a custom obtained, one need not even consult the regular superior[131]. In this manner the power to grant permission gradually passed into the hands of the local ordinary.

This entire legislation is changed by the Code. Now it is neither the bishop nor the regular superior who grants permission to outsiders to enter nuns' cloister in cases of necessity, but the superioress of the convent. However, she must have the approval of the local ordinary without further regard for the regular superior[132]. The ordinary must pass, first, upon the need itself, whether it is of such a nature as to warrant the admission of outsiders, secondly, upon the character of those to be admitted. A general approval may and ought to be given by the bishop at least for those cases that occur frequently[133].

The Council of Trent prescribed that the permission be given in writing[134]. The constitution "Apostolicae Sedis" required only a "lawful permission," "legitima licentia," wherefore

---

[129] Ferraris, v. *Moniales,* III 85-87; Pennacchi I 736.

[130] S. C. Conc., *Nullius,* 19 Junii 1597; in *Hieracen.,* 26 Jan. 1692 ad V, Ferraris, v. *Moniales,* III 88-89; Pennacchi I 737.

[131] S. C. Conc., in *Belluen.,* 21 Maii 1630, Benedictus XIV, *Op. Omnia,* XI 569. Similar decisions were given by the same C. in *Camerinensi,* 16 Dec. 1633; in *Perusina,* 10 Jan. 1637; *Montis Regalis,* 7 Aug. 1638; in *Neapolitana,* 18 Nov. 1645, ibid. 569-570; in *Bononiensi,* 17 Maii 1704; *Burgis S. Domnini,* 21 Apr. 1731; Decr. S. C. Ep. et Reg., 24 Aug. 1594; in *Camerinen.,* 7 Martii 1617, Ferraris, v. *Moniales,* III 90-93; S. C. Conc., in *Conversana,* 8 Maii 1751, ad VIII, Pennacchi I 738.

[132] Blat 590.

[133] Blat 590; cfr. S. C. Ep. et Reg., in *Parmensi,* 20 Nov. 1584; in *Interamn.,* 9 Sept. 1586; 27 Martii 1588; in *Placentina,* 6 Junii 1614, Lucidi II 154-155.

[134] Conc. Trident., sess. XXV, *de regularibus,* c. 5.

Pennacchi concluded that permission by word of mouth excused from censure[135]. Neither does the Code require that the approval of the bishop be given in writing. It may be advisable to obtain a written approbation in order that it can be proven, if one is called upon to do so, but a verbal approval will fully satisfy the requirements of the law.

Despite this provision for an habitual approval of the ordinary, unforseen conditions may arise that require immediate attention and will not suffer delay until the ordinary can be approached. In such cases the Code provides that the approval of the ordinary may be justly presumed. Neither should a superioress hesitate to apply this rule. Her experience in estimating cases of less urgency as well as the approval given by the bishop on those occasions must serve as a guide. If there is time, she might consult one or the other nun and then act as prudence dictates[136].

In none of the former papal constitutions is the nature of the necessity clearly specified. The Code, too, mentions merely "doctors, surgeons and others whose work is necessary" as persons who can lawfully be admitted. The reason is clear from the reply of the Congregation of Bishops and Regulars to the Bishop of Rhegium: no fixed rule can be laid down to determine the cases when it is lawful to enter the cloister, for time and places change and the nature of the cases varies according to circumstances. Therefore, it is necessary that a prelate in his prudence examine and carefully consider whatever occurs and then decide conscientiously, what appears expedient in the Lord[137]. But it is absolutely required that the necessity exist on the part of the monastery and not on the part of those that enter[138].

The best guidance regarding cases, when admission is justified and the precautions to be taken on such occasions will be found in the decisions of the Roman Congregations. In this respect Lucidi[139] will be followed.

---

135 Pennacchi I 738-739; D'Annibale, *Comment.*, 84.
136 Blat 590.
137 Lucidi II 152.
138 S. C. Ep. et Reg., in *Ravennaten.*, 9 Sept. 1611, Lucidi II 152.
139 Lucidi II 154-157.

In reply to the bishop of Parma the Sacred Congregation wrote November 20, 1584: "Here in Rome and in every other place where proper discipline is observed in nuns' convents, there is usually drawn up a list of persons whom the convent needs, as bakers, masons, carpenters, blacksmiths, porters (carriers) in certain cases, besides the doctor, surgeon and barber [for blood-letting]; these are given permission once for always, as long as it is not revoked, to enter the monastery for the exercise of their profession, with the precaution that only men of mature age and good character are chosen: Your Lordship must act in this manner in your diocese with the restriction that no other persons may enter but those who are necessary: thus it is ordained and prescribed in many places."[140]

Such authorized persons are forbidden to delegate others in their place, if they are not of the number who have obtained permission of the bishop[141].

The regular doctors and surgeons must be granted general permission to enter the enclosure even at night in case of urgent necessity, but for others who are not the regular physicians a special permission is required[142]. Therefore, the decree of a bishop forbidding the confessor and regular doctor to enter at night without special permission in each case was annulled[143]. They are to be attended not only on the way to the infirmary but as long as they are with the sick[144].

No nun is allowed to have her own special physician, but must be content with the one the convent usually engages[145], except in case of necessity[146].

The procurator and syndic are not permitted to enter[147], not even to accompany a priest who is to administer the sacraments[148] or the superiors who enter in cases of necessity, not-

[140] Lucidi II 154.

[141] S. C. Ep. et Reg., in *Interamn.*, 9 Sept. 1586, Lucidi II 154-155.

[142] S. C. Ep. et Reg., in *Ferrarien.*, 2 Julii 1599 et 13 Julii 1605, Ferraris, v. *Medicus*, 13.

[143] S. C. Ep. et Reg., in *Ferrarien.*, 10 Feb. 1593, Lucidi II 156.

[144] S. C. Ep. et Reg., in *Parmen.*, 26 Martii 1601, Ferraris, v. *Medicus*, 14.

[145] S. C. Ep. et Reg., in *Bononien.*, 6 Julii 1588, Lucidi II 156.

[146] S. C. Ep. et Reg., in *Catacen.*, 15 Feb., 1595, Lucidi II 156.

[147] S. C. Ep. et Reg., in *Lycien.*, 15 Martii 1595 et 4 Jan. 1610, Lucidi II 156.

[148] S. C. Ep. et Reg., in *Senogallien.*, 26 Jun. 1603, Lucidi II 156.

withstanding any contrary custom which was abolished by Gregory XIII[149].

If no other provision can be made, a servant may live in a room within the parlor, but outside the enclosure[150], and may enter the cloister to perform all necessary tasks[151].

Permission may be given to a notary and witnesses, if a lay-woman who dwells in the enclosure is sick and wishes to make her will or some other disposition of her property[152].

Outside of the preceding cases papal permission is required by the present canon that any person, man or woman, adult or infant, may enter or be admitted into nuns' enclosure[153]. Even bishops and regular superiors need this permission, except when they enter for the canonical visitation or for the administration of the sacraments as allowed in nn. 1 and 2 of this canon. Whatever conditions are laid down in the rescript allowing one to enter must be carefully observed. Thus Urban VIII ordained that the consent of the majority of the nuns assembled in chapter must be obtained, before use could be made of the permission granted by the Holy See[154].

There is no law forbidding that girls be educated in convents of nuns[155]. However, no pupils may be received without leave of the Holy See[156]. From a formulary commonly used in granting this permission one learns that the Congregation of Bishops and Regulars usually places the following conditions:

1) That the convent can and is wont to receive pupils and that there is no prohibition of it in the rule.

2) That the entire space allotted to the girls is completely separated from the part of the monastery which the nuns and novices occupy.

---

149 S. C. Ep. et Reg., in *Ariminen.,* 10 Jan. 1617, Lucidi II 156.

150 S. C. Ep. et Reg., in *Navarien.,* 5 Dec. 1600; in *Januen.,* 15 Martii 1606, Lucidi II 156.

151 S. C. Ep. et Reg., in *Perusina,* 9 Oct. 1618, Lucidi II 156.

152 S. C. Ep. et Reg., in *Catacen.,* 15 Feb. 1595, Lucidi II 157.

153 Pruemmer[2] 290; Leitner 412; Sole 288; Fanfani 125-126.

154 Urbanus VIII, const. *Sacrosanctum,* Matthaeucci 81; Ferraris, v. *Moniales,* III 56-57; Lucidi II 155.

155 S. C. Ep. et Reg., in *Hieracensi,* 31 Aug. 1575, Quaranta 449; Ferraris, v. *Moniales,* I 1.

156 S. C. Ep. et Reg., decr., 17 Maii 1603; in *Amerina,* 4 Jan. 1608, Monacelli, tit. XI form. I; Cappello, *De Visitatione,* II 436; Pruemmer[2] 290.

3) That the number of girls be limited according to the capacity of the convent, not to exceed half the number of nuns, not counting novices and lay-sisters.

4) That the pupil be furnished with all that is necessary and be received by the nuns in chapter and by secret ballot.

5) That she be above seven years and under twenty-five; and that as soon as she reaches the age of twenty-five, she leave immediately under pain of incurring ipso facto the penalties for violation of the enclosure[157]; furthermore her relatives are obliged to receive her, when she reaches that age or in any other case in which the ordinary or the nuns see fit to dismiss her.

6) That there are not more pupils than the number fixed according to n. 4.

7) That satisfactory security be given for the semi-annual payment in advance for board and tuition, which must net the convent a considerable income (emolumento considerabilique esse debeant utilitati); if the bondsman die or the bond lapse through any other accident, it must be renewed within a month, otherwise the girl must be dismissed.

8) She must enter alone, be dressed modestly and observe the laws regarding the cloister just as the nuns.

9) Once she leaves, she may not be received again in the same or any other convent, except for the purpose of becoming a nun.

10) The "pagella" must be executed within six months and preserved in the chancery. Any interpolation or erasure invalidates it[158].

Sometimes permission is granted that the nuns teach day-scholars. Then a dispensation is granted that the nuns may enter the school by a special door leading from the cloister[159]. Very exceptional were the concessions granted to a convent

---

[157] It is not true, then, that the Congregation "did not impose excommunication," as Bonacina, *De Clausura etc.*, q. IV p. IV n. 16 mantains.

[158] Lucidi II 481-482; cfr. Ferraris, v. *Moniales,* I 1-29; Bonacina, *De Clausura etc.*, q. IV p. IV nn. 15-16; Reiffenstuel lib. III tit. XXXV n. 41; Piatus, *Praelectiones,* I 372-374; Bouix I 668-669.

[159] S. C. Ep. et Reg., in *Placentina,* 18 Julii 1834, Lucidi II 161; 21 Apr. 1841, Bizzarri 463-465; S. C. Conc., 2 Apr. 1841; 22 Jan. 1847, Cappello, *De Visitatione,* II 436. Such a concession was made to the Visitation Convent at Georgetown in 1823 and Feb. 1, 1824. A. S. S. I 709.

of Dominican nuns of Modena by the Congregation of Bishops and Regulars December 31, 1840, and to the Salesian nuns of Padua[160].

Finally, no women may be received into the cloister as pensioners without leave of the Holy See[161].

Canon 2342, N. 1.

For the violation of nuns' enclosure by unlawful admission or entrance of outsiders excommunication without reservation was inflicted for the first time by the Council of Trent[162]. Under pain of excommunication reserved to the Holy See Gregory XIII forbade anyone to enter the enclosure on the pretext of some indult or privilege which he revoked; all who admitted them were excommunicated and deprived of their dignities, benefices and offices and became incapable of obtaining them in the future[163]. The same Pope declared that bishops and regular superiors, too, were not allowed to enter except in cases of necessity: if they entered on other occassions, bishops incurred interdict from entrance into church the first time, suspension the second, and excommunication the third; regular superiors were deprived of their offices and excommunicated for every offense[164]. These penalties were renewed by Benedict XIV in the constitutions "Cum sacrarum", "Per binas," and "Gravissimo animi moerore." Finally, Pius IX included in his constitution "Apostolicae Sedis", § 2 n. 6, the excommunication which is now received into the Code in almost the same words.

Canon 2342. The following incur ipso facto excommunication reserved simpliciter to the Holy See:

1. Those who violate the enclosure of nuns, of whatever class, condition or sex they may be, by entering into their monasteries without lawful permission; likewise those who

---

160 Lucidi II 170-174.

161 S. C. Ep. et Reg., 16 Julii 1884 ad I, *Collectanea S. C. de Prop. Fide* n. 1623; Hilarius a Sexten 188; Hollweck 225, footnote 12; Piatus, *Praelectiones,* I 365; Mocchegiani I 224; Cappello, *De Visitatione,* II 436.

162 Conc. Trident., sess. XXV, *de regularibus,* c. 5.

163 Gregoirus XIII, const. *Ubi gratiae.*

164 Gregorius XIII, const. *Dubiis.*

introduce or admit them; if they are clerics, they are furthermore to be suspended for a time to be determined by the ordinary according to the gravity of their guilt.

At the outset it must be noted that this excommunication is incurred only for violating the cloister *of nuns*[165]. This censure is of the same class as that inflicted for violating the cloister of male regulars. Therefore, what was said above regarding its reservation and absolution applies to this excommunication also[166].

They "violate" nuns' enclosure, who "enter[167] their monasteries," i. e., the limits of the cloister as defined by canon 597. These include the nuns' choir and the gardens reserved for them, but not the public church with its contiguous sacristy and the parlor[168]; nor the roof, since it does not lie within the enclosure, so that one who climbs upon the roof of a nuns' convent from a neighboring house, does not incur excommunication[169]. To constitute a "violation" of the enclosure, it is required that one be aware of the law, of its sanction and of the fact that he is trespassing upon the cloister. Ignorance of any or all of these points will excuse him from this censure, provided it is not "crassa vel supina."[170] But neither presumption[171], nor an evil intention[172], nor a pretext of a papal indult[173] is required, in order that one incur this excommunication[174]. Physical force or necessity, grave fear or

---

[165] Cfr. canon 597; Pennacchi I 716; Hilarius a Sexten 181; Moccheggiani I 218; Pruemmer II 105-106; Pruemmer[2] 290; Piatus, *Praelectiones,* I 363-364; Cappello, *De Censuris,* 107; Ayrinhac 266; Blat 695; Cerato 121; Sole 288; Leitner 412. Regarding the cloister of those who for special reasons do not take solemn vows vide supra p. 105.—Violations of the cloister of such congregations as have by special indult introduced papal enclosure are punished with the penalties mentioned in their respective rescripts. Vide supra pp. 105-106; Pennacchi I 717, 723-724; Pruemmer II 106; Piatus, *Praelectiones,* I 364; Appeltern 251; Cerato 121; Cavigioli 102.

[166] Vide supra p. 86.

[167] As to what constitutes "entering" vide supra pp. 87-90.

[168] Vide supra pp. 63-70; Cappello, *De Censuris,* 108-109; Sole 288; Blat 695; Cerato 122.

[169] Vide supra pp. 106-107; Cerato 122.

[170] Vide supra pp. 87-88; Cappello, *De Censuris,* 107.

[171] Vide supra pp. 87-88; Cerato 123.

[172] Vide supra pp. 88-89; Cappello, *De Censuris,* 107.

[173] Vide supra p. 89; Cappello, *De Censuris,* 107.

[174] Pennacchi I 723-724.

a great burden will excuse from the observance of the enclosure and from the penalty[175].

"Without lawful permission" those enter who neither have a papal dispensation nor are included under one of the sections of canon 600 or, if included, enter under conditions not allowed by that canon[176].

But what if a person enter under pretense of one of the reasons contained in canon 600, in reality for another? To illustrate, suppose he obtains permission to enter the enclosure to make necessary repairs on the building, his real motive being his curiosity to see the interior of the convent: does he incur excommunication? One must distinguish: if he really intends to perform the required task, he enters with lawful permission and is free from the censure; his second intention is more or less sinful according to its gravity. If, however, he does not at all intend to do any necessary work, but merely employs this occasion as a pretext to gain admission and satisfy his curiosity or whatever other purpose he may have, he enters without lawful permission and therefore incurs the penalty[177].

This excommunication is incurred by all violating nuns' enclosure "of whatever class, condition or sex they may be," provided they are baptized, as was said above page 88, footnote 69. This phrase introduces two changes in the law. First, unlike the penalty inflicted by the constitution "Dubiis" of Gregory XIII, bishops now incur excommunication even for the first unlawful entrance; for according to canon 2227 § 2 bishops are not liable to suspension and interdict unless expressly mentioned, but are subject to all other penalties[178]. The second change in this penalty is due to the omission of

175 Canons 2205 § 2 and 2218 § 2; vide supra p. 88. For this reason a public official would be free from sin and censure, if a so-called "convent-inspection" law obliged him to enter nuns' enclosure; but one would not be so easily excused, if the law left him a choice. Sole 26-28, 55; Ayrinhac 37-38, 51; Cerato 39-43.

176 S. C. Ep. et Reg., in *Ferrarien*, 6 Aug. 1601; in *Spoletana*, 1 Oct. 1601; in *Pisaurien.*, 14 Jun. 1630, Ferraris, v. *Moniales*, III 82; Hilarius a Sexten 182; Pennacchi I 724; Cappello, *De Censuris*, 108; Blat 588, 596; Cavigioli 102.

177 Bonacina, *De Clausura* etc., q. IV p. IV n. 18; Ferraris, v. *Moniales*, III 83; Pennacchi I 723.

178 Sole 77; Cappello, *De Censuris*, 10; Cerato 16; Pruemmer[2] 615; Ayrinhac 65.

the word "age." Under the law of Pius IX even children below the age of puberty, who had attained the use of reason, were subject to excommunication, if they entered nuns' enclosure[179]. By the omission of the word "age" boys and girls below the age of fourteen and twelve respectively are no longer liable to this censure, but are to be punished in other ways, as befits their years[180]. But all persons above the age of puberty, men as well as women, without any regard for their standing, ecclesiastical or social, who enter the cloister of nuns unlawfully, are by that very fact excommunicated[181].

If one who entered with lawful permission, through ignorance or for other reasons that will excuse him from the censure does not withdraw, as soon as those reasons cease, he sins by tarrying, but does not incur excommunication, since that is not the precise crime of "entering the enclosure" for which this censure is inflicted[182].

Besides those entering nuns' enclosure unlawfully, all those who "introduce or admit them" incur the same penalty. What is meant by "introducing or admitting" was explained above in the commentary of the second section of this canon pages 91-95. Only two points call for special treatment here. First, who are the persons that are liable to excommunication for introducing or admitting others into the enclosure of nuns? Bonacina[183] held that the abbess and other nuns, the regular superiors as well as all other persons were liable to this censure. Ferraris[184] inclined to the view that only the nuns fell under excommunication. The commentators of the constitution "Apostolicae Sedis" generally followed the latter's opinion[185].

---

179 Pius IX, const. *Apostolicae Sedis,* II 4; Pennacchi I 718; Hilarius a Sexten 182.

180 Cfr. canon 2230; vide supra p. 87; Blat 696; Cerato 121; Ayrinhac 266; Cappello, *De Censuris,* 108; Leitner 415; Sole 83-84.

181 Cfr. pp. 85-86; Sole 287-288; Leitner 415; Ayrinhac 266; Cerato 121-122.

182 Cfr. canon 2219 § 3; vide supra p. 90; Cerato 122.

183 Bonacina, *De Clausura etc.,* q. IV p. VI nn. 1-7.

184 Ferraris, v. *Moniales,* III 59.

185 Pennacchi I 740-744; Piatus, *Praelectiones,* I 378-379; Mocchegiani I 222. Hollweck, 225, footnote 11, held "a novice, a servant of the convent, the doctor, confessor etc.," might be guilty of "introducing" unauthorized persons.

Cappello[186], Cerato[187], Blat[188], Ayrinhac[189], and Biederlack[190] hold that outsiders also can "introduce," "admitting" being restricted to the superioress and janitress. Sole on the other hand says: "To introduce is to lead into, v. g., by opening the door, inviting, etc.; wherefore those outside the cloister do not incur excommunication, if they lend help to those entering."[191] But in the first place the Latin word "introducere" means "to lead or bring into a place, to conduct into or within," and can be said of one who is without as well as of one who is within[192]. Furthermore this is one of the few canons in which accomplices of a crime are expressly mentioned. Canons 2209 §§ 1-3 and 2231 would in themselves suffice to include those "introducing or admitting" intruders; but it was necessary to retain this phrase, since it had become a fixed phrase in Canon Law and its omission in the Code might easily have led to the assumption that accomplices were exempt from the penalty. These words have, it would appear, the same meaning as those in n. 2 of this canon: "superiors and others, whoever they may be." In that section these words were added to emphasize a decided departure from the former interpretation, according to which only the regulars were liable to the censure[193].

The other difficulty regarding the phrase of canon 2342 n. 1 under discussion is found in the word "them," "eos." Grammatically this pronoun refers to "violating," "violantes." Now the question arises: Do those introducing or admitting others incur this censure only if the persons introduced or admitted are themselves liable to the censure for entering; or do they incur it even then, when those introduced or admitted are not liable to it, inasmuch as they are below the age of puberty?

---

186 Cappello, *De Censuris,* 109.
187 Cerato 122.
188 Blat 696.
189 Ayrinhac 266.
190 Biederlack 239-240.
191 "*Introducere est intus ducere,* v. gr. ianuam aperiendo, invitando etc.; quamobrem excommunicationem non contrahunt stantes extra septa, si ingredientibus operam praestant." Sole 289.
192 Forcellini, v. *introduco*; cfr. Livius XL 25.
193 Vide supra pp. 90-91. Cfr. Cerato 17-18; Ayrinhac 41-46, 70-71; Sole 32-36, 84-85.

If one considers the grammatical construction and the corresponding words of the second section of this canon, it would appear at first sight that the former is the case, so that, if the person introduced or admitted is below the age of puberty, the one who introduces or admits him is free from the censure. This is the opinion of Sole[194] and Cavigioli[195]. Nevertheless, not only if the person introduced or admitted is above the age of puberty, but also if below it, the one introducing or admitting him incurs excommunication at least in a case where the boy or girl has the use of reason and knowingly violates the enclosure. The reason is found in canon 2230, which, indeed, exempts "impuberes" from penalties "latae sententiae," but not those above that age who co-operate in their crime. This view is accepted by Blat[196] and Leitner[197]. Cappello[198] and Biederlack[199] extend the censure to those introducing or admitting even infants, but the former's argument a pari has no weight.

Finally, if clerics, i. e., those who have received at least first tonsure, but not religious[200], enter the enclosure of nuns unlawfully or introduce or admit other unauthorized persons, they are to be suspended from office and benefice for a time which is not specified in the Code, but is left to the discretion of the ordinary of the place. This suspension is not a censure, but a vindicative punishment. It is, therefore, not incurred by the mere commission of the crime, but must be inflicted after due process of law[201]. It is meted out to them, because in their case there is the extra circumstance of their own state, which makes their crime more serious. Although religious are not included in the latter penalty, in their regard a wider range is granted both the ordinary of the place and their superior by virtue of canon 603.

---

194 Sole 289.
195 Cavigioli 104.
196 Blat 696.
197 Leitner 415.
198 Cappello, *De Censuris,* 109-110. Cfr. canon 2219 § 3.
199 Biederlack 239.
200 Cfr. Ojetti, v. *Clerici,* n. 1195.
201 Sole 289; Ayrinhac 267; Cerato 209-210.

2. Egress of Nuns.

Canon 601, § 1.

Boniface VIII forbade not only that outsiders enter the enclosure of nuns, but also that the nuns themselves leave their convent, except in case one became a source of danger to the health of the others or of scandal, or in case the abbess were obliged to appear in person at court to pay her respects to the king[202]. This law was re-enacted by the Council of Trent which forbade any nun to leave her convent "even for a brief period, under any pretext whatever, except for some lawful cause which is to be approved of by the bishop."[203] This prohibition was renewed by Pius V in his constitution "Circa pastoralis" and again in "Decori" which specified as the only reasons for which a nun was permitted to leave the cloister for a time, a great conflagration, leprosy or an epidemic; in the two latter cases the written approval of the local ordinary was required. In the constitution "Deo sacris" Gregory XIII made provisions that nuns be no longer compelled to go out to beg for their sustenance and by the constitution "Salutare" Benedict XIV revoked all privileges contrary to the preceding. Pius IX inflicted excommunication upon any nun leaving her convent, except as permitted by the constitution "Decori" of Pius V[204].

Canon 601, § 1. No nun, after profession, may, under whatever pretext, leave the monastery even for a short time, without a special indult of the Holy See, except in the case of imminent danger of death or other very serious evil.

This canon directly binds only *nuns*[205]. In the next place and indirectly those of *simple profession* preceding solemn vows[206]. Finally, novices[207] as well as postulants[208]. These

---

202 C. un., *de statu regularium,* III, 16, in VI°.

203 Conc. Trident., sess. XXV, *de regularibus,* c. 5.

204 Pius IX, const. *Apostolicae Sedis,* II 6.

205 Cfr. canon 488 n. 7.

206 Cfr. canon 578 n. 2; Sole 289; Ayrinhac 267-268; Blat 591; Leitner 414.

207 Cfr. canons 561-565; Hollweck 225, footnote 12.

208 Canon 540 § 3; Blat 591; Leitner 414; Sole 289; Ayrinhac 268; Fanfani 126. Nov. 7, 1916, it was declared that postulants may not leave convents subject to papal enclosure to visit parents or friends or for

last are expressly obliged to observe the law of enclosure by canon 540 § 3 and it would be preposterous to suppose that novices and simple-professed were free from this obligation. If any boarding-pupils are received into the cloister with papal dispensation, they, too, may not leave the enclosure as long as they remain pupils; if they do, they may not return without a new papal permission except to become nuns[209].

In order to cut off all subterfuges the Code adds "under whatever pretext." Except for the cases stated in this canon, no excuse can be framed that will justify any deviation from this rule[210]. Not "even for a short time": this phrase will be discussed in the treatment of canon 2342 n. 3.

December 22, 1880, the Holy Office declared that no particular custom, even if it were of immemorial standing, justifies a nun in leaving the monastery for a grave reason and with the permission of the bishop[211].

By "monastery" is here meant the enclosure within the limits designated by the bishop according to canon 597[212]. From the time a woman enters as a postulant she may not leave the cloister except in the cases allowed in this canon or by papal dispensation: she may not enter the public church[213] or the sacristy connected with it, nor even go up to the roof[214], since all these places lie outside the enclosure.

---

some other reason without leave of the Holy See. S. C. de Religiosis, 7 Nov. 1916, A. A. S., VIII 446. The present canon in no way limits the freedom of a postulant or novice (can. 571), or even of one who had taken temporary vows, but which have expired, to leave the convent *permanently* (can. 575), nor the right of superiors to dismiss a nun before solemn prefession (canons 571, 575, 647).

209 Vide supra p. 128.

210 Leitner 413; Blat 591; Fanfani 126.

211 S. C. S. Off., in *Ratisbonen.*, 22 Dec. 1880, ad III, *Collectanea S. C. de Prop. Fide* n. 1544.

212 Sole 289-290; Cappello, *De Censuris*, 111; Blat 591.

213 Except those required for the consecration of a nun, which takes place in the outer church. S. C. Conc., in *Hieracen.*, Jan. 1587, Pallottini, v. *Monasteria Monialium*, III 94-95; S. R. C., in *Bonon.*, 5 Julii 1698 et 27 Sept. 1698, *Decreta Auth. C. S. R.*, nn. 2001 et 2012.—The nuns of St. Paul's at Messina were accorded the special favor of being permitted to enter the outer church to decorate it, but behind closed doors. S. C. Conc., in *Messanen.*, Pallottini, *Monasteria Monialium*, III 96.

214 S. C. Ep. et Reg., in *Lycien.*, 16 Sept. 1609; in *Comen.*, 18 Sept. 1609, Ferraris, v. *Moniales*, III 11; Lucidi II 150; Mocchegiani I 228; Hilarius a Sexten 188; Cappello, *De Visitatione*, II 437; *De Censuris*, 111;

A word must be said about the parlor which is of peculiar construction. It consists of two rooms. One is intended to receive visitors and lies outside the enclosure: therefore, the nuns may not enter it[215]. The other lies within the cloister and is intended for the nuns only. These two rooms communicate with each other by means of a grille, i. e., a window with a close grate. The grille is covered with a heavy black curtain, so that the nuns can neither see nor be seen through it. This curtain may be raised only on certain occasions, e. g., when the bishop examines a postulant regarding her freedom from constraint, etc. At the grille the proper superior conducts the personal visitation and assists at the election of the abbess[216].

The door that leads from the parlor into the enclosure must always be locked and the key kept by the portress. At night[217] it must be locked with a second key which must be delivered to the superioress. The cloister-door may not be opened except to admit persons who enjoy a papal dispensation or who are permitted to enter by virtue of canon 600. A "rota" or revolving table is set in the wall near the door and serves the purpose of passing small articles into and out of the cloister, those of greater bulk being carried in through a larger gate. The "rota" must be constructed in such a manner as to shut off all view into or from the cloister[218].

No nun may speak with visitors, unless she first obtain permission of her superioress, and then, as a rule, only in the

---

Blat 591; Sole 290; Cavigioli 106-107.—The nuns of a Benedictine convent in the Diocese of Osimo were permitted to go up to the roof to hang out the altar-linens to dry, because they had no other place for the purpose; but the walls of the convent had to be built so high, as to cut off all view from neighboring buildings. Even then it was suggested that servants attend to the work. S. C. Ep. et Reg., in *Auximana,* 6. Sept. 1809, Bizzarri 410.

215 Sole 290; Cappello, *De Censuris,* 111.

216 Cfr. canons 506 § 2, 552 § 2 and 600 n. 1. "Ante cancellorum fenestellam", Conc. Trident., sess. XXV, *de regularibus,* c. 7; rubrica XXIII concilio Ravenati IV anni 1317 ab Archiep. adjecta, *Ss. Conc.* XI 1675-1676. Blat 536; Fanfani 37.

217 N. 177 of the *Normae* requires a statute prescribing that the door of the convent be locked *at sunset* and the key be delivered to the superioress for the night; Marsot, *Petit traite pratique des voeux et de l'etat religieux,* Paris 1920[12], 143, interprets "at sunset" as signifying the time after the last exercise of the community before retiring.

218 Cfr. Innocentius IV, bulla *Cum omnis vera Religio,* 6 Aug. 1247, *Bullarium Franc.* I 481.

presence of two other nuns[219]. Formerly there were very strict laws regulating the number of visits nuns might receive. Boniface VIII not only forbade entering the cloister of nuns, but also visiting them without necessity and lawful permission[220]. By a decree of the Congregation of Bishops and Regulars of May 7, 1590, Sixtus V forbade all religious to visit convents of nuns and sisters to converse with them or any other persons residing there except by leave of the Sacred Congregation. This prohibition was modified by Urban VIII, November 20, 1623, to the effect that the ordinary of the place could permit a regular to pay four visits a year to a nun related in the first or second degree. Parents and children of nuns were allowed to visit them not more than once a week, but not at all during Lent or Advent, nor on holydays, Fridays, Saturdays or Vigils[221]. The Code makes neither explicit nor implicit mention of these stringent regulations; therefore, we must conclude that they are abolished, unless contained in the constitutions[222].

Without permission of the Holy See a nun may not leave her convent to go to another of which she has been elected abbess[223], or to reform it or to establish a new foundation[224]. No nun may be sent to another convent for punishment or for correction[225]. If a nun is a source of scandal to the others and there is danger of her leading them astray, then some hold that she may be transferred to another convent[226]. However, this course seems precarious and is hardly advisable. It seems preferable to refer any such case to the Congregation of Religious, if need be, for her dismissal[227]. In all these and

---

219 Cfr. Innocentius IV, bulla *Cum omnis vera Religio,* 6 Aug. 1247, *Bullarium Franc.* I 477.

220 C. un., *de statu regularium,* III, 16, in VI°.

221 Cfr. Ferraris, v. *Moniales,* IV; Mocchegiani I 244-257; Piatus, *Praelectiones,* I 388-398.

222 Cfr. canon 6 n. 6; Charles Augustine III 320; Fanfani 127; Pruemmer[2] 292.

223 S. C. Ep. et Reg., *in Spoletana,* 31 Aug. 1830, Bizzarri 423; cfr. 208; 16 Julii 1884, ad III, *Collectanea S. C. de Prop. Fide* n. 1623.

224 S. C. Ep. et Reg., in *Sorana,* 20 Junii 1851, Bizzarri 596-598.

225 S. C. Ep. et Reg., 17 Maii 1603, Bizzarri 460, footnote 1; Pennacchi I 754, footnote 1; cfr. Pallottini, v. *Moniales quoad translationem.*

226 Card. De Lugo, cited by Benedictus XIV, *De Synodo Dioecesana,* lib. IX c. XV n. 8.

227 Pennacchi I 753-758.

similar cases the bishop has no authority to transfer a nun to a different convent even of her own order, although a just cause exists[228].

Strict as the law of enclosure is, it must have exceptions, for it could not oblige in opposition to the law of nature, in particular that of self-preservation. Most canonists held that the reasons specified by Pius V were not exclusive, but that others of a similar nature would justify nuns' leaving their convents[229]. There is no longer any reason to enter into this discussion, since the reasons that will warrant a nun's leaving the enclosure have been changed considerably. The present canon expresses them in the words "except in the case of imminent danger of death or other very serious evil." These words are so general that there is no occasion to restrict the danger to one that threatens the entire community, as was required under the former legislation; even if only one nun is exposed to the danger, she is free to leave the convent, if that is, morally speaking, the only means of escape open to her, e. g., a sickness which requires a difficult operation that cannot safely be performed in the convent[230].

In book XIII of his *De Synodo Dioecesana* Benedict XIV enumerates a number of cases for which under the former legislation permission of the Holy See was required that a nun might leave her monastery for the benefit of her health: because a change of climate was advisable, a series of baths at a health resort was necessary, etc.[231]. Would these cases

---

228 S. C. Ep. et Reg., 16 Julii 1884, ad II-III, *Collectanea S. C. de Prop. Fide,* n. 1623; Bonacina, *De Clausura etc.,* q. I p. I n. 4 et q. I p. IX nn. 10-14; Ferraris, v. *Moniales,* III 10-18; Hilarius a Sexten 188; Benedictus XIV, *De Synodo Dioecesana,* lib. IX c. XV n. 8; Mocchegiani I 228-229; Cappello, *De Censuris,* 112; Sole 290; Fanfani 126.

229 Bonacina, *De Clausura etc.,* q. I p. IX n. 6; Ferraris, v. *Moniales,* III 28; Reiffenstuel lib. III tit. XXXV nn. 29-35; Benedictus XIV, *De Synodo Dioecesana,* lib. IX c. XV n. 8; Hollweck 225, footnote 14; Hilarius a Sexten 189; Pennacchi I 751-753; Lucidi II 163; Cappello, *De Visitatione,* II 439; Piatus, *Praelectiones,* I 381-382; Ojetti, v. *Clausura,* n. 1167; Leitner 414.—That an epidemic is raging in the city where the convent is situated, is not yet a reason for the nuns to leave. If any are attacked by the disease, they are to be quarantined in a separate building which must be enclosed. S. C. Ep. et Reg., in *Avignonen.,* Sept. 1720, Bizzarri 311-320.

230 Leitner 414; Sole 290-291; Pruemmer[2] 291; Charles Augustine III 317; Cappello, *De Censuris,* 112.

231 Benedictus XIV, *De Synodo Dioecesana,* lib. XIII c. XII n. 29.

come under the name of "very serious evil," so that a nun would be allowed to leave her convent without permission of the Holy See? Abstracting from exceptional cases which develop very rapidly and then more easily warrant a nun's changing her residence, it would not seem so. For they are usually not so urgent as those for which the present canon provides and a delay of a month or two, until a papal dispensation can be obtained, will not aggravate the disease very much or seriously retard its cure[232]. If a nun desires to leave her convent, because it is situated in a climate that does not agree with her, not merely to recuperate, but to enter another convent where her health will not suffer and to spend the rest of her life there, it will be necessary to obtain leave of the Holy See, since only a temporary stay outside her own convent, not a transfer to another, is contemplated by this canon[233].

Leitner asks the question, whether nuns might leave their convents to vote. If their votes were necessary to avert a "very serious evil," it would be lawful in his opinion. Any other case, he believes, would have to be referred to Rome[234].

It is not possible to draw the line exactly between a case in which a nun may leave her convent without special permission of the Holy See and one in which such permission is required. The greater the distance from Rome the more easily a nun may make use of the permission granted by this canon. Whenever leave of the Holy See is required, a reply to a petition addressed to the Congregation of Religious will be obtained with greater

---

232 The Holy See has shown itself very ready to grant a dispensation in such cases. It requires a) that two doctors testify under oath that the change is necessary for the nun, and b) that she is willing to make use of the opportunity offered by the dispensation. It furthermore prescribes that, whenever she goes out, she be accompanied by a female relative or other respectable matron, that she avoid the society of men and that she conduct herself as befits her state. Cfr. Lucidi II 164-165; Linzer Theol. Quartalschrift (1884) XXXVII 626-627. Benedict XIV cites a case where an entire community left the convent for several months every year on account of its unhealthy environments during that period and returned, when the season became more healthful. Benedictus XIV, *De Synodo Dioecesana,* lib. XIII c. XII n. 29.

233 S. C. Ep. et Reg., 16 Julii 1884, ad II, *Collectanea S. C. de Prop. Fide* n. 1623. Biederlack 238.

234 Leitner 414. According to a letter from Archbishop Cerretti, made public by the National Catholic Welfare Council Oct. 25, 1920, such a dispensation was granted to nuns of Germany on the occasion of the recent elections.

despatch, if the bishop examine the matter and recommend the request, since such affairs are always committed to him for execution[235].

If a nun leaves her convent lawfully, she may remain only as long as the reason lasts or until the time for which leave was granted has elapsed. As soon as she can, she is obliged to return to her convent. However, a delay of a day or two would scarcely be considered a grievous matter[236].

Canon 601, § 2.

In order to remove all doubt whether a nun were lawfully permitted to leave her convent and to prevent too great laxity in granting the necessary permission, Boniface VIII reserved the right to grant this leave, even when sufficient reason existed, to the bishop[237]. The Council of Trent[238] and later Pius V[239] required that bishops give the permission in writing. Almost without exception authors maintained that in view of the clear words of these laws the permission of the bishop was necessary in every case and that the permission of the regular superior did not suffice, even if the nuns were subject to him[240]. Even those who held that the permission of the regular superior was sufficient admitted that the cause had to be approved of by the bishop and in this way the purpose of preventing too great ease in making exceptions was secured[241].

Canon 601, § 2. This danger, if time permits, must be recognized as such by the local Ordinary in writing.

If there is a just reason for a nun to leave the cloister, the cause must be submitted to the "local ordinary" for approval.

---

235 Benedictus XIV, *De Synodo Dioecesana,* lib. XIII c. XII n. 27.

236 C. un., *de statu regularium,* III, 16, in VI⁰; Pius V, const. *Decori;* Gregorius XIII, const. *Deo sacris;* Bonacina, *De Clausura etc.,* q. I p. IX n. 21; Ferraris, v. *Moniales,* III 36; Mocchegiani I 227; Cappello, *De Visitatione,* II 439; Biederlack 238; Cavigioli 107.

237 C. un., *de statu regularium,* III, 16, in VI⁰.

238 Conc. Trident., sess. XXV, *de regularibus,* c. 5.

239 Pius V, const. *Decori.*

240 S. C. Conc., in *Gerunden.,* 18 Nov. 1713, ad III, Pallottini, v. *Monasteria Monialium,* II 99; Bonacina, *De Clausura etc.,* q. I p. VIII n. 1; Ferraris, v. *Moniales,* III 29-31; Reiffenstuel lib. III tit. XXXV nn. 36-37; Mocchegiani I 227; Pruemmer II 109.

241 Cfr. S. C. Conc., in *Curien.,* 10 Apr. 1660, Pallottini, v. *Monasteria Monialium,* II 97; Piatus, *Praelectiones,* I 383; Hilarius a Sexten 190; Pennacchi I 759-761.

If he decides that the necessity is such as to warrant her leaving, she can conscientiously abide by it, for this approval is intended to forestall any self-deception as well as too great anxiety on the part of the nuns[242]. The approval given by the ordinary of the place is not properly permission to leave the enclosure: it is a necessary condition that must be fulfilled, before permission can lawfully be granted, so that a nun who would leave her convent without obtaining the ordinary's approval of her reasons would offend against the present canon[243].

The ordinary must give his approval "in writing," as was prescribed by the Council of Trent[244] and Pius V[245]. The reason for this requirement is presumably to supply the nun with the necessary testimonials that she is absent from her convent for a lawful reason.

"If time permits," this approval must be obtained. But, if the danger is so urgent as to give rise to well-founded fear that the evil will befall the community or the individual nun, before a reply could be received, there is no necessity, nor is it advisable, to postpone action. The greater the difficulty of communicating with the ordinary, the more readily the nuns may decide for themselves[246]. In this case Bonacina[247], with whom Ferraris[248] seems to agree, holds that they are obliged to inform the ordinary of the place, because the judgment is reserved to him and a cause that might appear to justify leaving the cloister in the eyes of the nuns, might not receive his approval and, therefore, they would be obliged to return. There is no foundation to this opinion, though it may be ad-

---

[242] Sole 291; Cappello, *De Censuris*, 112; Blat 591.

[243] Bonacina, *De Clausura etc.*, q. I p. VIII nn. 3-4; Ferraris v. *Moniales*, III 30-31; Pennacchi I 760; Hilarius a Sexten 189-190; Mocchegiani I 227; Piatus, *Praelectiones*, I 385; Cappello, *De Visitatione*, II 439; *De Censuris*, 112; Sole 291; Pruemmer² 291; Blat 591, 697; Biederlack 238.

[244] Conc. Trident., sess. XXV, *de regularibus*, c. 5.

[245] Pius V, const. *Decori.* Bonacina, *De Clausura etc.*, q. I p. VIII nn. 3-4; Cappello, *De Visitatione*, II 439; *De Censuris* 112.

[246] Bonacina, *De Clausura etc.*, q. 1 p. VIII n. 5; Ferraris, v. *Moniales*, III 32; Mocchegiani I 227; Hilarius a Sexten 190; Cappello, *De Visitatione*, II 439; Charles Augustine III 317; Biederlack 238.

[247] Bonacina, *De Clausura etc.*, q. I p. VIII n. 5.

[248] Ferraris, v. *Moniales*, III 32.

visable to acquaint the bishop of the fact and of their reasons in order to avoid any misunderstanding.

Formerly, if the convent was immediately subject to the Holy See or to the bishop, the permission of the bishop, or, if it was subject to regulars, of the regular superior with the approval of the bishop was required in the cases allowed by Pius V in the constitution "Decori."[249]. Is the permission of the regular superior besides the approval of the bishop still necessary? Canon 601 makes no mention of any permission. There can be no doubt that the individual nuns may not leave of their own accord. The vow of obedience will oblige them to obtain permission at least from their superioress, though in very urgent cases even this could be presumed. But it does not seem that they are bound to obtain leave from the regular superiors. For, whereas the Council of Trent[250] and the constitution "Decori" of Pius V were explicit in demanding the permission of the regular superior, the Code is silent on this point[251]. Such an obligation may be imposed by the constitutions.

Canon 2342, N. 3.

Boniface VIII[252] had indeed forbidden nuns to leave their convents and had commanded bishops and other superiors to enforce this law even to the extent of inflicting censures. However, he did not impose any censure which was incurred by the very leaving of the convent. Such a censure was first inflicted by the Council of Trent[253], and was renewed by Pius V in his constitutions "Circa pastoralis officii" and "Decori" and finally by Pius IX in the constitution "Apostolicae Sedis," § 2 n. 6, and now by the Code.

Canon 2342. The following incur ipso facto excommunication reserved simpliciter to the Holy See:

3. Nuns who leave the enclosure unlawfully contrary to the prescription of canon 601.

Cappello asserts that besides the solemn-professed nuns, also the simple-professed are subject to this censure, and seems to

---

249 Cfr. Pennacchi I 759-761.
250 Conc. Trident., sess. XXV, *de regularibus,* c. 5.
251 But cfr. canon 603 § 2.
252 C. un., *de statu regularium,* III, 16, in VI°.
253 Conc. Trident., sess., XXV, *de regularibus,* c. 5.

imply that novices and postulants, too, are liable to it, for he continues: ". . . yea, even novices and aspirants during their postulancy are bound by the law of enclosure, as canon 540, § 3 expressly states."[254] Sole speaks more clearly, saying: "'Nuns'; that is, with solemn vows. Still not only those who have made the simple profession for three years preceding solemn vows in accordance with canon 574, § 1, are bound by this excommunication, but also aspirants who, 'during their postulancy, are bound by the law of enclosure'; canon 540, § 3."[255] Capello's and Sole's view cannot be sustained. For, only those are "nuns," "moniales," who have taken solemn vows[256] and only they incur this censure[257]. The simple-professed religious of an order of nuns are "regulars," "regulares," not "nuns."[258] Now, according to canon 2219 § 3 it is "not permitted to extend a penalty from one person to another . . ., although a like or even a more serious reason be present." Therefore, simple-professed members of an order of nuns are not subject to excommunication, if they violate the law of enclosure that binds them also[259]. If simple-professed are free from this censure, the same is much more true of novices and postulants who are not by any means even religious[260]. There is no penalty fixed by the Code for cases

---

[254] "Moniales, i. e. votorum solemnium. Subjacentne huic censurae mulieres quae nonnisi votorum simplicium professionem ad triennium valituram sollemnibus praemiserint, ad normam can. 574, § 1? Affirmative respondendum est; imo etiam novitiae et adspirantes, dum postulatum peragunt, lege clausurae tenentur, uti can. 540, § 3 expresse statuit." Cappello, *De Censuris*, 111. In what appears to be a later impression of his book he corrects this view answering the same question thus: "Negative respondendum est, licet et ipsae, sicuti novitiae et adspirantes, dum postulatum peragunt, lege clausurae teneantur, uti can. 540, § 3 expresse statuit." Ibid.—On the following page he is speaking of permanent departure and of dismissal from the order, when he says: "Dicitur post professionem, et quidem sollemnem, nam, dum peragit postulatum vel novitiatum, imo exacto etiam temporariae professionis tempore, mulier aut sponte sua ad saeculum potest redire, aut a Superioribus iustam of causam dimitti."

[255] "'Moniales'; idest votorum sollemnium. Tenentur tamen hac excommunicatione nedum mulieres quae ad normam can. 574, § 1, votorum simplicium professionem ad triennium valituram sollemnibus praemiserint; sed etiam adspirantes quae 'dum postulatum peragunt, lege clausurae tenentur'; canon. 540, § 3." Sole 289.

[256] Canon 488 n. 7.

[257] Ayrinhac 267; Cerato 125; Blat 697; Leitner 514.

[258] Canon 488 n. 7.

[259] Cerato 125; Ayrinhac 267-268; Blat 697.

[260] Cerato 126; Leitner 415; Ayrinhac 267-268.

when simple-professed leave the cloister unlawfully. However, the superioress, by virtue of the authority she exercises in consequence of the vow of obedience, and the ordinary of the place and the regular superior by virtue of canon 603, are empowered to deal with such cases as also in regard to novices and postulants[261].

Nuns incur excommunication, if they leave the "enclosure" unlawfully. Cerato asks: "whether this excommunication refers to the unlawful egress of nuns out of the enclosure, as is said in canon 2342 n. 3; or the unlawful egress out of the monastery, as in canon 601"; and answers: "But, all things considered, it must certainly be held that excommunication strikes the unlawful egress out of the monastery." "However," he continues, "there can be no doubt that the nuns who leave only the cloister sin."[262] Cerato certainly did not consider that the word, "monastery," "monasterio," of canon 601 § 1 receives its interpretation from the word "enclosure," "clausura," of canon 2342 n. 3 and that the latter, not the former, contains the precise crime for which excommunication is inflicted. Canon 597 defines what the cloister is; canon 601 establishes the obligation of nuns not to leave their monasteries, a word frequently employed in papal constitutions to designate the enclosure[263]; and canon 2342 n. 3 inflicts excommunication on nuns who unlawfully leave the "enclosure." This is but a restatement of the former law and, therefore, must be interpreted like it[264]. Hence a nun who goes up to the roof of the convent, which, as Cerato himself admits[265], lies outside the enclosure, incurs excommunication, just as formerly[266].

---

261 One might be tempted to apply to novices and postulants what was said above, page 128, regarding pupils leaving the convent without permission. However, there is no warrant for it in the Code; it would be but another case of "extending a penalty from one person to another" (can. 2219 § 3), as Hollweck (p. 225 footnote 13) did.

262 Cerato 125.

263 Cfr. c. un., *de statu regularium,* III, 16, in VI°; Conc. Trident., sess. XXV, *de regularibus,* c. 5; Pius V, const. *Decori;* Gregorius XIII, const. *Deo sacris;* const. *Dubiis;* Benedictus XIV, const. *Per binas.*

264 Cfr. canon 6 n. 3.

265 Cerato 124, 126.

266 Lucidi II 150; Ferraris, v. *Moniales,* III 11; Sole 290; Cappello, *De censuris,* 111; Ayrinhac 268; Cavigioli 106-107.

A nun leaves the enclosure "unlawfully," if she leaves contrary to canon 601, which permits it only (a) by papal dispensation, or (b) on account of "imminent danger of death or other very serious evil." However, in the latter case canon 601 § 2 obliges the nun, if time permits, to have her reasons for leaving the monastery approved of by the ordinary of the place in writing. Does this oblige under pain of excommunication, so that, if a nun left the cloister for a sufficient reason but without obtaining the written approval of the bishop, provided there was time to obtain it, she incurs excommunication? Blat denies it, "because a nun leaving without that previous writing of the ordinary of the place does not act contrary to the prescription of the canon, since, as we suppose, a reason exists and the permission does not arise from that writing of the ordinary, but this contains only the approval of the cause, which is not required for the egress, but because the law does not leave the decision regarding its existence to private persons."[267] This view can hardly be accepted. For, first, it is not true that she does not act contrary to canon 601, since that canon in § 2 requires the ordinary's approval of the cause in writing. Then, if the Code meant not to inflict the censure, in case one neglected to obtain the written approbation of the ordinary, when time permitted, it would have stated it, the more so since under the former legislation in similar circumstances written permission of the ordinary was required under pain of excommunication[268]. This interpretation may appear rigorous; however, Blat himself gives the reason, why the Church demands the written approval of the local ordinary: that the law does not leave it to individuals to decide the existence of a sufficient reason, knowing how prone human nature is to justify any relaxation of the law[269].

"Leaving" the enclosure, so that a nun incurs excommunication, implies that her entire body be outside the limits of the

---

[267] Blat 697.

[268] Bonacina, *De Clausura etc.*, q. I p. IX n. 2; Pennacchi I 738-739; Hilarius a Sexten 189-190; Pruemmer II 109.

[269] This view seems to be accepted by Sole 291; Cappello, *De Censuris*, 112; Cerato 125; Biederlack 238.

cloister, similarly as was said regarding "entering" the cloister[270].

If a nun is lawfully outside her convent, she does not incur excommunication, if she leaves the house assigned to her for her residence during her absence from the monastery, since that house is not subject to the law of enclosure. The same is true, if she delays to return after the reason for her absence has ceased, because this is not the unlawful egress for which the penalty is inflicted[271].

Formerly those granting permission without sufficient reason as well as those accompanying and receiving nuns leaving their monasteries unlawfully were excommunicated and the nuns and their superiors lost all offices and became incapable of holding the same[272]. These penalties are not renewed in the Code. None of these persons, therefore, incur excommunication, unless they are the direct cause that nuns leave unlawfully[273]. But the ordinary of the place and the regular superior could inflict such penalties upon them, as they see fit[274].

3. Construction of the Cloister of Nuns.

Canon 602.

In the beginning of monasticism convents were built in deserts or other secluded spots. It was easy to maintain the privacy of the cloister under such conditions. Later, when necessity or other reasons introduced the building of monasteries within or near cities, this seclusion was obtained by the manner of construction. Once the law of enclosure was enacted by Boniface VIII, custom gradually developed a plan of building which made the seclusion of nuns complete. The windows were screened with lattice-work, "tubae ligneae," in

---

[270] Vide supra p. 90, where the question of "parvitas materiae" is also discussed. Cfr. Pallottini, v. *Monasteria Monialium,* II 7-8; Bonacina, *De Clausura etc.,* q. I p. I nn. 1-5, q. I p. IV n. 2; Ferraris, v. *Moniales,* III 10-18; Hilarius a Sexten 188; Blat 591; Cappello, *De Censuris,* 111; Sole 289-290; Ayrinhac 268; Biederlack 238.

[271] Bonacina, *De Clausura etc.,* q. I p. IV n. 3; Hilarius a Sexten 188; Cappello, *De Censuris,* 112; Cerato 126; Biederlack 238.

[272] Bonacina, *De Clausura etc.,* q. I p. IV nn. 1, 6, 7; Mocchegiani I 227-228.

[273] Cfr. canon 2209 §§ 1-3; Cappello, *De Censuris,* 112; Biederlack 238.

[274] Canon 603. Biederlack 238.

order to shut off all view of the nuns into neighboring buildings or of neighbors into the convent[275]. Even a window that gave the nuns a view into the parish church was ordered walled up[276]. The cloister was surrounded with high walls, so that neighbors could not look into the garden[277]. The Congregation of Bishops and Regulars commanded that all windows of a monastery of men that opened upon the garden of a nuns' convent be walled up[278]; windows even in the belfry of a neighboring church were ordered closed[279]; likewise all the windows in a convent of nuns through which they might see or be seen[280]; finally, no houses were allowed to be erected so high that they offered a view into the convent garden[281].

Canon 602. The enclosure of the monastery of nuns should be protected on every side in such a manner as to prevent, as far as possible, those within from being seen by, or seeing, persons outside.

In these few general words the Code renews those laws. The cloister, that is, the entire space reserved for the nuns according to canon 597 § 2 must be surrounded by a wall. This wall must, as far as possible, close off all view from the convent as well as into it. Windows facing a street or neighboring houses must be constructed in such a manner as not to allow the nuns any view into the houses of lay-people, which may be precluded by means of lattice, white or frosted glass, blinds and the like[282]. It may not always be possible, nor does the Church enjoy the power to enforce such regulations; wherefore it will be necessary at times to modify them. The words "as far as possible" give some latitude to the judg-

---

275 S. C. Conc., in *Verulana,* 2 Maii 1722, Pallottini, v. *Monasteria Monialium,* II 4; cfr. Benedictus XIV, *Op. Omnia,* XII 336; S. C. Ep. et Reg., in *Sorana,* 20 Junii 1851, Bizzarri 596.

276 S. C. Ep. et Reg., *Civitatis Castelli,* 22 Aug. 1815, Bizzarri 410-411.

277 S. C. Conc., in *Urbinaten.,* 10 Martii 1663, Bizzarri 596.

278 S. C. Ep. et Reg., in *Amerina,* 23 Dec. 1603, Bizzarri 596.

279 S. C. Ep. et Reg., in *Portugall.,* 19 Apr. 1605; in *Aquilana,* 31 Julii 1612, Bizzarri 596.

280 S. C. Ep. et Reg., in *Parmen.,* 28 Nov. 1636, Bizzarri 596.

281 S. C. Ep. et Reg., in *Interamn.,* 15 Maii 1612; in *Assisien.,* 11 Junii 1653; in *Conversana,* 8. Aug. 1653, Bizzarri 596.

282 Blat 591-592.

ment of the proper authorities. In the last instance it will be the bishop who must decide[283].

The protest that Charles Augustine raises: "But a little more light and air will not hurt the nuns,"[284] has no foundation in the law as interpreted by the Sacred Congregations. Zamboni cites a case where the Congregation of the Council decided that a small church be razed to allow sufficient space for the cloister of a newly erected convent of nuns[285]. In another instance the Congregation of Bishops and Regulars refused permission to a community of Tertiary Clares to take solemn vows and to establish papal cloister for want of a suitable garden[286]. It will be the part of the proper authorities to give such matters due consideration, when they choose a site for a convent.

4. Care for the Cloister of Nuns.

Canon 603, § 1.

The Council of Trent charged the bishops with enforcing its law of enclosure in convents of nuns—by their own powers in those subject to them, as delegates of the Holy See in those exempt from their jurisdiction[287]. This was renewed by Gregory XV in the constitution "Inscrutabili" and Alexander VII expressly conferred upon bishops the power to proceed against regulars, even if exempt, who violated the regulations laid down in his constitution "Felici."[288]

Canon 603, § 1. The enclosure of nuns, even those subject to Regulars, is under the vigilance of the local Ordinary who can correct and coerce, even with penalties and censures, the delinquents, not excepting male regulars.

Canon 597 § 3 authorizes the bishop to establish the limits of the cloister of all nuns within his diocese; canon 512 § 1 n. 1

---

283 Cfr. canons 597 § 3 and 603 § 1; Blat 591-592; Charles Augustine III 317-318.

284 Charles Augustine III 318.

285 S. C. Conc., in *Hieracen.*, 6 Dec. 1760, ad II, Zamboni v. *Monasterium Monialium,* I 56; Lucidi 11 233.

286 S. C. Ep. et Reg., in *Auximana,* 3 Dec. 1852, Bizzarri 596, footnote 1.

287 Conc. Trident., sess. XXV, *de regularibus,* c. 5.

288 Cfr. Pius IX, litt. encycl. *Quo graviora,* 8 Julii 1862, *Acta Pii IX,* vol. III pars I, 463-469; S. C. Conc., in *Marsicana,* Nov. 1587; in *Plocen.,* 10 Maii 1631, Pallottini, v. *Monasteria Monialium,* II 2-3; Benedictus XIV, *De Synodo Dioecesana,* lib. IX c. XV nn. 6-7; Lucidi II 228-244; Piatus, *Praelectiones,* I 387-388.

and § 2 n. 1, to visit it. These are corollaries of the power conferred upon him by the present canon. Consonant with the former legislation, the ordinary of the place is entrusted with the supervision of the enclosure, though the convent be subject to regulars. He is empowered to correct all abuses that may creep in; he can order the cloister wall raised[289], he can issue regulations regarding visits to the parlor and the like. He can also reprove and punish all who violate the general laws or his own regulations. Not even the regulars to whom the nuns are subject can plead exemption[290]. For this is one of the cases in which the law makes an exception as provided in canon 615. It does not matter whether the offense is notorious or occult, whether there is scandal for the people or not[291]. And, lest this power of the ordinary of the place become illusory, the bishop[292] is authorized to employ all the penalties at the disposal of ecclesiastical authority, not excepting censures, against all offenders including regulars[293]. Formerly the bishop exercised this power over convents subject immediately to the Holy See or to regulars as delegate of the Holy See[294]. By virtue of this canon he now acts with ordinary jurisdiction, not only over the nuns subject to himself, but also over all others, be they subject to the Holy See or to regulars[295].

Canon 603, § 2.

The constitution of Boniface VIII "Periculoso"[296] committed the custody of the enclosure of nuns subject to regulars exclusively to the regular superiors. When the Council of

---

289 Pallottini, v. *Monasteria Monialium,* II 53.

290 S. C. Conc., in *Olomucen.,* 7 Junii 1755, ad VII et VIII, Zamboni, *Monasterium Monialium,* I 54-55.

291 S. C. Conc., 9 Feb. 1622, Monacelli, I App. 427-429.

292 During a vacancy the vicar capitular or the administrator can inflict penalties. The vicar general, however, can not inflict any penalties, unless he is specially authorized by the bishop (cfr. canon 2220 § 2; Sole 61-62) or is the "official" or ordinary judge of the bishop's court (cfr. canon 1573 § 1).

293 Piatus, *Praelectiones,* I 387-388; Blat 592; Charles Augustine III 318.

294 Conc. Trident., sess. XXV, *de regularibus,* c. 5; Gregorius XV, const. *Inscrutabili,* § 2; Alexander VII, const. *Felici,* § 8; Benedictus XIV, *De Synodo Dioecesana,* lib. IX c. XV n. 6; Piatus, *Praelectiones,* I 387-388.

295 Blat 592; Charles Augustine III 318.

296 C. un., *de statu regularium,* III, 16, in VI°.

Trent[297], Gregory XV in the constitution "Inscrutabili" and Alexander VII in the constitution "Felici" authorized bishops as delegates of the Holy See to guard this cloister, it was not withdrawn from the jurisdiction of the regular superiors; they retained their powers conjointly with the bishops[298].

Canon 603, § 2. The custody of the enclosure of nuns subject to Regulars is confided also to the Regular Superior who can likewise inflict punishment on the nuns or his other subjects, if in this matter they be found guilty.

The Code reaffirms the jurisdiction of the regular superior. Like the bishop, he can correct abuses and lay down precautions to be observed. This power he possesses cumulatively with the ordinary of the place. He can also punish violations, but in this respect his authority is limited: whereas the bishop can punish *all* offenders against the law of enclosure, the regular superior can inflict penalties only upon the *nuns and the regulars subject to him.* The reason lies in the fact that only a subject can be punished. Now, none other than the nuns and the regulars come under the jurisdiction of the regular superior, whereas by virtue of canon 1566 § 1 the bishop can bring to account anyone guilty of an offense within his diocese, provided the delinquent is not withdrawn from his jurisdiction[299].

By virtue of canon 597 § 3 the bishop has the exclusive right to determine the limits of nuns' enclosure. He alone can give the required approval, when for reasons of necessity outsiders are to be admitted according to canon 600 n. 4 or when the nuns may leave the cloister according to canon 601. For all other matters touching the observance of enclosure in convents which are subject to regulars, the ordinary of the place and the regular superior have jurisdiction "cumulative," i. e., they have the same right to watch over the enclosure and enforce its observance. They need not act together, but may take whatever measures seem fit independently of each other. However, if

---

297 Conc. Trident., sess. XXV, *de regularibus,* c. 5.

298 Pius V, const. *Circa pastoralis,* § 8; cfr. schema const. *De Clausura,* c. V, prepared for the consideration of the Vatican Council.

299 Cfr. canon 1557.

either has taken a case in hand, by citing the delinquent, the other must leave it to him in accordance with canon 1568[300].

Papal cloister of nuns is almost unknown in the United States, since there are in this country only four convents of Visitation Nuns, in which it is observed. At first sight that enclosure may appear too rigorous. However, it must be remembered that, strict as it is, it has been tried by the experience of centuries. If the Church will not mitigate it, it is on account of the great benefits that flow from it.

It is true, the immediate reasons that prompted Boniface VIII to publish his constitution "Periculoso" have ceased. There were abuses, not general, indeed, but frequent enough to call for stringent measures. Thanks to the severity of that law, those abuses have been stamped out. Yet the Church maintains her former rigor, for she will not forego the sacrifices of heroic women and the noble example of obedience and devotion and mortification it entails, a sacrifice which, while it causes less heroic men to shudder, excites their unbounded admiration.

One frequently hears it said that women are thrust into the cloister by force and against their will or that, if they oblige themselves to perpetual enclosure voluntarily, they do so in a moment of youthful enthusiasm, that they soon weary of their seclusion from the world, only to repent of their hasty step in life-long misery; that they are confined within the cloister by the inflexible will of the Church. Is there any truth to these charges? The answer is given by the very law of the Church. The same Code which obliges nuns to observe perpetual cloister offers every possible guarantee for their freedom in entering the cloister and in remaining in it. Every person guilty of coercing another into entering a religious institute or into making religious profession incurs ipso facto excommunication[301]. If a woman is induced by force, grave fear or fraud to enter a religious institute or to take any religious vows whatsoever, her novitiate and her vows are invalid: she re-

---

300 Cfr. Pallottini, v. *Monasteria Monialium,* II 52-54, 78-87; v. *Regulares,* 12; schema const. *De Clausura,* c. V, prepared for the consideration of the Vatican Council; Mocchegiani I 237; Blat 592; Leitner 415; Charles Augustine III 318.

301 Canon 2352.

mains entirely free[302]. Neither is there any foundation for the fear that a candidate might take upon herself the obligation of perpetual cloister without sufficient knowledge of its burdens. Although at the time she enters she might be ignorant of what enclosure is, she will learn it both theoretically and practically, before she binds herself to it. For every candidate must reside as a postulant within the cloister for at least six months, before she is invested[303]. Then follows a year or more of novitiate[304]. During these eighteen months, or longer, she must observe the law of cloister, not by reason of a vow or other obligation, but solely to make the personal experiment, whether she is able and willing to take this obligation upon herself. At any time during these periods of probation she is free to leave both before the law and in conscience[305]. At the end of the novitiate she takes vows for three years: when they expire, she is again free to leave the convent, unless she chooses to take perpetual solemn vows[306]. In order to prevent any candidate from proceeding under duress, grave fear or deception, the bishop is obliged to inquire of each candidate individually before investiture and before each profession, whether she is free from all undue influence and whether she is aware of the importance of the step she is about to take: only if he is convinced that she is entirely free and understands the duties of religious life, may he permit her to be admitted to the novitiate or to temporary or perpetual vows, as the case may be[307]. If, despite all these precautions a nun, after taking either temporary or perpetual vows, finds the burden of religious life too heavy, she can still obtain a release from her vows by a lawful dispensation which will be granted, if sufficient reasons are presented[308].

These canons prove how scrupulously the Church protects the freedom of those who enter religion. If in a rare case force or fraud is employed in contravention of her laws, she is ready to restore the victim her liberty and to assist her to recover any damages she may have sustained.

---

302 Canons 542 n. 1 and 572 § 1 n. 4.
303 Canon 540 § 3.
304 Canon 555.
305 Canons 571 § 1 and 637.
306 Canon 575 § 1.
307 Canon 552.
308 Canons 638-642.

CHAPTER VII.

Episcopal Cloister.

Canon 604, § 1.

The canons discussed in the previous pages have reference only to members of orders with *solemn* vows. Until the year 1900 there was no *general* law concerning the cloister in congregations with simple vows. In that year Leo XIII ordained that bishops introduce total or partial enclosure in houses of *papal* institutes with simple vows[1]. Now the Code legislates regarding the cloister in *all* religious institutes.

Until the nineteenth century the Holy See did not recognize any other than papal enclosure[2]. When the civil laws of several countries, especially of France and Belgium, no longer permitted the observance of the laws of the Church for nuns, the Holy See permitted the latter to continue their religious life as best they could. Among other matters it released them from the observance of papal cloister, instead of which they observed such enclosure as the bishop of the diocese imposed upon them[3].

In the numerous congregations, especially of women, that began to spring into existence shortly after the French Revolution, the constitutions established a form of cloister that was less strict than that binding in houses of religious with solemn vows. In the draft of the constitution "De Clausura," that was to have been submitted to the Vatican Council, it was provided that in congregations of men papal enclosure and in congregations of women episcopal or partial cloister should be observed. In the constitution "Conditae a Christo," § II n. 4, Leo XIII prescribed that in congregations with papal approval either episcopal or partial enclosure was to be observed[4].

---

[1] Leo XIII, const. *Conditae a Christo,* 8 Dec. 1900, II 4.
[2] Lucidi II 246-250; Arndt 1-4; Bastien 4-6.
[3] S. Poenitentiaria, 23 Jan. 1821, Piatus, *Praelectiones,* I 364; S. C. Ep. et Reg., in *Parisien.,* 1 Aug. 1839, Bizzarri 86-87.
[4] Mocchegiani I 322-324; Bastien 154-156; Arndt 192-193.

Canon 604, § 1. In the houses also of religious Congregations, whether with papal or diocesan approval, the law of enclosure must be observed, so that no one of the other sex may be admitted there, excepting those mentioned in canon 598, § 2, and 600, and others whom the Superiors consider may, for just and reasonable motives, be admitted.

The Code now demands that a modified form of cloister be observed in all congregations of men as well as women[5]. This applies in the first place to all houses of religious congregations with only simple vows. It does not matter whether the institute has obtained papal approbation or commendation, or merely diocesan approval[6]: all are bound to observe a similar modified cloister[7]. The same enclosure must be observed in the houses of those religious orders whose members normally take solemn vows, but for special reasons make only simple profession, e. g., in France and Belgium[8] and in the convents of nuns in the United States except the four convents of Visitation Nuns of Georgetown, Baltimore, St. Louis, and Mobile[9].

The reasons for imposing such an obligation on these congregations are the same as in the case of regulars. In general their aim and duties are similar, especially as regards chastity, and, therefore, it is proper that a similar enclosure should protect them from the same dangers.

The cloister that obtains in houses of congregations must be fashioned after that of regulars. Therefore, what was said in the foregoing pages will to some extent apply to the enclosure in congregations. Yet it is not intended that the law should oblige with equal severity in the houses of either because of the difference between these two classes of religious institutes[10].

---

5 Fanfani 127; Leitner 415-416; Pruemmer[2] 289-292.

6 Cfr. canon 488 n. 3.

7 Cfr. Leo XIII, const. *Conditae a Christo,* II 4; Bastien 154; Arndt 193-194; Lanslots 117-118; Egger 36; Leitner 416; Fanfani 127; Charles Augustine III 319; Pruemmer[2] 289.

8 S. C. Ep. et Reg., in *Parisien.,* 1 Aug. 1839, Bizzarri 86-87; Mocchegiani I 322-323.

9 S. C. Ep. et Reg., in *Americana votorum,* 2 Sept. 1864, A. S. S. I 708-739; Leitner 416.

10 Leitner 416; Fanfani 127; Brandys 66; cfr. Bastien 154.

The extent of the cloister is defined by canon 597 § 2, with this difference (a) that the sisters' choir need not be enclosed, since there is not the same reason for them as for nuns; and (b) that the sisters' parlor need not be constructed as the nuns', since the sisters may enter the same parlor as their visitors. Section 3 of canon 597 would also seem to apply to congregations: in those of men the higher superiors, in those of women the bishop of the diocese must determine its limits.

Into said enclosure "no one of the other sex" may be admitted. For male religious this rule is the same as for male regulars[11]. The exception permitted in canon 598 § 2 is extended to congregations of men[12]. But in sisters' convents the cloister is far more lenient than in convents of nuns. Whereas not even women are allowed to enter the latter, the Code does not forbid women to enter the former; only men are excluded from them[13]. However, as Pruemmer remarks, care should be taken, lest through inconsiderate admission of women the religious spirit be lost[14]. Men may be admitted into sisters' convents under the same conditions as permitted in canon 600[15].

Exceptions to the rule laid down in the present canon may be made by the superior, not only by the higher, but also by the local superior, since the Code does not reserve this power to the former[16]. An exception must not be made arbitrarily; it must be prompted by "just and reasonable motives," e. g., to show a special mark of appreciation to great benefactors[17]. Whatever restrictions the constitutions of a congregation place upon a superior must be faithfully observed. In such cases no superior would be justified in neglecting the stricter obligation imposed by them, as they are not contrary to the Code and, therefore, remain in force[18].

---

11 Cfr. canon 598 § 1; Leitner 416; Fanfani 127; Charles Augustine III 319; Brandys 66-67.

12 Vide supra pp. 77-81; Leitner 416; Fanfani 128; Brandys 67; Charles Augustine III 319; Egger 37.

13 Leitner 416; Fanfani 128; Pruemmer[2] 292; Brandys 67.

14 Pruemmer[2] 292.

15 Vide supra pp. 104-129; cfr. *Normae* 171-172; Arndt 193; Bastien 156; Egger 37; Charles Augustine III 316; Fanfani 128; Leitner 416; Lanslots 118; Brandys 67.

16 Charles Augustine III 319; Brandys 67.

17 Charles Augustine III 319; Brandys 67; Biederlack 241.

18 Cfr. canon 489; Pruemmer[2] 290, 292; Brandys 67.

Canon 604, § 2.

The prescription of canon 599 applies also to houses of religious Congregation whether of men or women.

The special purposes of most congregations are works of charity conducted in connection with their convents, as schools, hospitals, etc. Wherever this is the case, partial enclosure prescribed under similar conditions for male regulars in canon 599 must be observed[19].

Canon 604, § 3.

In particular circumstances and for grave reasons, the Bishop can, except in the case of an exempt clerical Institute, safeguard the enclosure by censures; always, however, he must be vigilant in having it duly observed and in correcting any abuses that may arise in this respect.

As the earlier constitutions of the Popes committed papal enclosure of nuns to the custody of the bishop, so, too, Leo XIII entrusted the cloister of religious congregations approved by the Holy See to his vigilance[20]. By § 3 of canon 604 he is charged to watch over its keeping in all congregations, whether approved by the Holy See or by the bishop, whether of men or of women. No privilege of exemption that a congregation may have obtained will withdraw it from this jurisdiction of the bishop[21]. While he can enact laws for the better observance of the cloister, he is not authorized to impose a stricter enclosure than is contained in the Code and the constitutions. He could not, for example, oblige a community of sisters to observe total cloister after the manner of nuns with solemn vows. In congregations with papal approval this would amount to a change of the constitutions which is reserved to the Holy See[22]. In introducing such a change even in a diocesan institute he would do well to follow the example

---

[19] Vide supra pp. 101-103; cfr. Leo XIII, const. *Conditae a Christo,* II 4; Bastien 154; Egger 37; Lanslots 117-118; Leitner 416; Charles Augustine III 319; Biederlack 241; Brandys 66-67.

[20] Leo XIII, const. *Conditae a Christo,* II 4.

[21] Cfr. canons 615 and 618; Charles Augustine III 319; Leitner 416; Egger 37; Brandys 67-68.

[22] Canon 618 § 2 n. 1; cfr. canon 495 § 2.

of the Holy See, which does not grant an indult to introduce papal enclosure in a convent of simple-professed sisters without the consent of all the sisters[23].

The penalties contained in canon 2342 are inflicted only for violation of papal cloister in houses of religious with *solemn* vows[24] and do not affect those who violate the enclosure in congregations with *simple* vows. In fact, the Code does not inflict any penalty whatever for violation of episcopal or partial cloister in such institutes. However, the present canon authorizes the bishop to safeguard it even to the extent of employing censures, if he sees fit. His power is limited by two restrictions. First, he can never inflict a censure for violation of the cloister, if the congregation concerned is a clerical institute, i. e., one whose members for the most part are raised to the priesthood[25], and is exempt from the jurisdiction of the bishop[26]. Secondly, if the institute is not clerical or, if clerical, not exempt, the bishop can inflict censures for violation of the cloister, not by general law, but only "in particular circumstances and for grave reasons." Censures ought not easily be multiplied. Therefore, the bishop should be sparing in employing them, especially if other means will accomplish his purpose. However, when an abuse is very serious and the guilty persons will not readily amend their ways or the conditions are a scandal, the bishop ought to have recourse to such extreme measures[27].

Canon 679, § 2.

They shall observe the law of enclosure according to the terms of the constitutions, under the vigilance of the local Ordinary.

In societies whose members live in community without, however, taking vows of any kind there is also an obligation of enclosure and that "according to the terms of the constitu-

---

23 Vide supra p. 105.
24 Vide supra pp. 85-101; 129-134; 143-147.
25 Cfr. canon 488 n. 4.
26 Pruemmer[2] 292; Leitner 416; Charles Augustine III 319-320; Egger 37; Biederlack 241.
27 Pruemmer[2] 292; Charles Augustine III 319-320; Leitner 416; Brandys 67-68; Biederlack 241.

tions." Although members of such societies "must obey the enactments of canons 595-612, unless the constitutions ordain otherwise"[28], they are not bound to the enclosure enjoined by canons 604-607, but conformably to their constitutions. While it need not be as strict or extend as far as in congregations with simple vows, it should be modelled on canon 604. It remains under "the vigilance of the local Ordinary" in institutes that have obtained papal as well as diocesan approval. Consequently what was said in explanation of canon 604 § 3 can be applied to houses of societies of this nature[29].

---

[28] Canon 679 § 1. These words are omitted in the *Authorised English Translation.*

[29] Blat 656-657; Charles Augustine III 419.

CHAPTER VIII.

Egress and Visits of Religious.

Canon 605.

In the earlier monastic rules visits from those not belonging to the community could be received only with permission of the superior and in the presence of another monk. In the course of time custom has relaxed this rule somewhat. Permission of the superior, while still necessary, is often more or less general according to the office held by the individual.

In the "Normae" the Congregation of Bishops and Regulars suggested that constitutions order religious who receive visitors to be attended by another religious except, at least at times, when parents or other immediate relatives visit them[1].

Canon 605. All those who have the custody of the enclosure shall carefully see lest, through intercourse with outsiders[2], the discipline be relaxed and the religious spirit weakened by useless conversation.

The Code does not lay down minute rules governing visits which religious receive, as the variety of their engagements does not permit such. The present canon refers primarily to visits received in the parlor. All visitors must ordinarily be received there. If the constitutions contain special regulations for visits, they must be observed. Otherwise this matter is left to the judgment of the superiors whose prudence should prevent relaxation of discipline and danger of scandal or suspicion. Rarely will the porter be in a position where he can do more than refer any abuse or suspicion to the superior[3].

---

[1] *Normae* 175-176; Bastien 156-157; Lanslots 119.

[2] ". . . . lest discipline be relaxed and the religious spirit suffer through useless conversation with visitors," would render the words of the Code better than does the *Authorised English Translation*.

[3] Charles Augustine III 320.

Canon 606, § 1.

Religious Superiors must take care that the prescriptions of their constitutions be faithfully observed regarding the egress of subjects from the cloister (claustris), or their receiving visits from, or paying visits to, outsiders.

At no time was there any law that enjoined perpetual enclosure upon male regulars in the sense of absolutely forbidding them to leave their convents. Neither does the general law impose it upon religious congregations of men or of women, that take only simple vows. Such an obligation may arise from a special vow or a precept of the rule. Yet are they not free to come and go as they please. The duty of striving after perfection according to rule and constitutions, in particular the vow of obedience that requires them to remain under the authority and vigilant care of their superior, forbids them to go out except for a good reason approved by their superior and with his permission. To leave the convent otherwise means to refuse that obedience and, consequently, the service owing to the community. Therefore, as was already provided in the rules of the various orders, the Council of Trent forbade regulars to leave their monasteries; not even the pretext of going to a higher superior should exempt them from the obedience to their immediate superior[4]. In the decree "Nullus omnino" Clement VIII prescribed that a regular should not be allowed to leave his convent without a good reason approved of by his superior, having received his blessing and accompanied by another regular; upon his return he had to present himself to his superior to receive his blessing[5]. Although this decree was renewed by Urban VIII in his decree "Sacra Congregatio" of September 21, 1624, it does not seem to have been binding beyond Italy and certainly was never put into full effect[6]. The draft of the constitution "De Clausura," drawn up for the consideration of the Vatican Council, renewed most of the prescriptions of the decree "Nullus omnino."

---

[4] Conc. Trident., sess. XXV, *de regularibus,* c. 4.

[5] Clemens VIII, decr. *Nullus omnino,* nn. 19-21.

[6] Lehmkuhl in *Kirchenlexikon,* v. *Clausur,* III 444-445; Vermeersch, *De Religiosis,* II 60-61; cfr. I 111.

The Code does not directly specify the reasons a religious must have for leaving his convent and the precautions to be taken on such occasions, nor does it specify the reasons for the visits a religious receives or pays. These are matters that will vary considerably with the kind of work in which the institute is engaged and must be regulated by the constitution of each order or congregation[7]. Although the regulations of the Council of Trent and the decree "Nullus omnino" are not re-enacted by the Code, still several of them are intimately connected with the very idea of cenobitism and are incorporated into most rules or constitutions with such modifications as time and circumstances call for. These provisions laid down in the rule or constitutions must be observed and superiors are bound to enforce them. Therefore, it will not be out of place to present the general principles that must guide religious, both superiors and subjects, in this regard.

That the Code does not strictly impose upon male religious all the prescriptions of the decree "Nullus omnino," becomes apparent from a comparison of this canon with the next, where superioresses and local ordinaries are bidden not to allow sisters to go out alone except in cases of necessity. The reason lies very probably in this, that male religious, especially priests engaged in pastoral work, will frequently have affairs to attend to, that would render the presence of another embarrassing, even if he were a religious, a condition that will not easily arise in the case of sisters. Then, too, in a country like ours, where the number of religious in the individual house is often comparatively small, it would work a hardship upon the whole community, if a religious were obliged to take a companion with him every time he went out[8].

Permission to go out can not lawfully be granted by the superior except for a good reason, the weight of which depends very much upon circumstances. But an inferior who faithfully presents to his superior his reasons for going out and obtains his permission can feel perfectly safe in making use of same[9].

---

[7] Biederlack 241; Brandys 69; Blat 593; Pruemmer[2] 292.
[8] Bachofen 154; cfr. Butler, *Benedictine Monachism,* 308-309.
[9] Clemens VIII, decr. *Nullus omnino,* § 19; Bonacina, *De Clausura etc.,* q. II p. I n. 3; Piatus, *Praelectiones,* I 349.

Leaving the monastery without the superior's consent is unlawful; but, if it were only for an hour or two, it could not be considered a serious matter[10]. However, even a brief absence would become grievous, if thereby a religious neglected a grave duty, gave serious scandal or went out in direct violation of a special prohibition of his superior[11]. In the absence of aggravating circumstances Piat would not condemn the opinion of those who hold that there is no mortal sin, unless a religious remains away from his convent for the night or even for two or three days[12]. However, it is more probable that, even abstracting from particular circumstances, protracting an unlawful absence from the monastery over night or until late at night constitutes a grievous matter, for it appears to amount to a serious breach of discipline. This view gains weight from the fact that Clement VIII reckoned stealthy egress at night among the cases which superiors could reserve to themselves[13]. Neither would the case become a grievous sin in consequence of a statute, as Piat presupposes. For the statutes cannot oblige under pain of grievous sin in a small matter except on account of special cnrcumstances. Nevertheless, in some orders this case is treated as a grievous matter[14].

This unlawful leaving of the convent must not be confounded with the crime that would brand one as a fugitive from his institute. "A fugitive is one who, without the permission of the Superiors, deserts the religious house, but with the intention of returning to his Institute."[15] The verb "deserere" signifies more than merely leaving. Forcellini[16] says: "Etenim *relinquere* est simpliciter i. q. discedere ab aliquo

10 Suarez, tr. 8 l. I c. VI nn. 6, 7, 9; Bouix *Tr. De Jure Reg.* II 563-565; Sleutjes 286, and Vermeersch, *De Religiosis,* I 177 take the view that unlawfully leaving the convent is ex genere suo a grievous sin, though it may be only venial because of the short stay outside the convent. Bonacina, *De Clausura etc.,* q. II p. I n. 2, holds that it is ex genere suo only venial. Bastien 156; Piatus, *Praelectiones,* I 347.

11 Piatus, *Praelectiones,* I 347. Cfr. Sleutjes 286.

12 Piatus, *Praelectiones,* I 347. Cfr. Sleutjes 286.

13 Clemens VIII, decr. *Sanctissimus Dominus Noster,* 26 Maii 1593, Vermeersch, *De Religiosis,* II 613.

14 Cfr. *Constitutiones Generales O. F. M.* (1913) n. 125.

15 Canon 644 § 3.

16 Forcellini, v. *desero.*

et in alium locum se conferre; *deserere* est derelinquere aliquem cum consilio nocendi; illud genus verbi, haec species; quare saepius reperitur *relinquere* positum pro *deserere;* non *deserere* pro *relinquere.*" As Pruemmer[17] justly remarks, "a fugitive differs from an apostate only in this that the former intends to return, the latter not." Now there is a far greater difference between an apostate and one who goes out stealthily: an aspostate shakes off the yoke of community life completely and quasi-permanently; a fugitive also separates himself from the community completely and more or less openly, yet only for a time; but one who leaves his convent by stealth does not break off his connection with the community; he may, on the contrary, attend all the community exercises; he leaves secretly and unlawfully; for the rest his leaving could easily be permitted by the superior even without a very serious reason[18]. Finally, canon 2386 deprives a fugitive ipso facto and without any sentence of whatever office he may hold and suspends him, if he is in major orders; besides it ordains that he be punished by his higher superior in accordance with the constitutions or, if they make no provision, according to his guilt. Such severe penalties presuppose a grievous fault which can hardly be said to exist, if one leaves his convent without lawful permission, but only for a very brief space of time.

It must be noted that under the Code, as also under the former law, no censure is incurred for unlawfully leaving one's convent. The only penalty, if penalty it can be called, was that contained in the decree of Clement VIII "Sanctissimus Dominus," which enumerated among the sins that could be reserved by religious superiors "going out of the monastery or convent at night and by stealth, even without the intention of apostatizing."[19] "Going out at night and by stealth" means leaving one's convent without lawful permission and knowledge of his superior at such an hour of the night as to cause surprise and wonder at the sight of a religious outside his convent at that hour. Going out under these conditions must

---

17 Pruemmer² 329.

18 Piatus, *Praelectiones,* I 205; Pruemmer² 329.

19 "Nocturna ac furtiva e monasterio seu conventu egressio, etiam non animo apostatandi." Clemens VIII, decr. *Sanctissimus Dominus,* § 1 n. 2, Vermeersch, *De Religiosis,* II 612-613.

always be suspicious and could not be excused from grievous fault[20]. The reservation of this case is not retained in the Code. It is left to the constitutions or the judgment of the superior to deal with a case of this kind.

The Council of Trent ordered: ". . . . Nor shall it be lawful for regulars to withdraw from their convents, even under the pretext of repairing to their own superiors; unless summoned by them. And whoever shall be found to be without the order aforesaid in writing, shall be punished as a deserter of his Institute by the Ordinaries of the places . ."[21] It must be noted that this decree says "even under *pretext* of repairing to their own superiors." If a religious were grievously wronged by his immediate superior and redress were possible in no other way than that he go at once and personally to his higher superior, he is not to be treated as an apostate, since he does not sin nor withdraw from obedience to his superiors by his appeal. The intention of the Council was to forbid regulars under some trifling, unfounded and suspicious pretext to seek an occasion to roam about and to free themselves from the obedience due their superior, as sometimes happened. It was therefore, that the Council commanded that such religious be punished as deserters of their institute, albeit they leave their monastery or convent under said pretext without lawful permission. It did not mean to cut them off from every avenue of redress through their higher superiors in cases of real and extraordinary wrong, present or imminent, the less so since permission cannot be asked of one from whose injustice relief is sought. In such cases the tacit consent of the superior can be presumed. Statutes of religious institutes, which contain a similar prohibition, have no other meaning. The same holds good of recourse to the Holy See.

But a religious who is driven to seek redress from a higher superior in this manner, must be so manifestly and seriously wronged, that it is evident or can easily be proven, that he has no *other* means of relief. In order to justify his recourse and to shield himself against the suspicion of desertion, he

---

20 Cfr. Vermeersch in *Catholic Encyclopedia,* v. *Cloister,* IV 61; Bonacina, *De Clausura etc.,* q. II p. I n. 2.

21 Conc. Trident., sess. XXV, *de regularibus.* c. 4.

should, if at all possible, ask leave of the superior who wronged him to go to the higher superior; if it be refused him, let him seek trustworthy witnesses to this fact, as was provided in the constitution of Sixtus V "Ad Romanum spectat" of October 21, 1588[22]. If, however, asking for this permission meant to invite greater wrongs, he could go at once to the higher superior for the necessary relief, because no one is obliged to expose himself to such injustice[23].

It is a rare case, however, in which this course need be followed. For seldom will the injury that a religious suffers at the hands of his immediate superior be so great and unbearable and the religious' need of redress so urgent, that the ordinary course of appeal at the canonical visitation or by letter will not suffice.

Section 19 of the decree "Nullus omnino" absolutely forbade *general permissions* to go out. There can be no doubt that this decree applied only to Italy and the adjacent islands and custom certainly allowed general permissions. Neither does there seem to be anything improper in this, since they usually are granted for cases that arise from the work appointed for the religious by his superior. Further, if a general permission could not lawfully be granted at least in such cases, the religious would often be compelled to resort to presumed permission and this would easily lead to never ending scrupless on the one hand and great laxity on the other[24]. As a rule, express permission ought to be obtained for every instance, if possible; otherwise, in general for cases that occur frequently. However, permission can often be presumed, and this even at night, in such cases as sick calls and the like[25].

[22] Sixtus V, const. *Ad Romanum spectat,* § 19, Vermeersch, *De Religiosis,* II 270-274. In § 20 of this constitution the following regulation was contained: If a regular came to Rome on the plea that he came to appeal from his superiors to the Holy See, but could not show in writing that he had permission from his superior, he was not to be received in any monastery, until the Sacred Congregation had determined his standing.

[23] Ferraris, v. *Apostasia,* nn. 29-41, who cites a number of authorities in support of his view: Lezana, t. I c. 16 nn. 8-9; Ameno, *De Delictis,* tit. 2 § 1; *Apostasia* 27 et 31; Pignatelli, tom. X consult. 24 nn. 27-28; Bonacina, *De Clausura etc.,* q. II p. XI § 1 n. 9; Matthaeucci, *Officialis quoad apostatas,* nn. 16-17. Benedictus XIV, *De Synodo Dioecesana,* lib. XIII c. XI n. 14.

[24] Bachofen 153-154.

[25] Piatus, *Praelectiones,* I 347-348; Bastien 156.

The constitution "Nullus omnino" also ordained that a janitor be appointed to guard the cloister door; he should not allow anyone to leave except by permission of the superior and in company of another religious appointed by the superior. Finally, upon the return of the religious, the superior should ask an account of him for the time of his absence[26].

As was stated above, the Code does not renew these regulations nor does it give any special directions in this matter, but refers the religious to their respective constitutions. The latter will reflect the spirit of the institute. Whatever they prescribe must be faithfully observed. The same applies to paying and receiving visits. In canon 606 § 1 the Code lays the obligation of enforcing them directly upon the superiors. That they may be enabled to fulfill their obligation, their subjects are bound to submit these matters to their judgment and allow themselves to be guided by them[27].

Canon 607.

The Superioresses and the local Ordinaries shall attentively see that the religious[28], except in the case of necessity, do not go out singly from the house.

Canon 606 § 1 has reference to all religious, men as well as women. Nevertheless a special canon is devoted to the religious decorum that sisters should observe, whenever they leave their convents. They should never go out alone, but always have another member of their own congregation or at least some respectable lay-woman as a companion[29]. However, in exceptional cases of great urgency or for special reasons a sister may be permitted to go out alone, for instance, if it were difficult to obtain a companion and there was no danger of scandal and the like[30]. In this matter the sisters may abide by the decision of their superioress who is immediately charged by the Code to provide for all cases[31].

---

[26] Clemens VIII, const. *Nullus omnino,* §§ 18-20; cfr. Piatus, *Praelectiones,* I 348-349.

[27] Blat 593; Leitner 417; Pruemmer[2] 293; Egger 37; Brandys 69.

[28] "Sisters" would render "religiosae" more correctly.

[29] Leitner 417-418; Blat 594; Brandys 70.

[30] Leitner 417; Blat 594.

[31] Leitner 417.

If the ordinary of the place is especially commanded to watch over the observance of this canon, it does not follow that each individual exception must receive his sanction: time and circumstances may prevent it. If exceptions were made too frequently, it would be his duty to check the abuse[32].

Finally, it must be observed that this canon refers only to "sisters," "religiosae," who do not observe perpetual enclosure, and to nuns who by way of exception do not make solemn profession and are not, at least generally speaking, bound to perpetual enclosure[33].

Canon 606, § 2.

It may at times be necessary or advisable that a religious be permitted to remain outside of his institute for a length of time. But a prolonged absence and freedom from the accustomed environments and restraints of the convent, which should go far to assist him in his manner of life, may easily prove a source of danger to the religious himself, of ill-repute to his institute and of scandal to the faithful. Therefore, Clement VIII in his constitution "Nullus omnino", n. 32, revoked all patents granted to regulars to remain away from their convents, commanded that all who enjoyed such permission be recalled and that no similar concessions be granted again except for weighty reasons to be approved by the Holy See. For what length of time a superior could grant leave of absence without the consent of the Holy See was not certain. Ferrari[34] thought permission of the Holy See was necessary, if a regular intended to stay outside a monastery of his institute for more than two months. Pruemmer[35] states that according to a statute of the Dominicans the provincial could for sufficient reason permit a subject to live outside the convent for four months.

Canon 606, § 2. It is not lawful for Superiors, saving the dispositions of canons 621-624, to permit their subjects to remain outside the house of their own Institute, except for

32 Brandys 70; Biederlack 242.
33 Leitner 417.
34 Ferrari, *De statu rel.*, 168, quoted by Pruemmer II 100.
35 Pruemmer II 100.

a just and grave cause and for as brief a period as possible according to the constitutions; but for an absence of more than six months, unless for motives of study, the permission of the Apostolic See is always required.

This paragraph refers only to a stay of a religious *outside a house of his own institute.* If he is to be sent to another house, though of another province, monastic congregation and the like, there is no need of such permission. He then remains under the full jurisdiction of his superiors; if he is not transferred *permanently* to this house or province, the local superior is given such authority over him as is necessary. For cases of this kind there are special regulations in the constitutions of each institute.

Neither does this paragraph treat of the so-called "indultum exclaustrationis" or the "indultum saecularizationis," by which a religious is released temporarily or permanently from obedience to the superiors of his institute. By the former he is placed under obedience to the local ordinary as long as he remains dispensed from living in the community; by the latter he is freed entirely from all obligation arising from his vows or the rule of his institute[36].

The Code repeats the former provision which forbade superiors to permit their subjects to live outside a house of their institute. Still the prohibition is not absolute. Besides the cases provided for in canons 621-624, where the conditions are laid down regarding the manner in which religious, mendicants as well as others, may be sent to collect alms for the community, others can and will arise, in which superiors are justified in permitting subjects to remain outside a house of their own institute. But they must observe the following conditions: (a) They must have "a just and grave cause." The adequacy of the reason will depend upon many circumstances: the longer the intended absence, the weightier must be the reason. Assisting parents and other near relatives in their last illness, going in search of one's lost health and the like constitute sufficient reason to justify such an absence. (b) "For as brief a period as possible": leave of absence can

[36] Cfr. canons 638-642.

only be given for the duration of the reason; as soon as it ceases, the religious is bound to return to his convent. (c) "According to the constitutions": whatever restrictions the constitutions make, may further limit the power of the local or provincial superior and must be taken into consideration or the permission could not lawfully be granted[37].

If it becomes necessary that the absence of a religious from his institute extend beyond six months, no superior of the institute, not even the general, can grant leave. For every such case special permission of the Holy See is required. The period of absence is to be reckoned according to canon 34 § 2 from minute to minute[38]. If the absence is interrupted by a return to a house of the institute for a short space of time, e. g., for a week, the period continues, if the absence is for the same purpose; for such an interruption does not morally break the continuity of the absence. To seek to evade the law by a bare fulfillment of its letter would not be justifiable[39].

Only in one case may the superior permit a religious to remain outside a monastery of his institute for a longer period than six months without leave of the Holy See. That is for the purpose of pursuing special studies[40]. Following in the footsteps of Alexander III[41] the Third Lateran Council forbade regulars to leave their monasteries in order to study civil law or the natural sciences[42]. The Council of Trent ordained that regulars who frequent universities live in monasteries[43]. July 21, 1896, the Congregation of Bishops and Regulars issued an institution. "Perspectum est Romanos Pontifices," dealing with the question of religious attending universities in charge of the Italian government[44]. Pius X extended the regulations of that instruction to the whole world[45].

---

[37] Pruemmer[2] 292; Blat 593-594; Egger 38; Leitner 417; Fanfani 129.
[38] Pruemmer[2] 292; Blat 594; Egger 38; Leitner 417; Fanfani 130.
[39] Blat 594; Brandys 69.
[40] Blat 594; Egger 38; Leitner 417; Biederlack 242; Brandys 69.
[41] C. 3, X, *ne clerici vel monachi saecularibus negotiis se immisceant,* III, 50.
[42] Vide Conc. Later. III, app. p. 27 c. 2, *Ss. Conc.,* X 1421.
[43] Conc. Trident., sess. XXV. *de regularibus,* c. 4.
[44] A. S. S. XXIX 359-364.
[45] Pius X, litt. encycl. *Pascendi,* 16 Julii 1907, A. S. S. XL 642; motu proprio *Sacrorum Antistitum,* 1 Sept. 1910, A. A. S. II 658-659.

Like that decree of the Sacred Congregation, the Code does not forbid religious to take up any branch of study. How far it is from the mind of the Church to prevent religious from acquiring knowledge of any science that can be of any service to them, can be seen from this, that the Code does not require that permission of the Holy See be obtained, if such studies take a religious out of a house of his institute. While it grants the greatest liberty in this respect, it nevertheless prescribes certain precautions against aimless roaming about during an absence from one's institute granted for the purpose of study. According to canon 587 § 4 religious whom the superior grants leave of absence for the sake of study must reside in a house of their institute; if this is not possible, they must stay in some religious institute of men, in a seminary or other pious house in charge of priests, that has the approval of ecclesiastical authority[46]. Almost on the eve of the day that the Code went into effect, April 30, 1918, the Consistorial Congregation published the decree "Nemo de sacro clero,"[47] in which special rules are laid down regarding the attendance of secular and religious priests at lay universities. (1) No clerics of a religious institute may attend a lay university, unless they are already ordained priests and their character and talents hold out the hope that they will do honor to their state; (2) the only purpose for which they may be sent is to provide suitable teachers for the education of youth; (3) priests attending such universities are not exempt from the examinations prescribed in canon 590 for the younger priests, lest their profane studies absorb all their interest to the neglect of the ecclesiastical sciences[48]; (4) their course of studies completed, they remain entirely subject to their superior and may not accept a position as professor without his consent or against his wishes[49].

---

46 Blat 594; Egger 38; Leitner 417.
47 A. A. S. X 237-238.
48 Cfr. canon 129.
49 Leitner 399; Blat 571-572.

ALPHABETICAL INDEX.

VITA.

Valentine Theodore Schaaf was born at Cincinnati, Ohio, March 18, 1883. He received his elementary education at St. Joseph Parish School and his classical training at St. Francis Seraphic College (now St. Francis Preparatory Seminary), Cincinnati, whereupon he entered the Order of Friars Minor August 15, 1901. After his religious profession he pursued the prescribed courses in philosophy and theology in the monasteries of his Province at St. Bernard, Ohio, Louisville, Kentucky, Cincinnati, Ohio, and Oldenburg, Indiana, and was raised to the priesthood June 29, 1909. The following nine years he devoted to teaching the classics at St. Francis Preparatory Seminary. In the fall of 1918 he entered the Catholic University of America and attended the lectures of the Rt. Rev. Philip Bernardini, J. U. D., in Canon Law, of the Very Rev. Edmund T. Shanahan, Ph. D., S. T. D., J. C. L., in Dogmatic Theology, and of the Very Rev. Patrick J. Healy, S. T. D., in Church History.

Universitas Catholica Americae

Washington, D. C.

S. Facultas Theologica

1920–1921

No. 13

CANONES

DEUS LUX MEA

CANONES

QUOS

AD DOCTORATUS GRADUM

IN

JURE CANOINCO

Apud Universitatem Catholicam Americae

CONSEQUENDUM

PUBLICE PROPUGNABIT

VALENTINUS THEODORUS SCHAAF, O. F. M.

PROVINCIAE S. JOANNIS BAPTISTAE CINCINNATENSIS

JURIS CANONICI LICENTIATUS

HORA XI. A. M. DIE XXXI. MAII A. D. MCMXXI

I.	Canones	5–7
II.	Canones	15–24
III.	Canones	36–42
IV.	Canones	43–50
V.	Canones	51–61
VI.	Canones	90–95
VII.	Canones	111–117
VIII.	Canones	145–151
IX.	Canones	366–371
X.	Canones	471–478
XI.	Canones	518–530
XII.	Canones	572–578
XIII.	Canon	597
XIV.	Canones	598–599
XV.	Canon	600
XVI.	Canon	601
XVII.	Canones	602–603
XVIII.	Canones	604–607
XIX.	Canones	632–636
XX.	Canones	726–730
XXI.	Canones	762–769
XXII.	Canon	804
XXIII.	Canones	893–900
XXIV.	Canon	1017
XXV.	Canones	1047–1057
XXVI.	Canones	1060-1064
XXVII.	Canon	1077
XXVIII.	Canon	1078
XXIX.	Canones	1089–1091
XXX.	Canon	1092
XXXI.	Canones	1094–1099
XXXII.	Canones	1110–1117
XXXIII.	Canones	1188–1196
XXXIV.	Canones	1239–1242

XXXV.	Canones	1250–1254
XXXVI.	Canones	1572–1579
XXXVII.	Canones	1642–1645
XXXVIII.	Canones	1672–1675
XXXIX.	Canones	1676–1678
XL.	Canones	1687–1689
XLI.	Canones	1690–1692
XLII.	Canones	1701–1705
XLIII.	Canones	1726–1731
XLIV.	Canones	1770–1781
XLV.	Canones	1825–1828
XLVI.	Canones	1868–1877
XLVII.	Canones	1892–1897
XLVIII.	Canones	1960–1965
XLIX.	Canones	1993–1998
L.	Canones	2147–2156
LI.	Canones	2199–2208
LII.	Canones	2226–2235
LIII.	Canones	2252–2254
LIV.	Canones	2278–2285
LV.	Canones	2306–2311
LVI.	Canon	2319
LVII.	Canon	2335
LVIII.	Canon	2350
LIX.	Canon	2366
LX.	Canones	2385–2386

Vidit Sacra Facultas:

JOANNES A. RYAN, S.T.D., p. t. Decanus
PETRUS GUILDAY, Ph.D., p. t. a Secretis.

Vidit Rector Universitatis:

†THOMAS I. SHAHAN, S.T.D.

www.ingramcontent.com/pod-product-compliance
Lightning Source LLC
LaVergne TN
LVHW050235080826
844660LV00012B/538